I0235252

Fernando of Cordova

A Biographical and Intellectual Profile

TRANSACTIONS

of the

American Philosophical Society

Held at Philadelphia for Promoting Useful Knowledge

VOLUME 82, Part 6, 1992

Fernando of Cordova
A Biographical and Intellectual Profile

JOHN MONFASANI

THE AMERICAN PHILOSOPHICAL SOCIETY

Independence Square, Philadelphia

1992

Copyright © 1992 by The American Philosophical Society
Publication of this work was supported in part by the
Haney Fund of the American Philosophical Society.

Library of Congress Catalog
Card Number: 92-72642
International Standard Book Number 0-87169-862-9
US ISSN 0065-9746

In Memory of My Parents

ALESSANDRO MONFASANI
11 November 1906 – 1 July 1973

and

CLEMENTINA MONFASANI
25 August 1914 – 7 November 1985

TABLE OF CONTENTS

Preface ix
Abbreviations x

Introduction 1
First Appearance in the 1440s and Prior Life 3
In the Entourage of Cardinal Juan Carvajal 17
In the Service of Cardinal Bessarion......................... 23
The Pontificate of Sixtus IV................................ 41

APPENDICES

1. A List of Authentic, Doubtful, and Misattributed Works
   of Fernando of Cordova 55
2. Papal Documents concerning Fernando of Cordova 57
3. Calendar of Documents on "Fernandus de Medina Diocesis
   Cordubensis" and "Fernandus de Corduba" at the Spanish
   College in Bologna, 1442–1446.......................... 64
4. A Report on Fernando of Cordova in Siena, July 1446 67
5. Letter of the Sienese Government to King Alfonso V of
   Aragon, 21 July 1446, concerning Fernando of Cordova 69
6. Fernando of Cordova at the University of Vienna, September
   1448 71
   A. Fragment of University *Acta* concerning Fernando of
      Cordova 71
   B. The *Propositiones* Argued by Fernando of Cordova 73
7. Preface of Fernando of Cordova to Cardinal Guillaume
   d'Estouteville for the *Adversus Hereticos Qui Fraterculi dela
   Opinione Appellantur* and the Table of the Sections
   (*tractatus*) in the Treatise 83
8. Preface of Fernando of Cordova to Cardinal Francesco
   Todeschini-Piccolomini for the *De Misterio Pallii* 89
9. Henricus de Zoemeren, Cardinal Bessarion, and the
   University of Louvain 93
10. The Verdict of the Papal Commission on Pere Deguí (Petrus
    Dagui)'s *Ianua Artis Magistri Raymundi Lull*, Rome, 1484.... 95
11. The Tomb of Fernando of Cordova at S. Maria di Montserrat,
    Rome 100

Bibliography 101
Index of Documents and Manuscripts 111
Index of Names and Subjects.............................. 113

PREFACE

I had never intended to write a book on Fernando of Cordova. I gathered material on Fernando merely as background for a section of a monograph on the Plato–Aristotle controversy of the fifteenth century. Only when I started to write did it finally dawn on me that my material on Fernando had outgrown my initial conception and needed to appear separately. I first thought of a large article, but even that format proved too constricting for the amount of material I had. So I am very grateful to the American Philosophical Society for coming to my rescue and accepting this work in its publication series.

Since I have worked on Fernando of Cordova intermittently since the early 1970s, virtually every travel grant and fellowship I have received contributed in some way to the completion of this project. Especially important were a travel grant from the Research Foundation of the State University of New York in the summer of 1975, a recent Ph.D. Fellowship from the American Council of Learned Societies in the spring of 1977, a fellowship in 1982–1983 at Villa I Tatti, the Harvard University Center for Renaissance Study in Florence, and a travel grant from the American Philosophical Society in the summer of 1987.

Of the many colleagues and friends who have encouraged and aided me in my research, Paul Oskar Kristeller deserves a special mention for this study of Fernando of Cordova. By his advice, criticism, and encouragement, he fostered this study from beginning to end. Without his erudition and generosity, this would be a much poorer book.

ABBREVIATIONS

ASV   Archivio Segreto Vatican, Vatican City

BAV   Biblioteca Apostolica Vaticana, Vatican City

Bibl.   Biblioteca, Bibliothèque

BN   Biblioteca Nazionale

CAG   *Commentaria in Aristotelem Graeca*, Berlin

CCSL   *Corpus Christianorum. Series Latina*, Turnholt

CSEL   *Corpus Scriptorum Ecclesiasticorum Latinorum*, Vienna

CTC   *Catalogus Translationum et Commentariorum: Mediaeval and Renaissance Latin Translations and Commentaries*, ed. P. O. Kristeller, F. E. Cranz, and V. Brown, Washington, D.C.

DHGE   *Dictionnaire d'histoire et de géographie ecclésiastiques*, Paris

DTC   *Dictionnaire de théologie catholique*, Paris

GW   *Gesamtkatalog der Wiegendrucke*, Leipzig-Stuttgart

M   MS Florence, BN, Magl. XXXI, 17 (see note 257, page 42)

PG   J. Migne, *Patrologia Graeca*

PL   J. Migne, *Patrologia Latina*

INTRODUCTION

Part charlatan, part *Wunderkind*, and part learned scholastic, Fernando of Cordova burst upon the European scene and into the historical record in 1444-1446 when he traveled to different parts of Europe disputing *de omni scibili*. He astounded audiences by his command of the subject matter in all the university faculties, his mastery of oriental languages, his skill in painting, music, and instrument making, and his expertise in knightly warfare.[1] Viewed by contemporaries as a preternatural wonder and even the Anti-Christ—and more recently as a Giovanni Pico della Mirandola *ante litteram*[2]—Fernando patently possessed a prodigious memory[3] and, just as obviously, a flair for self-advertisement. In the standard accounts, he disappears from sight after 1444-1446, when he was supposedly about twenty years old, only to return comet-like twenty years later in 1466 as a Roman curialist active in several controversies. He passed from the scene, in almost periodic fashion, with his death twenty years later in 1486.

My interest in Fernando stems from his involvement in the Plato-Aristotle controversy of fifteenth-century Italy. But his significance extends beyond the controversy. He is a major representative of Spanish university culture in the first half of the fifteenth century. His philosophical, theological, and scientific writings cover a wide range of topics important to his age. And his biography has a special value because of what he did and whom he impressed in his travels in the cities, courts, and universities of Europe.

While studying Fernando for the Plato–Aristotle controversy, I compiled a dossier of data which throws new light on his *curriculum vitae* and his writings. It is this information that I share here.

---

[1] The standard study is Bonilla y San Martín's in 1911, which does not totally replace the earlier studies of Havet (1882) (I used the reprint in Havet [1896], 2:310-38); and Morel-Fatio. See also Lohr (1967-1974), 23:407; and Di Camillo, 231-41, 243-44, 247-48.

[2] See Bonilla y San Martín, 122-23; Thorndike (1934): 486-87. Note that Thorndike's reference to cod. 281 of Merton College, Oxford, is a misattribution corrected by Thorndike-Kibre, 1496; and by Lohr (1967-1974), 23:407.

[3] As one contemporary put it, for Fernando to read anything was for him to memorize it (Havet [1896], 337; Bonilla y San Martín, 60-61n.): "waz er list und wie schnell er daz list, so verstet er es doch alles und behelt es auch in gedaechtnüsz."

FIRST APPEARANCE IN THE 1440s
AND PRIOR LIFE

Scholars have lamented Fernando's failure to live up to the brilliant promise of his youth. But there is a certain continuity between the *Wunderkind* of the 1440s and the polymath-turned-curialist of the 1460s. In fact, this continuity is one of the keys to understanding Fernando despite our fragmentary knowledge of his biography and the loss of some of his writings. Fernando's own sepulchral epitaph of 1486 stresses this continuity.[4] It records not only the time when "the schools of all nations stood dumbstruck before his intellectual brilliance and dialectical acumen," but also the fact that he produced (in his later years) a considerable body of literary "monuments," reflective of a learned culture which we can trace back to his youth.

The earliest notice of Fernando cited in the literature is the remarkable letter of recommendation Lorenzo Valla wrote for him to King Alfonso of Aragon.[5] Valla dated the letter Naples, 25 July. We can add the year 1444.[6] Valla described a lad of no more than seventeen or eighteen[7] who

---

[4] See Appendix 11.

[5] Our sole source for the letter is *Epistolae Principum Rerumpublicarum ac Sapientium Virorum*, 362–69; it is now to be read in Valla (1984), 258–62. Previously, the standard edition had been Sabbadini (*Chronologia*, 1891), 108–11 (reprinted in Valla [1962], 2:414–17). The letter has been reprinted many times: *Principum et Illustrium Virorum Epistolae*, 364–69; Cancellieri, xiii–xviii; Morel-Fatio, 523–26 (from Sabbadini [*Chronologia*, 1891]); Bonilla y San Martín, 53–55 (from Sabbadini [*Chronologia*, 1891]); and Soria, 293–97 (from Sabbadini [*Chronologia*, 1891]).

[6] Sabbadini (*Chronologia*, 1891) first dated the letter to "after 1442," but in the "Correzioni ed aggiunte" in the same publication, viii, he opted for 1445. Mancini, 185, preferred 1444, and has been followed in this dating by Morel-Fatio, Bonilla y San Martín, and Regoliosi (in Valla [1984], 232). But neither Mancini nor those who agree with him have given evidence to support this date. However, we have a Neapolitan document of September 1444 which speaks of Fernando as newly arrived from Spain (Mauro, 28n.). There is also strong circumstantial evidence. King Alfonso was not in Naples when Valla drafted his letter of 25 July; but the king must have been staying at a site not very far away since Valla assumed that his letter and Fernando would have no trouble finding the king in a day or two ("etsi propediem visurus auditurusque hominem es"). The only year which meets these conditions for 25 July is 1444, when Alfonso was at Fontanelle, a site about five kilometers southeast of Sorrento; see Jiménez Soler, 213. In late July 1442 Alfonso was far away, up towards Pescara and L'Aquila, and in late July 1443 he was again in the Abruzzi region (Jiménez Soler, 194, 204–05); in late July 1445 and 1446 he was in Naples (Jiménez Soler, 219, 235). In late July 1447 Valla himself was no longer living in Naples.

[7] Valla (1984), 261: "duodevicesimum agens annum aut modo ingressus undevicesimum, nondum malas signante lanugine."

had demonstrated in three days of disputation in Naples a complete command of the university curriculum in arts, law, medicine, and theology.[8] He could recall the words of his opponents better than they could themselves. Moreover, he claimed to know not only Hebrew, but also Arabic and Aramaic (these, I presume, are the languages which Valla called Punic and Chaldean).[9] Not surprisingly, Valla judged Fernando's Latin in need of some polish and further acquaintance with the classics. Valla also recommended that Fernando learn Greek.[10] The next year in northern Europe, when he was free of Valla and other humanist critics, Fernando did not hesitate to pass himself off as a master of classical Greek and Latin.

Valla's breathless description of Fernando accords well with those of many witnesses to Fernando's "performance" in these years. Unfortunately, these reports do not fully jibe with each other and with other evidence concerning his age.

We have two dates to choose from for his birth, i.e., either a date ca. 1422 or a date ca. 1426. According to Valla, in 1444 Fernando was seventeen or eighteen years old, which would mean that he was born ca. 1426. Valla's estimate agrees with almost all of the sources connected with Fernando's trip to northern Europe a year and a half later, who describe him in 1445-1446 as about eighteen or nineteen years old.[11] In harmony with this dating, witnesses to his visits to Genoa and Siena mid-1446 made him out to be nineteen years old.[12] Two years later, in August 1448, he asserted to the theological faculty of the University of Vienna that he was twenty-two years old,[13] which fits with a birth date ca. 1426.

---

[8] Valla (1984), 260: "Nihil in grammatice est, nihil in dialecticis, nihil in physicis, nihil in metaphysicis, nihil in moralibus, nihil in geometricis, nihil in astronomicis, nihil in medicinis, nihil in musica, nihil in theologia, nihil denique in iure quod ignoret; ignoret, dico? immo quod non habeat in promptu memoriterque reddat ac pene decantet."

[9] Valla (1984), 260: "Quid autem illa studio ac lectione comparata (praeter ea de quibus iudicare non possum, hebraeam, punicam, caldaicam linguam)?"

[10] Valla (1984), 261: "Verum, ut sincere de homine iudicem et nihil vel quod adest ei vel quod abest omittam, lingua latina, facultas poetica tanta ei adest quantam Hispania docere aut aliqua provincia potuit. Breviter summa, ut dicitur, manus in eo desideratur (solum namque in Italia nitor ille dicendi, ornatus orationis, vis eloquentie viget sive in prosa sive in carmine), praesertim iactis fundamentis in Graeca lingua." Valla then gives a sample list of Latin classical texts that Fernando still had to read.

[11] Two sources, the letter of the student of St. Bernard (Delisle, 194; Bonilla y San Martín, 73 n. 1) and the letter to the chancellor of Brabant (Havet, 336; Bonilla y San Martín, 60n.), have him about nineteen years old in December 1446; three sources, Mathieu d'Escouchy (Havet, 316; Bonilla y San Martín, 66 n. 1), the *Bourgeois de Paris* (Havet, 318; Bonilla y San Martín, 64 n. 1), and Georges Chastellain (Havet, 320, 327; Bonilla y San Martín 75), make him about twenty years old on that date.

[12] Giacomo Bracelli had him just past his twentieth year in June 1446 (Resta, 279; Balbi, 59); Leonardus of Siena has him in his twentieth year in July of that year (see Appendix 4, this volume).

[13] Uiblein, 1:230: (30 August 1448) "quidam iuvenis, ut asseruit, 23 annorum."

However, according to the inscription on Fernando's tomb, he died in 1486 in his sixty-fifth year,[14] which would mean that he was born about 1422 and not about 1426. A source for Fernando's visit to France lends comfort to this earlier date since it reports that Fernando was twenty-two or twenty-three in 1445.[15] Finally, we have several papal documents of 1448 and 1449 concerning benefices for him where no mention is made of his being under the canonical age for the priesthood (twenty-six completed years) and therefore in need of a dispensation to receive the benefices.[16] This silence suggests that Fernando was twenty-six years old by 1448 and not in need of any dispensation. Yet, even if we assume, as I think we ought, that Fernando exaggerated his youthfulness to amaze his audiences even further, he would still have been only about twenty-three years old in 1445–1446 when he astounded "the schools of all the nations."

As for Fernando's education, the author of the only other monograph on him, A. Bonilla y San Martín, suggested the University of Salamanca.[17] I know no text that actually confirms this guess,[18] but there is one which increases its likelihood: when Fernando registered as a member of the *Natio Rhenensium* at the University of Vienna in October 1447, he called himself a *sacre theologie et artium professor Salamantinensis universitatis*.[19]

What we can confidently assert is that Fernando began his European career in 1444 with a very specific philosophical orientation. Our prime witness for Fernando's visit to the University of Paris in 1445 listed the scholastic authorities that Fernando knew by heart.[20] They were Thomas Aquinas and the mainstays of the Augustinian-Franciscan school, i.e., Alexander of Hales, St. Bonaventure, and John Duns Scotus. Some

---

[14] See Appendix 11.

[15] A notice in a register of the municipal archives of Châlons-sur-Marne (Havet, 320; Bonilla y San Martín, 58 n. 2).

[16] See Appendix 2, docs. 1–3. Doc. 3, dated 30 Sept. 1449, is the most important since in it the pope grants Fernando several benefices. Doc. 2 grants Fernando a legal privilege which in itself would not require any mention of age. Doc. 1 is a supplication for a legal privilege and again would not necessitate any mention of age.

[17] Bonilla y San Martín, 49.

[18] It was mainly on the basis of this guess that Beltrán de Heredia (1:136–37) included Fernando in his *Bulario de la Universidad de Salamanca*.

[19] University of Vienna, 1:256, for 13 October 1447: "Venerabilis dom. Vernandus [sic] de Cordua Hispanus, sacre theologie et artium professor Salamantinensis universitatis et archidiaconus de Atza ecclesie Osmensis." He was not required to pay the matriculation fee since none is listed next to his name, which heads the list of those incorporated into the Rhenish nation at the start of the fall semester.

[20] ". . . hat in gedachtnüsz und chan auswendig nachent die ganzen wibel [= "il a en mémoire et sait par coeur presque toute la Bible," tr. Havet] und maister Nicolaum von Lira, und was sand Thoman von Aquino, Alexander von Alis, Scotas, und Bonaventara un [sic] vil ander maister geschriben haben" (Havet, 336; Bonilla y San Martín, 60n.).

months later, our Genoese source added Augustine, Averroes, and Albert the Great to the list of authorities memorized by Fernando.[21] Since Averroes was a standard author, and since the two Dominicans, Albert and Thomas, had incorporated a good deal of Neoplatonism into their writings, these early lists of Fernando's favorite authorities anticipate fairly well the authors and the Platonic (or Neoplatonic) themes one finds in the extant writings of his later life. William of Ockham and the nominalists are conspicuous by their absence from these lists of authorities. Fernando did note his agreement with Ockham on a point in the *Propositiones* which he argued at the University of Vienna in 1448,[22] but that was a sop to the nominalists in what, as we will see below, was a theologically Scotist and philosophically realist document. By education and outlook, Fernando was already a medieval Platonist when he left Spain.[23]

What is less certain but worth noting is the possibility that Fernando was a student at the Spanish College in Bologna before Valla met him in 1444. We can document at the Spanish College from December 1442 to September 1446 one "Fernandus de Medina diocesis Cordubensis," a medical student otherwise known as "Fernandus de Corduba,"[24] who probably was the "Fernandus de Corduba" hired by the University of Bologna to teach medicine in the academic year 1447–1448.[25] The existence of two Fernandos of Cordova active in Italy in the mid-1440s learned in theology and medicine (the Fernando of the Spanish College had initially come to Bologna to read theology) would seem unlikely. Furthermore, over a five-year span, i.e., from late 1442 to late 1447, none of the evidence for the whereabouts of our Fernando conflicts with his hypothetical presence at Bologna as a student at the Spanish College.[26] Having Fernando resident in Bologna would explain why in November 1445, in France, he claimed to have been already "on embassy" in Italy for two years.[27] Yet, the identification has its problems. For one, in 1447–

---

[21] In a letter of 15 June 1446, Giacomo Bracelli reported: "Sepe illi [*i.e.,* Fernando] Augustinus in ore est, sed Thome Scotique et quem magistrum sententiarum vocant tanta familiaritas tamque expedita recitatio ut non tam meminisse quam legere videretur." Bracelli's letter was first published in full by Resta, 278–80; and then by Balbi, 58–62.

[22] See Appendix 6B, §§ 64–65.

[23] For the establishment of Scotism in Spain see Vásquez, esp. 201–03 and 207 for Salamanca; cf. also Andres, 19ff., esp. 23–25.

[24] See Appendix 3.

[25] Dallari, 1:24, under the rubric *Lecture Universitatis:* "Lecture Universitatis / Ad lecturam Medicine / M. Fernandus de Corduba."

[26] The six documents in Appendix 3 place Fernandus de Medina in Bologna in December 1442, September 1443, September 1445, and September 1446. We can place our Fernando at Naples in July 1444, in France in November–December 1445, and in Genoa and Siena in June–July 1446.

[27] According to the letter to the chancellor of Brabant (Havet, 337; Bonilla y San Martín, 60n.): "Ez sein auch ieczo zwai jar vergangen, daz er schied von Hysponia, als er dann gesent was von dem chünig von Castell und ieczo gebesen in obern Walschen landen, und hat geantburt offenperlich nachet in allen uni-

1448, when "Fernando de Corduba" was supposed to teach medicine at
Bologna, our Fernando was in Germany as a member of the entourage
of the papal legate, Cardinal Juan Carvajal (see the following chapter).
For another, it is difficult to square Fernando's claim in November 1445
to have been on embassy in Italy for two years with the fact that Fernandus de Medina had been at the Spanish College at least since late
1442. On the other hand, Fernando's claim in late 1445 of having spent
two years on embassy in Italy also contradicts his assertion to Valla in July
1444 that he was newly arrived from Spain. Obviously, we should take
Fernando's assertions *cum grano salis.* But if he was telling the truth in
1445 and had spent the previous several years in Italy as he told the
French (what would he gain from lying?), residency at the Spanish College would certainly provide a good explanation of what he was doing
there.

If our Fernando is Fernandus de Medina—and I advance this identification merely as a possibility awaiting verification or elimination—then I
should also note that the only Medina I could locate in the diocese of
Cordova is Medina Azzahra, the site of the ruins of a Moslem palace
about ten kilometers from Cordova.[28] That is close enough for someone
to be called "de Corduba"; but in fact "de Medina" may simply be a
patronymic.[29]

At one point or another the sources of the 1440s call Fernando a master
or doctor in each of the four medieval university faculties. The title which
he himself consistently used was "doctor of theology." According to a
report from Siena in 1446, he "received the doctorate in arts when he
was in his tenth year [i.e., when he was nine years old], the doctorate in "the sacred page" in his thirteenth year [i.e., when twelve years
old], the doctorate in medicine in his fifteenth year [i.e., when fourteen

versiteten oder hochen schulen." Havet's translation and note are useful (313):
"Il y a maintenant deux ans passés qu'il est parti d'Espagne, envoyé par le roi
de Castille; il a été dans les hauts pays welches,[1] oú il a répondu publiquement
dans presque toutes les universités ou hautes écoles [[1] «In obern Walschen
landen.» Le nom de *Wälsch* en allemand s'applique tantôt à tous les peuples de
langue romane, Français, Italiens, etc., tantôt aux Italiens en particulier]." Cf.
Grimm, 13.1:1327ff., esp. 1331–35.

[28] Perhaps because of the difficulty of finding a Medina in the diocese, Piana
changed the name to Metina (see the reference to the index of Piana [1966] in
Appendix 2); but I do not see how this solves the problem. No Metina existed,
as far as I know, in the diocese of Cordova. "Metina" is only a medieval Latin
variant of Medina in any case.

[29] Concerning his lineage, one report calls him a "militis filius" (Delisle, 195;
Bonilla y San Martín, 73 n. 1), while several sources call him a knight at arms
(see n. 49 below). In each of the lower corners of his sepulchral monument (see
Appendix 11) an angelic *putto* holds a coat of arms which consists of an eagle
spread-wing with its head in left profile. Two diagonal lines, each running from
the top of one wing to the bottom tip of the other wing, cross in the middle of
the eagle to form a cross of St. Andrew spanning the whole eagle. At each of the
four extremities of this cross is another small cross of St. Andrew formed by the
addition of a small diagonal.

years old], [and] in his twentieth he was dubbed a knight by the King of England."[30] Even though it omits mention of a degree in law,[31] the chronology reflected in the Sienese report must have left Fernando's audience flabbergasted—just as Fernando intended it to do. It certainly violates by large margins the common medieval statutes on the minimum age for the different university degrees.[32] Even if we discount these ages as just more braggadocio from Fernando about his precocity, the fact remains that the papal court accepted Fernando as a doctor of theology and, if he is Fernandus de Medina, that the University of Bologna recognized his medical degree since it hired him to teach medicine in 1447–1448. A Masters of Arts was, of course, a prerequisite for either of these degrees. Only Fernando's law degree lacks some kind of external corroboration, but since he successfully debated doctors of law at Naples in 1444 and Siena in 1446, he obviously had competence in the discipline by the early 1440s. The Sienese report makes it clear that Fernando claimed to have achieved these degrees before coming to Italy. Since he said he was nineteen years old when he spoke in Siena and fourteen when he received his last degree (in medicine), he therefore claimed to have gained this last degree in 1441.

Returning to Fernando's arrival in Naples in 1444, we need to consider another source besides Valla's letter, namely, the Aragonese *cedole della Tesoreria*. These registers were destroyed in World War II; but even before the Germans blew up the Neapolitan Archivio di Stato, Camillo Minieri Riccio's misleading summary of one *cedola* had already caused considerable mischief[33]:

In questo mese di settembre [*the register is for the year 1444*] viene di Spagna maestro Ferrando de Cordova, maestro in arti ed in teologia, e re Alfonso lo riceve nella corte in qualità di suo confessore e gli fa pagare una pensione di ducati 50, e nello stesso tempo altri ducati 18 per comprarsi due libri di teologia.

Accepting this notice at face value, scholars have not flinched from the implausibility of King Alfonso of Aragon selecting the freshly arrived young Castilian as his confessor.[34] Yet Valla never hinted that Fernando was a priest. A subdeacon could be a doctor of theology,[35] and that, in fact, is the highest ecclesiastical title we can document for Fernando,[36]

---

[30] See Appendix 4.

[31] He had already claimed a degree in both laws, i.e., Roman and Canon law when traveling in France in the previous year; see *infra*.

[32] See Rashdall, 1:247, 303, 462, 472, 474.

[33] Minieri Riccio, 245 (= 53 in the offprint I used), combining two items found on ff. 48v and 56v respectively of vol. 8 of the *Cedole di Tesoreria*.

[34] For example, Morel-Fatio, 530; Bonilla y San Martín, 53; Croce, 92–93; Soria, 39–40; and Ryder, 83–84.

[35] Rashdall, 1:479 n. 1.

[36] I have no firm evidence that Fernando was a subdeacon in 1444; but see below for his appointment as a papal subdeacon in the 1460s. In 1312 Clement V set eighteen years completed as the minimum age for a subdeacon; see Naz, 1076. If born in 1422, Fernando would have been twenty-one or twenty-two years old when Valla met him.

though it is very probable that in subsequent years he did become a priest.[37] Fortunately, before the destruction of the Aragonese *cedole della Tesoreria*, Alfredo Mauro discovered that the relevant text actually ran as follows:[38] "Item doni a mestre Ferrando de Cordova, maestre en arts e en theologia, novament vengut al senyor Rey dels parts de Spanya L duc., los quals lo dit senyor graciosament li mana dar etc." In other words, the *cedola* records *only* that King Alfonso gave Fernando of Cordova, a doctor of arts and a master of theology, freshly arrived from Spain, a gift of 50 ducats. Mauro also correctly distinguished our Fernando of Cordova from two other Fernandos: Fernando Valenza, the royal confessor, whom Alfonso wanted to have made a cardinal; and Juan Fernando, a doctor of theology who served Alfonso as an emissary to the papal court.[39] The *cedola* published by Mauro confirms that Fernando visited Naples in 1444 and that Valla's letter of recommendation had good effect. The *cedola* also corroborates Valla's report that Fernando claimed to have come directly from Spain, though the next year in France he asserted that he had lived in Italy the previous two years. It is also worth noting that neither Valla nor the *cedola* speak of Fernando as representing King Juan II of Castile, which is what he claimed to have been doing the next year in France. Perhaps he had received some kind of recommendation from the Castilian king, but it is hard to believe that his story about representing the king was anything other than another one of his exaggerations.

According to Poggio Bracciolini, Fernando reciprocated Valla's support in 1444 by rescuing him from the Inquisition.[40] Since the inquisitional proceedings against Valla in Naples are generally dated to the spring of 1444,[41] either Poggio's report is inaccurate or Valla's run-in with the Inquisition needs to be dated to the summer of 1444 or later.[42] Valla himself was ambiguous when he responded to Poggio's assertion. He said that either Fernando was an ingrate and not the friend he claimed to be

---

[37] In doc. 7 of Appendix 2, Fernando received a Spanish benefice because the previous holder did not become a priest within the specified time. The presumption therefore is that Fernando already satisfied this requirement.

[38] Mauro, 28n., where he quotes from f. 48v of vol. 8.

[39] Ibid., 22ff. (Valenza is the "Ferrando Catelano" whose life is found in Vespasiano da Bisticci's *Vite*). Ryder, 83–84, confuses the three Fernandos, but does give new information concerning them.

[40] Bracciolini, 1:251: "Scis te iam Neapoli ignis periculum tanquam haereticum adisse. Scis te opera doctissimi viri Vernandi [*sic*] Corduben., cui in hoc malas habeo gratias, ab eo discrimine liberatum" (*Invectiva V*, reprinted from the Basel, 1538 *Opera*); and 2:874: "qui primum Neapoli ignis periculum adiit . . ., sed intercessione doctissimi viri Ferrandi Cordubensis ab ea poena fuisse ademptum" (*Invectiva IV*, ed. Fubini).

[41] Mancini, 193; Fois, 366 and 377. See also Zippel.

[42] I know no document fixing Fernando's whereabouts between July 1444 in Naples and November 1445 in France unless we place him in Bologna as Fernandus de Medina.

or Poggio lied when he said Fernando spoke against him;[43] but he did not deny that Fernando was in Naples at the time of his difficulties with the Inquisition.

Whatever were Fernando's activities in Naples, by late 1445 he had embarked on a trip to northern Europe. He was ostensibly on a diplomatic mission for King Juan II of Castile,[44] but all the sources concentrate on his amazing displays of erudition and manual dexterity. Indeed, the repertoire of accomplishments he now claimed quite exceeded the already daunting list we have from Valla in Naples the previous year. In addition to asserting a mastery of the whole medieval university curriculum[45] as well as Arabic, Hebrew, and Aramaic,[46] Fernando also vaunted his abilities in Latin and Greek.[47] And there was more. Arriving at the

<hr />

[43] Valla, *In Poggium Antidotum IV*, in Valla (1962), 1:342: "Quare tibi nec de Ferdinando Cordubensi respondeo, qui si tecum de me, quem ait sibi amicum et de se bene meritum, male loquitur, ingratus est nec officio probi viri fungitur; sin verum amicum agit, tu potius ementitus es."

[44] See n. 27 above and the report of the student of St. Bernard in Paris (Delisle, 195; Bonilla y San Martín, 73 n. 1): ". . . quia missus a suo principe visere patriam et principes." The letter to the chancellor of Brabant (Havet, 337; Bonilla y San Martín, 60n) further asserts that Fernando wrote a letter to the French king urging the maintenance of peace.

[45] The student of St. Bernard: "Est enim in artibus liberalibus subtilissimus magister ita ut parem in discuciendo rationes profundissimas artis dyaletice et phisice super terram non repererit. . . . Non est inventus in geometria ei similis. . . . Et quid de aritmetica et astrologia proferam? . . . In utroque iure, scilicet, civili et canonico, sed et in medicina doctor est precipuus. Postremo in sacra pagina doctor eximius existens . . ." (Delisle, 194; Bonilla y San Martín, 73 n. 1); Matheiu d'Escouchy: "docteur en theologie et medecine, en loix et en decret" (Havet, 316; Bonilla y San Martín, 66 n. 1); the *Bourgeois de Paris*: "il est maistre en ars, maistre en medecine, docteur en loix, docteur en decret, docteur en theologie" (Havet, 318; Bonilla y San Martín, 64 n. 1); the register of Châlons-sur-Marne: "maistre en ars, docteur en loys et en decret, docteur en theologie, docteur en medecine, astrologien" (Havet, 320; Bonilla y San Martín, 58–59 n. 2); and the letter to the chancellor of Brabant: "maister in den freien künsten, lerer in geistlichen und weltlichen rechten, maister in der erznei und lerer in der heiligen gescrift" (Havet, 336; Bonilla y San Martín, 60n.).

[46] The letter to the chancellor of Brabant: "Er chan auch fünf sprach screiben, lesen, und reden, daz hist Lateinisch, Hebraisch, Kriechish, Caldaish, Arabish, und ist gebesen in miner kamer und hat die benenten sprach gescriben . . ." (Havet, 337; Bonilla y San Martín, 60n.); the register of Châlons-sur-Marne: "parlant grec, ebreu, caldeen et latin et françois" (Havet, 320; Bonilla y San Martín 58–59 n. 2); and the *Bourgeois de Paris*: "Il parle latin trop subtil, grec, ebreu, caldicque, arabicque et tous autres langaiges" (Havet, 318; Bonilla y San Martín, 64 n. 1).

[47] For his Greek and "latin trop subtil" see the previous note. For Latin also see the student of St. Bernard: "poeta et grammaticus excellentissimus extitit, adeo ut grammaticam septem dierum spacio evoluto perlustraverit et retinuerit . . . floribus rethorice et verborum vetustate adornatus, michi experto credatis, ita ut laurea meretur coronari et extolli" (Delisle, 194; Bonilla y San Martín, 73 n. 1); the letter to the chancellor of Brabant: ". . . chan er ganz . . . die ganzen rethoricam, daz ist die kunst von hoeflichait der red . . . spricht auch selbs, daz er in der jugent in siben tagen gelernet hab daz Doctrinal Allexander, daz er auch

court of King Charles VII of France with a train of eight horses, he answered successfully all the questions put to him concerning "knightly arts and works."[48] And to show that he was a true *chevallier en armes* and not merely a *clerc*, he also gave a terrifying display of his skill with the *espee à deux mains*.[49] Furthermore, he professed expertise in painting,[50] and the ability not merely to play all musical instruments, but also to manufacture them.[51] Rather than Giovanni Pico, Fernando brings to mind Hippias of Elis, the fifth century B.C. Greek Sophist who appeared at Olympia showing off his oratory, singing his poetry, and displaying the clothes made with his own hands.[52]

Report of Fernando's success at the royal court no doubt preceded him

---

noch in gedaechtnusz behelt" (Havet, 337; Bonilla y San Martín, 60n.). The fact that two separate witnesses cited as an example of Fernando's great Latinity his claim that as a child he learned Alexander of Neckham's *Doctrinale* indicates well the difference in Latinity between the Parisian masters and Quattrocento humanists such as Lorenzo Valla. In June 1446, Giacomo Bracelli remarked that in astrology Fernando was "non contentus Latinis codicibus . . . ad Arabicos quoque auctores, quorum etiam nomina nobis inaudita sunt, aliquando confugerit," and in Scripture that he knew not only "quid Catholici sentiant sed que sit insuper Hebreorum interpretatio" (Resta, 280; Bracelli, 61–62); but Bracelli is silent on Fernando's Greek and Latin.

[48] The letter to the chancellor of Brabant (Havet, 337; Bonilla y San Martín, 61n.).

[49] Mathieu d'Escouchy (Havet, 316; Bonilla y San Martín, 66, n. 1); and the *Bourgeois de Paris* (Havet, 318; Bonilla y San Martín, 64 n. 1; and now also available in an English translation: Shirley, 360–62), who tells of his display of martial skills in Paris. The register of Châlons-sur-Marne also called him a "chevalier en armes" (Havet, 320; Bonilla y San Martín, 58, n. 2), while the student of St. Bernard put the name into Latin: "miles extat in armis" (Delisle, 195; Bonilla y San Martín, 73 n. 1). Canon law permitted clerics while traveling to bear arms: "Nulla arma induant clerici nisi itinerantes" (*Decret.* 2, c. 23, q. 8); see Thamiry.

[50] The student of St. Bernard: "Pictor est eciam peroptimus" (Delisle, 195; Bonilla y San Martín, 74n.); and the *Bourgeois de Paris*: "si savoit jouer de tous instrumens, chanter et deschanter mieulx que nul autre, paindre et enluminer mieulx que oncques on sceust a Paris ne ailleurs" (Havet, 318; Bonilla y San Martín, 64 n. 1).

[51] For the *Bourgeois de Paris* see the previous note; the register of Châlons-sur-Marne: "musicien et moult abile" (Havet, 320; Bonilla y San Martín, 59, n. 1 from the previous page); Mathieu d'Escouchy: "se cognoissoit en l'art de musique plus que nul aultre, jouoit de tous instrumens tant bien que nul ne l'en pooit passer, bailloit les raisons et instructions comment ilz se devoient faire" (Havet, 337; Bonilla y San Martín, 66 n. 1); the letter to the chancellor of Brabant: "Er can auch musicam, die kunst des gesanges und seczung der don, und auch nicht alain auf allen saiten spilen und don spilen, sunder er chan si auch darzu machen" (Havet, 337; Bonilla y San Martín, 61n.; and the student of St. Bernard: "Musicus etenim est et omnium instrumentorum ipsius artis expertissimus" (Delisle, 194; Bonilla y San Martín, 73 n. 1).

[52] Plato *Hipp. Min.* 368b ff. Interestingly enough, after he saw Fernando perform in Siena the next year, the humanist Agostino Dati also compared him to the fifth-century Greek Sophists (Dati, f. 10v).

to Paris.[53] When he arrived in the city towards the first week of December, he promptly petitioned the rector of the university for permission to hold a disputation in four days time *de omni scibili*.[54] We have no less than eight separate accounts of the sensation he caused.[55] However, on 9 December 1445 the university voted to have him jailed because despite twice promising to respond *in omnibus scientiis*, Fernando was now asking to be excused on account of illness and the need to reach the court of the Duke of Burgundy before Christmas.[56] In meetings with individual scholars and various groups of the university community, Fernando probably gave demonstrations of his intellectual prowess,[57] and perhaps even encouraged the view that he possessed superhuman powers,[58] not to speak of knowing more than all the university masters combined. He also claimed to have written commentaries on Ptolemy's *Almagest* and much of the Bible, especially the *Apocalypse*.[59] Not without provocation, the university authorities determined to test him. On 11 December, before a great assembly of students and masters in the College of St. Bernard, Fernando was interrogated by the rector of the university about the rumors circulating "in tota villa Parisiensi . . . et in magnum dedecus et vitium totius Universitatis dicta fuissent."[60] Fer-

[53] I am assuming that all these demonstrations of martial skill took place at the royal court rather than at Paris. He doubtless flaunted other accomplishments while at the royal court.

[54] The letter of the student of St. Bernard (Delisle, 194; Bonilla y San Martín, 73 n. 1): ". . . in omni scientia arguere volentibus ultro se offert responsurum, et quod maius est, domino rectori Universitatis Parisiensis supplicuit et supplicari fecit ut quatuor dierum spacio Universitati de quoqunque scibili sibi concederetur respondendi facultas ut virum se ostenderet peritum et profundum."

[55] To wit, (1) the records of the university, (2) the letter to the chancellor of Brabant, (3) the letter of the student of the College of St. Bernard, (4) the *Journal d'un bourgeois de Paris*, (5) the chronicle of Mathieu d'Escouchy, (6) the register of Châlons-sur-Marne, (7) the poem of Georges Chastellain, (8) the account of John Trithemius in the *Chronicon Sponheimense* (ad annum 1501) and in the variant version overlooked by Fernando's biographers, the *Annales Hirsaugienses* (see *infra*).

[56] See Denifle and Chatelain, 2:632–33.

[57] The author of the letter to the chancellor of Brabant speaks of Fernando writing foreign scripts in his presence and of having heard him respond many times to doctors on every kind of subject (Havet, 337; Bonilla y San Martín, 60n.); and the *Bourgeois de Paris* reports that Fernando spoke before several assemblies (see the interpretation of this passage by Havet, 324).

[58] For example, the student of St. Bernard; ". . . mater nostra Universitas istud insolitum et quasi supernaturale in hoc iuvene considerans . . . intra se sillogizans an divinitus aut magice in minima etate constitutus his dotibus insignitus fuerit [*text as corrected by Delisle*]" (Delisle, 195; Bonilla y San Martín, 73–74 n. 1). The letter to the chancellor of Brabant also leaves the impression that such discussions were going on before the meeting of 11 December, with "many saying that he was the Antichrist."

[59] The Parisian correspondent of the Chancellor of Brabant thought the *Almagest* was a book of medicine; see Havet, 313 n. 2 and 337; Bonilla y San Martín, 61: "Er hat auch ieczo gescriben über ain puch in arztei, genant Almagesti Tholomei und über ainen grozzen tail der bibel und gar vil über apocalipsim."

[60] Denifle-Chatelain, 2:633.

nando responded to a series of theological articles as the Parisian masters probed for grounds to charge him with heresy, fraud, or even magic.[61] After he left Paris, an assembly of masters did decide that Fernando's knowledge exceeded human capacities, and that he therefore was either the Antichrist or a disciple of the Antichrist.[62] They also sent the Duke of Burgundy a letter warning him against believing this Spanish *doctor*.[63] But all this occurred after Fernando had taken his leave of Paris. In the assembly of 11 December in St. Bernard, Fernando responded to his questioners so meekly and with such orthodox sentiments that no charge could be laid against him.[64] The university had no choice but to release him, but not before extracting a promise that he would return to debate *in omni facultate* in two months time.[65] He may have returned; but we have no text documenting a second visit.[66]

According to Mathieu d'Escouchy, Fernando achieved an equally brilliant success at the court of Duke Philip the Good in Ghent.[67] D'Escouchy also states that Fernando was not able to continue on from the Burgundian court to England as planned. Instead, according to one report, he turned towards Germany, where he was arrested during Lent at Cologne, for heresy and diabolic possession.[68] Fernando himself claimed to have visited England when he spoke in Genoa in June 1446 and again in Siena in July of the same year.[69]

In the spring of 1446, Fernando turned up in Genoa, claiming to have

---

[61] The student of St. Bernard specifically says that he was questioned "de profundissimis theologie questionibus" (Delisle, 195; Bonilla y San Martín, 74n.); the letter to the chancellor of Brabant speaks of his being questioned concerning "strange and wild statements" (Havet, 337; Bonilla y San Martín, 61n.); but Mathieu d'Escouchy, relating what he heard from an eye-witness, reports that Fernando was examined "sur pluseurs [sic] sciences" (Havet, 316; Bonilla y San Martín, 67n.).

[62] Mathieu d'Escouchy in Havet, 316; and Bonilla y San Martín, 67n.

[63] Samaran-Van Moé, 125.19ff. This letter is the source of the notice which Havet found in Boulay, 5:534. See also Denifle and Chatelain, 2:633.

[64] Denifle-Chatelain, 2:633: "aliqualiter de omnibus se excusavit, et si aliqua ab eo minus bene dicta fuissent, reputavit pro non dictis et satis reverenter loquens se posuit in manibus Universitatis in omnibus corrigendis." According to the letter to the chancellor of Brabant, he humbly excused himself by claiming to be an "ignorant child" ("und nennet sich albeg ein ungelercz kind"; Havet, 338; Bonilla y San Martín, 61n.).

[65] The letter to the chancellor of Brabant (ibid.); and the university register in Denifle and Chatelain, 2:633.

[66] If Fernando subsequently went to England (see *infra*), then a stop at Paris on the way back would have been possible.

[67] See Havet, 317; and Bonilla y San Martín, 67n. Havet, 327, points out that Georges Chastellain must have seen Fernando at Ghent.

[68] The register of Châlons-sur-Marne (Havet, 320; Bonilla y San Martín, 59 n. 1 from the previous page).

[69] For the Siena report see Appendix 4. The Genoese report (see the next note) adds a further complication in that it has Fernando visiting England and Germany *before* going to France and then Italy. Since we can prove he was in Italy before France, the sequence in the Genoese report remains suspect.

already traversed England, Germany, and France, and to have also won fame as a disputant in Padua, Venice, and Milan.[70] On 6 June 1446 he gave a virtuoso performance disputing against all comers on twenty-eight questions concerning the arts, medicine, theology, and philosophy.[71] The Genoese chancellor, Giacomo Bracelli, immediately afterwards wrote a letter extolling Fernando's achievement.[72] On the other hand, another humanist in Genoa, Antonio Cassarino, wrote a letter to a friend expressing nothing but disgust at the praise the Genoese had lavished upon this pompous *barbarusculus*.[73]

From Genoa Fernando traveled southward to Siena, where, on 21 July 1446, he held a disputation in the cathedral *in quovis doctrinarum genere sibi fuissent proposita* and bested the town's "canonists, jurists, medical doctors, humanists (*doctores eloquentiae*), mathematicians, and theologians."[74] The next day the Sienese jurist Mariano Sozzini declared in a

---

[70] Letter of Giacomo Bracelli, 15 June 1446: "Adolescens quidam Ferdinandus nomine, civis Cordubensis, vixdum vicesimum annum egressus, peragrata Britannia ac Germania in Gallias primum, deinde in Italiam venit; nullaque fuit aut celebris schola aut urbs illustrior in qua non aliquod insigne disputationis certamen ediderit. Cum Patavii, Venetiis, Mediolani magnum nomen iam sibi comparasset, Genuam venit . . ." (Resta, 279; Balbi, 59).

[71] The letter of Bracelli: "Octo et viginti questiones preposite illi sunt, quarum etsi pars maxima ad medicinalem et theologicam materiam pertinebat, non arithmetica tamen aut geometria vel astrologia pretermissa . . . Cum ad phisica transitum est, Aristotiles, Averrois, Albertus pari promptitudine in medium afferebantur" (Resta, 279–80; Balbi, 59–60). Bracelli also voiced amazement at Fernando's memory.

[72] Resta, 278–80; Balbi, 58–62.

[73] Dated 11 June 1446 and addressed to Iacopo Curlo, the humanist and calligrapher at Naples. Cassarino's letter was first edited by Sabbadini ("Note," 1891), 302–05; and is best read today in Resta, 281–83. Cassarino apparently did not know that Fernando had already been to Naples.

[74] A. Dati, *De Immortalitate Animi*, Bk. 7, in Dati, f. 10v (to standardize the spelling and to approximate more closely Dati's probable usage, I have silently changed "ae" diphthongs to "e"): "Ferdinandus Cordubensis superioribus annis, vir magno ingenio et omnium disciplinarum eruditione apprime instructus et Hispanus nequaquam indisertus more quo<n>dam Leontini Gorgie ac veterum sophistarum, in nostre urbis fano eo, quod, ut plerique sentiunt, C<h>ristianorum omnium templa superat, aliquando sese ad omnia responsurum professus est quecunque in quovis doctrinarum genere sibi fuissent proposita. Aderant iuris pontificii, legalis prudentie, medicine, eloquentie, mathematice institutionis, divine quoque sapientie doctores ac professores percelebres. Varia ac longior multis de rebus habita disputatio est. Et cum plerosque in disputando concertatores superasse videretur ut quasi inferiores terga darent, postremo Petro Russio, nostri etatis philosophorum ac theologorum facile principe, cum in mentionem rationalis anime ventum esset, disserente, discessit tandem nequaquam superior. Sed cum multa et subtiliter explicuisset et dixisset, composite illud absurdius affirmare ausus est, nunquam Aristotelem Peripateticum preterquam in Metaphysicis libris idque uno tantum loco [*Metaph* 12.1070a25ff.] animi immortalitatem asseruisse, quasi vero philosophorum omnium pene summo id aut obscurum aut ambiguum foret, quod qui ignorat, non modo philosophus habendus non est, sed et turpiter ab eruditis omnibus irridendus, quod, scito,

lecture at the University of Siena that Fernando, *vir potius divinus quam humanus*, had disputed *per integram diem*.[75] According to the Sienese humanist Agostino Dati, only the Sienese biblical scholar and Aristotelian Pietro Rossi was a match for the young Spaniard.[76] More importantly, Dati spent half of his report refuting Fernando's claim in the disputation that Aristotle never asserted the immortality of the soul except once in the *Metaphysics*.[77] Clearly from his first years in Italy, Fernando was critical of Aristotle and shared John Duns Scotus's doubts about Aristotle's belief in the immortality of the soul.[78] Though Dati did not expand upon Fernando's argument, I suspect that Fernando had compared Aristotle's virtually non-existent support of the immortality of the soul with Plato's position on the same issue. Fernando so impressed a medical scholar at Siena, one Leonardus, that he recorded details of Fernando's visit in one of his manuscripts, and then acted as a host to him when he returned the following year.[79] Finally, as an expression of their ad-

---

Gorgie, in quo tanta doctrine venditatio erat, magnis de rebus disserenti facile usu venit, refellente illum parente philosophorum Socrate, qui se nihil scire profiteretur, quamquam sapientissimus Apollinis oraculo fuerat comprobatus. Magna mea quidem sententia acutissimo veterum omnium ac doctorum pene doctissimo omnium Aristoteli facit iniuriam quisquis illum asserat tam pauca, tam strictim, tam negligenter ea de re locutum, in qua tum investiganda, tum etiam pronoscenda tanquam gravissima omnium, que quidem in omni philosophia tractantur, precipua sapientis exercitatio sita esse debet. Nam qui vel ignoraverit vel negaverit vel denique dubitaverit manere post mortem animos, is proculdubio hominum vitam prorsum labefactat atque confundit et bonorum ac malorum finem, unde omnis philosophandi ratio pendet, radicitus convellit, funditus evertit. Multa Ferdinandus memoriter atque eleganter. At fugit illius memoriam crebra in plerisque locis de anime immortalitate Aristotelis commemoratio. Et in libris quam Περὶ ψυχῆς, quod est De anima, scripsit, idipsum pensioribus verbis sepius contestatur." Cf. Bandiera, 195–96n.

[75] See Nardi, 72 n. 4, quoting from Sozzini's *Commentaria super Secunda Parte Libri Quinti Decretalium*, c. *Pendimus, De Sententia Excommunicationis*, num. 208, f. 267va of the Parma, 1574 edition: "Hesterna die, 12 Kalen. Augusti huius anni 1446, studio vacare non potui propter egregiam, notabilissimam, et admirandam disputationem quam Ferrandus Cordibensis [*sic*], vir potius divinus quam humanus, a primis litteris usque ad theologiam inclusive per integram diem fecit."

[76] See n. 74 above and Fioravanti (1980), 124. See also Dati, f. 165v, where in reporting Fernando's praise of Rossi, Dati speaks again of Fernando: ". . . Petrus Russius Senensis, vir nobilitate, ingenio, virtute prestans, huius etatis philosophorum facile princeps, et harum denique rerum omnium [*philosophical matters*] optimus quidam censor ac iudex, in hanc nos opinionem [*concerning the doctrine of species*] adduxisset. Huic enim maximam adhiberi fidem cum alia multa cohortata sunt, tum Ferdinandus Cordubensis submonuit, qui in tantum Petro Russio tribuit, audientibus nobis, ut eo plane eruditiorem ac maioris doctrinae attestaretur sese vidisse neminem. Magna hec quidem laus est et a magno quoque viro profecta. Lustravit namque Ferdinandus quasi alter quispiam Apollinis disiunctissimas terrarum regiones quascunque ingeniis hominum et liberalibus disciplinis atque ingenuis artibus florere cognovisset."

[77] See n. 74 above.

[78] See Luger, 32–37, 60–74; Gilson (1952), 485–86; and Poppi, 193–91.

[79] See Appendix 4.

miration, the members of the Sienese Signoria dispatched to King Alfonso of Aragon a glowing recommendation of Fernando, who had said he was proceeding on to Naples.[80]

Whether Fernando went to Naples on this occasion I do not know. Most authorities have him disappearing from public view after 1446 as suddenly as he had entered it in 1444. In the sixteenth century, Trithemius completed his account of Fernando's wonderous *Wanderjahr* by explaining that Fernando then sailed off to Majorca, where he lived as a hermit until his death.[81] More plausibly, Bonilla y San Martín suggested that Fernando remained in Italy until he reappeared again in the late 1460s.[82] He was right.

---

[80] See Appendix 5.

[81] Trithemius (1601), 2:585–86, *ad annum* 1501: "Contempsit autem post annos paucos omnem scientiam huius mundi et pro Christi amore saeculo valedicens ad insulam navigavit Maioricam, factusque eremita solitarius omnipotenti deo usque ad mortem in sancto proposito servivit . . . Eius fuit discipulus et omnium haeres voluminum Libanius Gallus, omnium huius tempestatis doctorum quos noverim facile doctissimus." I owe this reference to the kindness of Prof. Paola Zambelli, who considers "Gallus" to be a fiction of Trithemius. It is the addition of this tale about Fernando's later life that is the only significant difference between the account in the *Annales Hirsaugienses* and that in the *Chronicon Sponheimense* used by previous students of Fernando (in Trithemius [1601], 2:415).

[82] Bonilla y San Martín, 80.

IN THE ENTOURAGE OF
CARDINAL JUAN CARVAJAL

In documenting Fernando's appearance at the University of Paris in 1444, Denifle and Chatelain called attention to two supplications in the Vatican archives.[83] In the first, dated 13 January 1442 and addressed to Pope Eugenius IV, one "Fernandus Alfonsi," cleric of Cordova, supplicates for the confirmation of certain benefices in the dioceses of Cordova and Seville, for which he had earlier litigated at the Roman Curia.[84] "Fernandus Alfonsi" is not credited with any academic title and is not characterized in any way which would force us to identify him with our Fernando. However, our Fernando is unquestionably the "Fernandus de Cordoa [sic], magister in sacra theologia" of the second supplication.[85] This document carries the date 1 February 1448 and asks Pope Nicholas V to grant Fernando and his procurators special privileges in suing for benefices at the papal court. It also describes Fernando as presently resident in Germany in the service of the papal legate, Cardinal Juan Carvajal. This last bit of information proves that the supplication concerns our Fernando. Leonardus of Siena, one of our sources for Fernando's disputation at Siena in 1446, tells us that Fernando stayed in Siena—indeed, as a guest in Leonardo's house—on 20 September 1447 as part of the entourage of the papal legate to Germany, Cardinal Juan Carvajal. The papal registers also record two papal letters of September 1449 granting Fernando expectatives and benefices, the first of which gave him the same legal standing as a member of the papal household (*familia* in Latin).[86] By the late 1440s, Fernando had become a denizen of the papal court.

Fernando apparently owed this transformation to his acceptance into the *familia* of his fellow Spaniard, Cardinal Juan Carvajal in 1446 or 1447. We know of this relationship only because Carvajal took Fernando along with him during his legation to Germany and Hungary from September 1447 to the spring of 1449.[87] As we have seen, Leonardo in Siena noted

---

[83] Denifle and Chatelain, 2:632 n. 5; cf. Bonilla y San Martín, 46.

[84] ASV, Suppl. 379 (olim 372), f. 127v. I wish to thank Dr. Concetta Bianca for sending me a transcription.

[85] See Appendix 2, doc. 1.

[86] See Appendix 2, docs. 2 and 3.

[87] It is this period with Carvajal that creates the largest stumbling block to identifying our Fernando with the Fernando of Cordova at the Spanish College in Bologna who was scheduled to teach medicine at the university in the academic year 1447–1448. The roster of teachers for 1447–1448 edited by Dallari (1:24) is dated 9 October 1447 (1:24) and the academic year at Bologna began on

his presence in the cardinal's entourage. But we have much richer evidence from the north.

Doubtless from what Fernando himself told him, Juan de Lucena relates in his *Dialogus de Felicitate* how Fernando impressed the Holy Roman Emperor:

Frederick, King of Hungary, thus honored the educated: one day when he heard that most distinguished youth Fernando of Cordova dispute and since he marveled that a twenty-year old had mastered so much learning, he had him paint his portrait, and every time that he entered Fernando's room he raised his cap to him as to Apollo's oracle.[88]

No example of Fernando's paintings survive, but we have the theses which he argued at the University of Vienna in September 1448. According to the *Acta* of the theological faculty, Fernando wanted to give his usual performance disputing *de omni scibili* against all comers almost as soon as he arrived in Vienna in the fall of 1447.[89] We have seen that he enrolled in the Rhenish nation at the university in October 1447. Probably because he was a member of Cardinal Legate's *familia* and perhaps because he was accepted as already a doctor of theology, he did not have to pay the customary tax for this privilege.[90] Fernando made the offer to dispute on 7 November 1447, having already gained the support of Emperor Frederick and Cardinal Carvajal for the event.[91] Despite this

---

18 October (Dallari, 1:viii), at which time our Fernando was demonstrably in Vienna. One can conceive of three possible, but doubtful scenarios that would save the identification of the two Fernandos: first, that the roster is wrong and that Fernando never taught in 1447-1448; second, that the Fernando of the Spanish College was not the Fernando of the Bolognese teaching roster; and, last, that our Fernando made a commitment to teach at Bologna when Carvajal's entourage passed through the city in September and that he returned to Bologna later in 1447 having failed to hold a disputation at Vienna in November 1447. (The next notice I have of Fernando in Vienna is not until August of 1448, though on 1 February 1448 the Vatican believed him to be in Germany; see Appendix 2, doc. 1.)

[88] Edited in Paz y Mélia, 102: "Federico, Rey de Hungaria, así honró los letrados que oyendo un dí disputar á Fernando Cordubés, jouen claríssimo, maravillado que la edat veyntenaria inglutiese tanta sciencia, lo fizo pintar en su sala de cada vez que intrava, alçava el capello aś como al oráculo de Apolo."

Since Lucena completed the work in 1463, as proved by his letter of dedication, he probably heard the story from Fernando himself. The fact that Emperor Frederick III is said to have called Fernando a twenty-year old confirms that the date of the episode was 1447-1448 and not some time later.

[89] See Uiblein, 1:228-29.

[90] See note 19, page 5.

[91] Uiblein, 1:228-29: "(1447 November 7) Item in crastino Leonardi congregata fuit facultas super hoc articulo: Ad audiendum desiderium cuiusdam qui a facultate petit aliquid iuxta mandatum domini regis ut asserit . . . qui tandem adiecit, quod de informacione sua forte in tantum sibi non esset necessarium, sed quod dominus rex sibi demandasset, qui et cum domino legato interesse vellet. Item desideravit idem, quod questio sibi assignaretur per facultatem quecumque vel si placeret facultati ipse recipere vellet materiam, quam magistri

support and even though Fernando claimed that Paris and other universities had permitted him such a display,[92] the theological faculty of
Vienna insisted that he could only argue on theology and that he must
submit his propositions for approval to them beforehand, after which
they would assign one of their number to respond to him.[93] Fernando
demurred and the disputation did not take place. However, the next
year, in August 1448, he did agree to these terms[94] and committed himself to disputing on a theological question on Monday, 16 September.[95]
He published his theses, but when the appointed day approached he
asked for and received a postponement until Thursday, 19 September.[96]
Emperor Frederick, nobles, and several bishops were among the dignitaries who attended on 19 September.[97] Such display disputations by
foreign visitors were not new to the University of Vienna. The humanist
Enea Silvio Piccolomini held one there three years earlier before the
assembled masters and the high nobility, including Emperor Frederick
and Duke Sigismund.[98] In any event, on 20 September 1448, the day
after Fernando spoke, the assigned respondent, Georg Tudel of Giengen,
a *bacchalarius formatus* in theology, gave his answer, and though Cardinal
Carvajal actively joined in the debate on Fernando's side, Georg Tudel
refuted Fernando good and proper—at least that is how the acts of the
Viennese theology faculty recorded the affair.[99]

Fernando was supposed to stick to theology. Nonetheless he violated
the agreement and proposed six classes of propositions dealing with
theology, metaphysics, physics, ethics, logic, and sophistic. As the acts
of the theological faculty put it: "[Fernando] mixed into his proposal
many things which are unknown and rare in our schools as well as other

---

in theologia iam pre manibus haberent in scolis legenda. Item quia varii ad talem
actum veniunt arguentes, desideravit, quod responderet sic, ut poneret conclusiones in omni facultate, ita quod quilibet haberet materiam sue facultatis, in qua
posset replicare."

[92] Uiblein, 1:229: "quia in aliis universitatibus et precipue Parisiensi ille
modus respondendi sibi admissus esset. . . ."

[93] Uiblein, 1:229.

[94] Uiblein, 1:230.

[95] See Appendix 6A, § 4; the acts of the theology faculty in Uiblein do not
report this earlier agreement.

[96] Appendix 6A, § 4.

[97] Uiblein, 1:231.

[98] We do not have the text of Piccolomini's arguments but rather of his respondent, Hermannus Edlawer, which has been edited by Lhotsky, 263–73; see
also ibid., 139–40.

[99] On Tudel see Aschbach, 1:526–27; and Uiblein, 2:645–46; he is also mentioned in an excerpt from the *Acta facultatis artium* dealing with a university legation of February 1464 published by Kink, 1.2:100. On Georg Tudel's success
against Fernando and Carvajal see Uiblein, 1:231: "racionibus et autoritatibus for-
tibus dicta improbavit Fernandi, cui Georgio dominus cardinalis arguit et conse-
quenter magister Fernandus, qui tamen nihil evicit aut probavit, magistro
Georgio formalibus responsionibus resistente, et sic actus fuit conclusus cum
magno honore universitatis et facultaltis theologice etc."

irrelevancies from the arts [*i.e., from subjects in the arts curriculum*]."[100]
Four-fifths of what he had to say, however, did concern theology.[101] His
respondent, Georg Tudel, made sure to answer him only on this part of
his propositions.[102]

Fernando argued that Christ—not only as the divine word, but also
as a human being—achieved the *summum bene essendi gradum*, which I
take to mean that Christ as a man achieved the supreme level of
grace.[103] That Christ had achieved the supreme level, or grade, of grace,
such that it could not be increased by God's absolute power, was a traditional tenet of Scotist theology.[104] Fernando's *Propositiones*, in fact,
resonate with Scotist themes and arguments. Like Scotus, Fernando
denied that the Word was the act of the intellect of the Father,[105] while
insisting, in Augustinian terms repeated by Scotus, that the Son was the
supreme art or product of the Father.[106] He further sounded the Scotist
theme of the eternal filiation of Christ.[107] Finally, he agreed with Scotus
that persons of the Trinity existed on the basis of *absoluta*, not *relativa*.[108]
As a sop to the Ockhamists in the audience, Fernando said he agreed
with the *Venerabilis Magister* that to be accepted by God we need no other
grace than the charity which is the Holy Spirit.[109] Since Fernando knew
this opinion of Ockham from the latter's commentary on the *Sentences*,
he also knew and therefore implicitly rejected Ockham's criticism in the
same work of Scotus's arguments concerning the *summa gratia* of Christ
as a derogation of God's absolute power.[110] Indeed, in the metaphysical

---

[100] Uiblein, 1:230: "Immiscuit autem sue positioni plura difficilia abolita et
inconsueta in scolis nostris et aliqua impertinencia ex artibus etc."

[101] See Appendix 6B; 58 of its 89 sections are in its first part on theology.

[102] For Tudel's text see the manuscript descriptions in the introduction to
Appendix 6.

[103] See especially § 60 which is a gloss on § 1; see also Uiblein, 1:230: "Et sic
feria quinta ante Mathei determinavit hanc questionem: Utrum Christum sive ut
patris sive ut humanam naturam suppositantem summum bene essendi gradum
per caritatem consequi posse sit affirmandum."

[104] See John Duns Scotus, *Opus Oxoniense*, 3, d. 13, qq. 1–4 (in Duns Scotus,
14:447–53); Minges, 2:359–60; and Costa.

[105] See Appendix 6B, §§ 3, 11, 12, 26; see John Duns Scotus, *Reportata Parisiensia*, Prolog., q. 1 (Duns Scotus, 22:23–24); *Opus Oxon.*, 1, d. 11, q. 1 (Duns
Scotus, 10:826); Minges, 2:192–93; and Wetter, 358–88.

[106] See Appendix 6B, §§ 20, 37–40; John Duns Scotus, *Report. Paris.*, Prol.,
q. 1 (Duns Scotus, 22:23–24).

[107] See Appendix 6B, § 54; Minges, 2:346–37; and Manteau-Bonamy, 131–61.

[108] We cannot assume that the Viennese masters were uniformly hostile to
Duns Scotus; there was a tradition of favorable interest, especially in his Mario-
logy; see Binder, who concludes (760): "Die angeführten Theologen der mittelalterlichen Universität Wien waren keine reinen Thomisten oder Nominalisten,
auch keine ausgesprochenen Scotisten, sondern mehr oder weniger Eklekiter."

[109] Appendix 6B, § 41; John Duns Scotus, *Opus Oxon.*, 1, d. 26 (Duns Scotus,
10:291–354); Minges, 2:225–30; and Wetter, 287–95.

[110] Appendix 6B, §§ 64–65; and William of Ockham, *Scriptum in librum
primum Sententiarum. Ordinatio*, 1, d. 17, q. 1 (= William of Ockham, 3:440–66).

propositions, Fernando threw down the gauntlet to the nominalists by embracing the realist view that the universals existed outside our minds.[111] He also criticized those whom he called the *terministae* for the way they treated God's essence and existence.[112]

Although they are inadequate for drawing any firm conclusions, two of Fernando's metaphysical propositions seem to reflect Thomist influences.[113] They contend that God's quidity (*quod est*) is His act of existence (*esse*) and that this identity of *quod est* and *esse* does not hold in creatures.[114]

Fernando criticized Plato twice: first, in the physical propositions, for saying that after death human souls return to suitable planets[115]; and then, in the ethical propositions, for wanting to expel poets from his ideal commonwealth.[116] Rather than reflecting hostility toward Plato, the inclusion of these two propositions demonstrates a special interest in him.[117] I doubt that either of these opinions of Plato was of much concern to the scholastics at Vienna in 1448. Most probably Fernando brought them up because he wanted to parade before the collected dignitaries his "knowledge" of Plato.

We do not have the text of Fernando's disputation to see how he argued his *Propositiones* in detail. But the propositions themselves further confirm that Fernando came out of a realist, "Platonizing" tradition sympathetic to Scotism.[118]

What else Fernando did in the north I do not know, but we have no reason to doubt that he returned with Carvajal to the papal court in the spring of 1449, when Pope Nicholas V was in Spoleto.[119] It was surely no accident that in September 1449 we find Fernando at the Curia actively pursuing benefices.[120]

---

[111] William of Ockham, *Scriptum in Librum Primum Sententiarum. Ordinatio*, 1, d. 17, q. 8, "Utrum sit dare summam caritatem cui repugnet augmentari" (William of Ockham, 3:546–68), where Ockham quotes and refutes (547, 558–65) the *quaestio* of Duns Scotus cited in n. 104 above. Ockham denied that God could create a charity that which He could not make greater, i.e., a supreme grade (e.g., ibid., 557–558); but, as Adams, 2:739, notes, he did concede (William of Ockham, 3:567) that *de potentia dei ordinata* there was no charity greater than Christ's.

[112] Appendix 6B, § 71.

[113] Appendix 6B, §§ 68 and 70.

[114] See the handy survey of medieval discussions of essence and existence in Wippel, 392–407.

[115] Appendix 6B, § 70.

[116] Appendix 6B, § 75.

[117] Similarly, his passing criticism of St. Bonaventure and John of Ripa (Appendix 6B, § 42) belies the fact that he knew these authors well and was himself a representative of the same Franciscan Platonizing tradition of which they were members.

[118] Another characteristic which the Viennese propositions reveal is Fernando's sloppiness in citing his authorities (cf. his citations of Aristotle and Augustine *passim*), concerning which trait see *infra*.

[119] Gómez Canedo, 125.

[120] See Appendix 2, docs. 2 and 3.

IN THE SERVICE OF
CARDINAL BESSARION

By the late 1440s, Fernando was well known in curial circles. In his invectives against Valla in 1452, Poggio Bracciolini referred to Fernando a number of times.[121] One of the references is especially pertinent here: "Quid loquar de doctissimo ac excellentissimo in artibus liberalibus ac theologia viro Fernando Cordubensi, qui praesens est in Bononiensi curia . . . ?"[122] The *Bononiensis curia* to which Poggio refers can only be that of the papal legate in Bologna, Cardinal Bessarion.[123] Poggio was writing in 1452, but Fernando had to have entered Bessarion's service before the cardinal left for Bologna in early 1450 since that would have been the only way Poggio in Rome would have known that Fernando was serving Bessarion. So Fernando had gone from the household of one cardinal to that of another.

Whether Fernando stayed with Bessarion continually through the 1450s up to his reappearance in the 1460s is a question we cannot answer, though I would suppose that he stayed in Bologna until Bessarion returned to Rome in 1455 at the death of Pope Nicholas V.[124] What we can say is that when he reappeared, in the 1460s, he again showed himself to be a client of Cardinal Bessarion.

Before we can take up the evidence for that relationship, however, we have to proceed through an extraordinary series of papal documents from 1460 to 1463 which show Fernando in Rome seeking benefices in Spain. The first of these documents is the supplication Fernando addressed to Pope Pius II on 6 March 1460 requesting the right to hold incompatible benefices.[125] On 27 October 1460 he did succeed in extracting a new benefice from Pius II.[126] But the real interest of this last document is that it identifies Fernando as a professor of theology at the University of Rome. Since he is not called that again after early 1461,[127] he

---

[121] See n. 40, p. 9.

[122] Poggio Bracciolini, *Invectiva II in L. Vallam*, in Bracciolini, 1:230. The passage continues: ". . . in Bononiensi curia, qui te non solum stultum, indoctum, insanum, sed etiam haereticum iudicat, qui cum tuas iactantias legisset, infinitos in illis errores deprehendit. Tua opuscula adeo laudat ut nullum ex eis esse dicat in quo non aliqua haeresis labes admisceatur."

[123] The most extensive study of Bessarion in Bologna is that of Nasalli Rocca.

[124] For the possibility that Fernando spent some time teaching in Burgos, see the introduction to Appendix 2.

[125] See Appendix 2, doc. 4.

[126] Ibid., doc. 5.

[127] He is called a professor of theology in documents of 16 Dec. 1460 and 31 Jan. 1461 (ibid., docs. 6 and 7), but not in that of 18 August 1461 (ibid., doc. 8).

probably stopped teaching at the university soon after that year. The academic year 1460–1461 may, in fact, have been the only year he taught. Then on 16 December 1460, less than two months after the prior document, Pius allowed Fernando to surrender his claim to certain Spanish benefices in return for a large pension from the new holder of these benefices.[128] The next month, on 31 January 1461, we find Fernando still busily collecting benefices, as he supplicated the pope this time for a parish in Leon.[129] On 18 August 1461, he supplicated for and received benefices in the diocese of Cuenca.[130] He was still in litigation concerning these benefices two years later when, by a letter of 14 July 1463, the pope sanctioned an arrangement whereby Fernando surrendered these benefices in return for a canonry in the cathedral of Cuenca.[131]

This blitz of documents does not mean that Fernando indulged in benefice hunting for only a few years. Rather the documents are the remains of what was probably a fairly constant pursuit which the fortuitous survival of the documents and my ability to identify them have allowed us to follow in detail for the early 1460s. We have already seen a similar succession of papal documents in 1448–1449. Further methodical searches in the Vatican's Archivio Segreto will no doubt produce others, but, at the moment, our best evidence concerning Fernando after the early 1460s are his extant writings.

The earliest of these works is a collection of testimonia in favor of Plato, the *De Laudibus Platonis ex Testimoniis Tum Sacrorum Interpretum, Tum Ethnicorum adversus Quosdam Doctrinam Eius et Vitam Carpere Solitos*,[132] which served as the opening salvo of the campaign of the Bessarion circle against George of Trebizond's anti-Platonic *Comparatio Philosophorum Platonis et Aristotelis*. Fernando addressed the *De Laudibus* to Cardinal Bessarion. The *codex unicus*, MS I 22 of the Biblioteca Vallicelliana, Rome, bears the date 28 January 1467 in its colophon, but this is probably a scribal rather than an authorial colophon. Nonetheless, the date cannot be far distant from the time when Fernando finished the work. Niccolò Palmieri wrote his refutation of the *De Laudibus* as soon as he was charged by the pope to examine it,[133] and he was demonstrably given this order

---

[128] Ibid., doc. 6.

[129] Ibid., doc. 7.

[130] Ibid., doc. 8.

[131] Ibid., doc. 9.

[132] An edition of the *De Laudibus Platonis* will be part of my forthcoming study of the Plato–Aristotle controversy.

[133] In the preface to Pope Paul II, Palmieri speaks of being charged by the pope with examining Fernando's treatise only the day before: "Pridie, beatissime pater, dum ante pedes sanctitatis tue prostratus essem et que gesta sunt contra hereticos impios apud Castrum Polim retulissem, iussit tua sanctitas libellum cuiusdam docti viri ac opinione apud homines non mediocri diligenter percutere . . ." (an edition from the *codex unicus*, Montserrat 882, will appear in the forthcoming study on the Plato–Aristotle controversy); cf. also Monfasani (1976), 217–18.

in the second half of 1466[134] (in any case, he died on 25 October 1467).[135] Moreover, the *codex unicus*, dated 28 January 1467, carries autograph additions which prove that Fernando was closely associated with its preparation and final form.

The sequel to the *De Laudibus* is the lost *De Duabus Philosophiis et Praestantia Philosophiae Platonis supra Aristotelis*. Fernando had completed most, if not all of the *De Duabus Philosophiis* by the first half of 1469. We know this because of another work he wrote in this period, the *De Artificio*, in which Fernando mentions that the *De Duabus Philosophiis* was nearly completed.[136] Since the *De Artificio* addresses Bessarion as the cardinal bishop of S. Sabina, it was not written earlier than 8 October 1468, which is the day Bessarion received this *titulus*.[137] On the other hand, the *De Artificio* cannot be later than August 1469 since it is highly improbable that Fernando would have continued to promise, as he does in the *De Artificio*, a work settling the Plato-Aristotle controversy (i.e., the *De Duabus Philosophiis*) after his patron, Bessarion, had published the *In Calumniatorem Platonis* doing precisely that. Bessarion's work appeared about August 1469.[138] So Fernando completed the *De Artificio* between October 1468 and August 1469, and by that time he had also nearly finished writing the *De Duabus Philosophiis*.

Bessarion did not want Fernando to finish the *De Duabus Philosophiis*. He had initially assigned Fernando the task of collecting Latin *testimonia* (i.e., the material of the *De Laudibus Platonis*) even though Fernando really wanted to write the major Platonic response to George of Trebizond's *Comparatio*.[139] When Fernando persisted in this desire, Bessarion ordered him to leave off the *De Duabus Philosophiis* and to write instead a work that had nothing to do with the controversy, the *De Artificio*.[140] Nonetheless, Fernando finished the *De Duabus Philosophiis*. The 1474 inventory of Bessarion's library records the following item: "Ferandi [*sic*] de comparatione philosophorum, in diversis quinternionibus."[141] The same inventory reports another item, "Ferdinandi in quibus differunt

---

[134] The proceedings against the Fraticelli to which Palmieri referred in the text quoted in the previous note took place over the late summer and autumn of 1466; for literature on this well-known episode, see Monfasani, 1991.

[135] See the note of Palmieri's *famulus*, Andrea Guazzalotti, in MS BAV, Chis. A. IV. 113, ff. 116v–117r; on Palmieri see Monfasani, 1991–1992.

[136] Bonilla y San Martín, v, lin. 22: ". . . ad multam partem eius operis tractationem perduxeram."

[137] Eubel, 2:8.

[138] See Monfasani (1976), 219.

[139] In the preface to the *De Laudibus Platonis*, Fernando remarked that he was putting off the refutation of Trebizond because Bessarion had ordered him to produce the collection of *testimonia*.

[140] Bonilla y San Martín, v, lin. 18ff.: "nam de duabus philosophiis . . . disserentem me subito et cursu suo revocavit voluntas tua, quippe qui iussisti intermittendum esse opus et in artificium omnis et investigandi et inveniendi scibilis calamum esse referendum."

[141] Labowsky, 239, num. 918; see also ibid., p. 119.

Aristoteles et·Plato," which may be a separate fascicle of the same work.[142] Whatever the truth of this supposition, "Ferandi de comparatione philosophorum" does not appear in the subsequent inventories of Bessarion's library and was presumably destroyed after the deposit of the library in Venice. Unfortunately, as was the case for several other writings of Fernando, Bessarion's copy seems to have been the unique copy.

After Bessarion died, Fernando lost interest in the *De Duabus Philosophiis* and the Plato–Aristotle controversy. The deaths in quick succession of both Bessarion and George of Trebizond deprived the controversy of its main protagonists and probably removed any sense of urgency that their associates might have felt in the matter.[143] We have no subsequent references to the *De Duabus Philosophiis*; and none of Fernando's later writings concern themselves with the issues of the *De Duabus Philosophiis*, or, for that matter, of the *De Laudibus Platonis*.

The *De Artificio* preserves most of what we know of the *De Duabus Philosophiis*.[144] But the *De Artificio* is important in its own right. It is, in fact, Fernando's largest extant philosophical work.[145] As its full title reveals, the *De Artificio Omnis et Investigandi et Inveniendi Natura Scibilis* purports to offer *the* method of investigating and discovering everything that is naturally knowable. Probably as far back as the 1440s Fernando believed he possessed such a method. One witness to Fernando's visit to Paris in 1445 implies as much when he states that Fernando offered to debate *de quocunque scibili*[146] and that Fernando *omne scibile luculenter*

---

[142] Labowsky, 238, num. 915 (b). Labowsky, 305, num. 419, suggests that this work is the same as that listed in the inventory of 1543 as "De differentiis quibus Plato ab Aristotile discidet, in papiro." This is not unlikely, but since the inventory does not name the author, it is at least conceivable that this item refers to Pletho's *De Differentiis*. Also, the possibility remains that the *De Differentiis* listed in the two inventories is a work of Fernando distinct from the *De Duabus Philosophiis*. Labowsky, 289, also wonders if this is the work listed as num. 962 in the 1543 inventory: "Ferdinandi Cordubensis opusculum quoddam, in papyro."

[143] See Monfasani (1976), 228–29.

[144] I discuss these hints in the forthcoming study of the Plato–Aristotle controversy.

[145] Bonilla y San Martín edits and analyzes the work. See also the discussion of Carreras y Artau, 2:283–84, 647–49. The dedication copy is the elegant parchment MS Venice, Bibl. Marciana, Zan. lat. 481 (= 1915), which bears Bessarion's coat of arms; see Gasparrini-Leporace and Mioni, 89, num. 92, and tav. 53. This copy is reported in the inventories of the Biblioteca Marciana of 1474 (Labowsky, 234, num. 813), of 1546/47 (ibid., 347), and of c. 1575 (ibid., num. 708); cf. also ibid., 289, num. 950. The other two known manuscripts of the treatise are Vatican, Vat. lat. 3177, a paper codex of 62ff. in a late fifteenth-century hand (see Kristeller [1963–1992], 2:317), and Madrid, Bibl. Nacional, 9250 (see Kristeller [1963–1992], 4:534), from the seventeenth century, upon which Bonilla y San Martín primarily based his edition (see his description, iii n. 1). *Pace* Bonilla y San Martín, at several points the variants of the Marciana manuscript and its copy, the Vaticanus, strike me as clearly preferable to the ones he chose, e.g., at the beginning, iv n. 2; v n. 4; and ix n. 2.

[146] Delisle, 94; Bonilla y San Martín, 73 n. 1.

sapit.[147] These phrases suggest that Fernando had developed his *ars* quite early in Spain under Lullian influences. Fernando attacked Ramon Lull by name in the *De Artificio*,[148] but, as we shall see, his work is much indebted to the Lullian *Ars* for inspiration and content.[149] We have no way of knowing whether, and to what extent, Fernando's *artificium* changed from the 1440s to the 1460s. We should also note that the text of the *De Artificio* is marred to an unusually high degree by inaccuracy in citing authors[150] and by a general carelessness in the final preparation of the text.[151] These traits mar other works of Fernando,[152] and indicate

---

[147] Delisle, 95; Bonilla y San Martín, 74n.

[148] Bonilla y San Martín, vii–ix. Cf. Menéndez y Pelayo, 1:553. For Fernando, Lull "virum hunc laicum mere fuisse et omnium literarum expertem, per humorem malenconicum elevatum habuisse ingenium, quo ubi fundamentis careas eruditionis atque doctrinae et fantastico ingenio coniungas, nihil periculosius esse possit ut in extremos et fidei orthodoxae adversos labaris errores, quod et in eo viro deprehensum est" (Bonilla y San Martín, ix, lin. 7–10).

[149] See *infra*. Indeed, from the sixteenth century onwards Fernando actually had a reputation as an important disseminator of Lullism. This misconception started with Henricus Cornelius Agrippa, who probably based himself on Trithemius. In the preface to his *In Artem Brevem Raymundi Lulli Commentarii*, Agrippa averred (H. A. Agrippa, 2:315): "Notum est Ferdinandum Cordubam Hispanum per cuncta ultra et citra montes gymnasia omnibus studiis hac arte celebratissimum extitisse." The first to contradict this myth was Antonius, 1:324.

[150] For example, at Bonilla y San Martín, vii, lin. 1–4, he cites Alfarabi's *De scientiis* as a letter *ad regem Albohacem de Marruecos* attempting a universal art of knowing. But this work attempts no such thing; and it is not a letter; nor is its addressee or dedicatee known; see Steinschneider, 83–85; on p. xvi, l. 10, he claims to be following Alfarabi when, in fact, he is excerpting Algazel's *Logic*; on p. iv, l. 4, he cites Plato's *Parmenides* for the doctrine of the *primum in aliquo genere* which it does not contain.

[151] Even the dedication copy of the *De Artificio* is marred by a large number of blank spaces where the scribe could not read Fernando's autograph. Apparently, Fernando did not bother to correct it.

[152] For example, even though Fernando had the *codex unicus* of the *De Laudibus Platonis* in his hands, and even made some marginal additions in it, the manuscript is filled with obvious errors, which I discuss in my edition of the work. But peculiar citations are noticeable in other writings. For instance, in the *De Misterio Pallii*, MS Florence, Bibl. Naz., Magl. XXXI, 17, f. 130r, he cites Cardinal Bessarion's translation of Eusebius of Caesarea's *Sermo de epifania* apropos the Hebrew cloak called the *ephod* (see n. 255, p. 42). However, Eusebius left no such sermon *de epiphania*, and Bessarion never translated any work of Eusebius. Bessarion did translate St. Basil the Great's sermon *de nativitate domini* (preface in Mohler, 3:452–53), but neither this sermon nor that of Gregory Nazianzenus *de epiphania* (PG, 36: 311–14) nor those attributed to Gregory of Nyssa with the same title (PG, 46: 577–600, 1128–49) contain anything concerning the *ephod*. In the *De Iure Medios Exigendi Fructus* (printed Rome [1484]), f. (41v), Fernando cited another non-existent work of Eusebius, a *sermo de sacerdotali veste* (see p. 46). Earlier in the same work, on f. (33r), Fernando cited apropos of Aristotle's *Metaphysics* the commentary of John Philoponus, the *Excerpta super Metaphisicam* of Themistius, and Alexander Peripateticus' *De Sillogismis Hypotheticis*. But all three references are very problematic (see n. 283, pp. 46–47). The same may be said of his citation of Eustratius' commentary on Aristotle's *Nicomachean Ethics* (see p. 47).

that he worked very rapidly. Consciously or unconsciously, when citing authors, he did not always distinguish memory from fancy.

The justification for the *De Artificio* is the realist philosophical principle of the *primum in aliquo genere*, which was much used by some medieval philosophers, especially Thomas Aquinas, and which became a mainstay of the philosophical thought of the Florentine Platonist Marsilio Ficino.[153] Fernando argued that there had to be a universal method of investigation underlying the different modes of investigation peculiar to the various arts and sciences because only a *primum* uniting in itself all the diverse perfections of its genus can account for the very existence of the multiplicity of perfections in the genus.[154] Hence, there must be a "single art of everything knowable," which unites in itself the "diverse arts in diverse sciences and knowables."[155] Fernando's *artificium* was this *unica ars*.

In essence, Fernando had written a *Topica*. He divided the *De Artificio* into six tractates, but, in fact, it falls into two halves,[156] which we may call, using Ciceronian terminology, invention and judgment.[157] The more important and interesting of the two parts is the first, on invention, where Fernando gives his taxonomy of the categories (*termini*). Having laid down two rules that are reciprocal, i.e., that there are as many demonstrations of a positive proposition as there are *convenientiae* between its subject and predicate, and that there are as many demonstrations of a negative proposition as there are *differentiae* between its subject and predicate,[158] Fernando then proceeded to detail all the possible categories of which *convenientiae* and *differentiae* can be predicated. And he did so with a specific metaphysical scheme in mind as he split the *termini* into those transcending being, those coextensive with being, and those "inferior" to being.[159]

Explaining that "there are many questions on some things transcending being,"[160] Fernando first posited twenty-five "terms transcend-

---

[153] For this concept in medieval and Renaissance philosophy see Geiger, 244ff. and 470–71; Fabro (1950), 142–43; Kristeller (1953), 152ff.; and Mahoney.

[154] Bonilla y San Martín, v–vi.

[155] Bonilla y San Martín, vi, lin. 12–13.

[156] This disparity between the real and the purported organization of a work is something one finds in other writings of Fernando. In the *De Iure Medios Fructus Exigendi* he even failed to produce the whole second half which was announced in the very title of the work and which was promised in the introduction.

[157] Cic. *Top.* 6.

[158] Bonilla y San Martín, x, lin. 27ff. Fernando adds this proviso to his rules (x, lin. 32ff.): "observata tamen illa Posteriorum analetica [*sic*] regula, ut convenientia, quae medium argumentationis est, vel aequalis sit utrique extremitati, vel sit inferior maiore extremitate, et superior minore: alioquin altera praemissarum falsa esset, nec intentam probare conclusionem posset."

[159] I found no comparable scheme in Schulemann.

[160] Bonilla y San Martín, xii, lin. 18–19: "multae sunt quaestiones de aliquibus ens [ente *correxi*] transcendentibus."

ing being."[161] These terms were "common to being and nothing" and, consequently, could stand (*supponere*) "for nothing or for something."[162] Fernando never explained why there could only be twenty-five such terms. What is clear, however, is that Fernando treated "nothing" almost as if it were something. For instance, he argued that "perfection" is a term transcending being because:[163] "By definition it lacks nothing . . . 'To lack nothing,' however, suits 'nothing' as much as 'being.' For in the same way that stone lacks nothing to be stone . . . so does nothing lack nothing to be 'nothing.'" Again, "permanence" is a transcendental because "nothings" can be said to persist in nothingness.[164] Pointedly, Fernando considered "one" a term transcending being because Parmenides and Plato said that "one is before being."[165] He thus implicitly identified "one," "non-being," and "nothing." Quite consistently, he included among the transcendental *termini* the disjunction, *esse–non esse.*[166]

Fernando intended his categories to serve a metaphysics where non-being played an important role. He surely was familiar with the broad medieval tradition of negative theology going back to pseudo-Dionysius. Directly or indirectly, he may have also been influenced by John Scotus Eriugena's *Periphyseon* (*De Divisione Naturae*), where the first division is between being and non-being.[167] Eriugena, however, was really concerned with relative rather than absolute non-being,[168] while Fernando is innocent of any such distinction. Perhaps Fernando had read Plato's *Sophist*, where it is argued that non-being exists[169]; but this would be a

---

[161] Ibid., xiii, lin. 19ff. Since each of these terms can be accepted *permixtim* with any of the others, there are really 625 *differentiae*, i.e., the original 25 plus 600 more (25 × 24). The twenty-five terms transcending being are *perfectio, quantitas, potentia, permanentia, quies, vis, inclinatio, esse vel non esse, instinctus, meditatio, terminus, principium, gradus, gradus negatio, ordo, distinguibilitas, intentio prima, intentio secunda, unitas, numerus, positivum, privativum, habitudo, quaesitura, mensura.*

[162] Ibid., xiv, lin. 13ff.

[163] Ibid., xiv, lin. 19ff.: "in sua ratione includat id, cui nihil deest . . . nihil autem deesse ita conveniat nihilo sicut enti. Nam quemadmodum lapidi ut sit lapis nihil deest . . . ita nihilo, ut sit nihil, nihil deest."

[164] Ibid., xxvii, lin. 17ff.: "Permanentia . . . quarto loco a nobis enumerata est. Eius est ambitus atque transcendentiae qua ceteri superiores. Nam et enti et nihilo convenire potest dum nihilia in nihilitate permanent sicut entia in entitate."

[165] Ibid., xxxv, lin. 4.

[166] Ibid., xxxi, lin. 30ff.

[167] *De Divisione Naturae*, in Scotus Eriugena, 1:36.22 (= *PL*, 122:441A).

[168] See Moran, 212–40; Cappuyns, 328–30; and Bett, 98. John himself states (Scotus Eriugena, 1:40.10 sq; *PL*, 122:443C): "Nam quod penitus non est nec esse potest nec prae eminenentia suae existentiae intellectum exsuperat, quomodo in rerum divisionibus recipi valeat non video nisi forte quis dixerit rerum quae sunt absentias et privationes non omnino nihil esse sed earum quarum privationes seu absentiae seu oppositiones sunt mirabili quadam naturali virtute contineri ut quodam modo sint."

[169] Plato *Soph.* 236e ff. and 256e ff.

hazardous assumption. Fernando's twenty-five terms transcending being and his assertion that "one is before being" point to a Neoplatonic metaphysical hierarchy; but, again, we cannot be sure of the structure of this hierarchy since Fernando referred to "one" only very briefly and nowhere suggested that it was the basis of his metaphysical system. In fact, no coherent picture of Fernando's metaphysics emerges from the *De Artificio*. Instead we are left with a series of disconnected definitions and further subdivisions of the *termini* and their modes. But we should not be surprised. Fernando was writing a *Topica*, not a *Metaphysica*; and, contrary to the opinion of Menéndez y Pelayo[170] and the brothers Carreras y Artau,[171] he did not confuse the two. Though Fernando based his *Artificium* on his metaphysics, he did not identify his *Artificium* with metaphysics, at least not in the *De Artificio*.

The second level of Fernandian categories consisted of terms coextensive with being. There were two kinds of terms at this level. In the first set of these terms, the *passiones entis*, Fernando placed the five traditional scholastic transcendentals (*res, unum, aliquid, verum, bonum*).[172] The second group, Fernando specifically tells us, were what the Scotists called the *modi intrinseci entis*.[173]

In the last level of *termini*, the *inferiores ente*, Fernando listed the ten Aristotelian categories. Under the heading of substance he did not shrink from going on for ten pages naming every kind of angel, planet, sea, mountain, river, and animal known to him.[174] Why he left out plant life I do not understand. In any event, at the end of the section he felt qualified to claim that "by this *artificium* you will find not merely three thousand, but more than sixty thousand arguments for a single question or truth which has to be demonstrated."[175]

In many ways, Fernando anticipated Rudolph Agricola's highly successful *De inventione dialectica*. Like Agricola, Fernando developed a system of categories for discovering arguments within the context of a universal two-part logic. However, Fernando's categories are more original than Agricola's and reflect a philosophical and scientific perspective as opposed to Agricola's more rhetorical orientation. Indeed, Fernando reduced to a mere two and a half pages Boethius's system of *loci* which dominates Agricola's *De Inventione*.[176] Furthermore, Agricola never wrote

---

[170] Menéndez y Pelayo, 1:554, where he speaks of Fernando's "identificación continua de la *Lógica* y de la *Metafísica*" and of his "realismo extremado."

[171] Carreras y Artau, 2:284 and 647, where the *De Artificio* is characterized as a "lógica ontologica."

[172] Bonilla y San Martín, xlii, lin. 17–18. Fernando called the traditional transcendentals *simplices entis passiones* as opposed to the *disiunctae passiones entis*.

[173] Ibid., xlii, lin. 15–16 and xliii, lin. 2ff.

[174] Ibid., xliii, lin. 20ff.

[175] Ibid., lvii, lin. 18 sq.

[176] See ibid., lxii–lxiv, where Fernando discusses the "argumenta a sedibus ipsis et locis argumentorum," which "maxime oratori possunt convenire" (lxii.1–3). He immediately specifies that he is talking "de sumptis ex locis secundariis maximarum," which he divides into ten species.

an accompanying manual on judgment,[177] while Fernando, ever the good scholastic, dedicated the second half of his treatise to explaining syllogisms, *consequentiae*, and dialectical rules.[178] He even urged his readers to consult his now lost *Dialectica* for more detailed information.[179] Bonilla y San Martín believed that the *practica* to which Fernando also referred was another lost work, but it seems to me that in all instances where Fernando referred to *practica*, he meant no more than the practice sessions he planned to have with Bessarion.[180]

The *De Artificio* is clearly Lullian in inspiration. Fernando specifically asserts that his work is the universal art of discovery which Lull promised but failed to deliver.[181] Not by chance Rudolph Agricola also attacked Lull for pretending to teach the universal art of discovery.[182] However, whereas one is hard put to identify substantial points of contact between Agricola and Lull, Fernando admits at one point that he is borrowing from Lull.[183] Indeed, the most original part of the *De Artificio*, the list of twenty-five *termini* transcending being seems modeled on Lull's nine transcendental *dignitates*, or *principia transcendentia*.[184] It was precisely because he was such an expert on Lull that in 1484 Fernando

---

[177] At the start of the *De Inventione Dialectica Lucubrationes* (R. Agricola, 8–9), after distinguishing the *pars inventionis* from the *pars iudicandi*, he states: "Sed nos de priore illa, quae ad inveniendum pertinet, his libris loquemur."

[178] Fernando reasoned that since by his *artificium* one could find "not only the middle terms in every science but everything knowable in every science" and since "the *ratio* of finding middle terms comes from consequences, antecedents, and repugnants, it is therefore right that we transmit the art of finding all consequences, antecedents, and repugnants" (Bonilla y San Martín, lxi, lin. 2–9). Nor did he ignore rules of dialectics, listing, for instance, eighty-five rules for *comparatio* (e.g., num. 1: "bonum diurnius est magis eligendum quam minus tale;" Bonilla y San Martín, lxix.11–12).

[179] Bonilla y San Martín, lxi, lin. 15, 19, 42. Bonilla y San Martín never takes note of this separate work in his introduction.

[180] See Bonilla y San Martín, 121 n. 1. Note that Fernando put all the references either in the future tense or in a way that referred to the future. At the end Fernando reiterated the need for *exercitatio* (ibid., lxxvi, lin. 30ff.).

[181] For example, Bonilla y San Martín, vii, lin. 11 sq.: "Fuit et novissime Raymundus Catalanus, orbi notissimus, quem constat suo Artificio omnia polliceri et divina et humana sine aliquo discrimine . . . (ix.3ff.) Hunc autem virum constat omnia non modo cognitu possibilia, sed et intellectu impossibilia arbitrari sub eius Artificio comprehendi posse. . . ." For Lull see Platzeck (1962); Johnston; and Bonner, esp. 1:59–70 for Lull's *Art*.

[182] R. Agricola, 181–82.

[183] Bonilla y San Martín, xli–xlii (at xli.14 read *utrum*, not *unum*), where Fernando repeats Lull's ten *regulae*; see Raymundus Lullus, *Lectura super Artem Inventivam* (Lull, 5:360ff.; and Platzeck [1962], 1:275ff.). Lull based these rules on Algazel; but Fernando claimed to be putting in good order what Lull had taken from Alfarabi.

[184] The following table of correspondence is suggestive:

Dignitates Lulli	Termini transcendentes Fernandi
1. Bonitas	(1. Perfectio)*
2. Magnitudo	2. Quantitas
3. Duratio	4. Permanentia

was appointed to a papal commission to judge the orthodoxy of the first Lullist work printed outside of the Iberian peninsula.[185]

But there are also fundamental differences between Lull and Fernando. Unlike Lull, Fernando offered no mechanical *ars combinatoria* of symbols by which one could arrive at truth.[186] Nor did he follow Lull in pretending that his system allowed one to discover and prove Christian mysteries.[187] Even more fundamentally, Fernando did not imitate Lull in explicitly identifying his *Artificium* with metaphysics.[188] For Lull such an identification was essential in order for his system to work. Only if the logical and ontological orders were really the same, could Lull's mechanical *ars combinatoria* produce results.[189] For Fernando, on the other hand, not the identity between logic and metaphysics, but the principle of the *primum in aliquo genere* provided the ontological base of his *Artificium*.[190] To be sure, this principle only makes sense within the context of a Platonic metaphysics based on the notion of ontological participation and the assumption that universals have an objective existence at least in the mind of God. But Thomas Aquinas and other scholastics held similar views without identifying logic and ontology. [191]

What has been overlooked in the *De Artificio* is the influence of Scotism. A special characteristic of John Duns Scotus's metaphysics was the importance he attributed to transcendentals, and especially to the class of transcendentals which he called "pure perfections."[192] *Perfectio* stands at the head of the *termini* Fernando listed as transcending being.[193] Fernando's interpretation of St. Anselm's famous definition of

4. Potentia	3. Potentia
5. Sapientia	(1. Perfectio)*
6. Voluntas	(1. Perfectio)*
7. Virtus	6. Vis
8. Veritas	(1. Perfectio)*
9. Gloria	

* *Bonitas, Sapientia, Voluntas,* and *Veritas* are among the modes of Fernando's first transcendental term, *perfectio* (Bonilla y San Martín, p. xvi, lin. 22-23, 33); but we might be dealing here with Scotist as much as Lullian influence; see *infra.*

[185] See *infra.*

[186] Fernando even joked about this aspect of Lull's system; see Bonilla y San Martín, viii, lin. 34-35.

[187] The title of Fernando's work is very clear on this; his *Artificium* promised only to find what was *natura scibilis;* see also the latter part of his attack on Lull in n. 148, p. 27.

[188] This is a false assumption of Menéndez y Pelayo and the brothers Carreras y Artau; see nn. 170-71, p. 30. Bonilla y San Martín does not explicitly confront the issue.

[189] On Lull's extreme realism see Platzeck (1962), 1:131-33, 183-86; Johnston, 54-55, 169-70, and *ad indicem* ("realism"); Carreras y Artau, 1:484-85 (cf. also 2:74-75 on Pere Deguí); Probst, 83-86; and Yates, 1:55.

[190] See p. 28.

[191] See Gilson (1965), 146-49.

[192] See Wolter, 163ff.

[193] Bonilla y San Martín, xiv-xx. Reflecting its importance for him, Fernando's

perfectio simpliciter as *quaecumque est melius ipsum quam non ipsum* follows closely Scotus's interpretation.[194] Fernando's list of eleven disjunctive transcendentals, which he called the *coordinatio perfectionum simpliciter*, approximated very closely in name and number the disjunctive transcendentals one finds in Duns Scotus.[195] I believe that for Fernando, just as for Duns Scotus, the transcendentals were fundamental for proving the existence of God and establishing our knowledge of Him.[196] That is why Fernando created the scheme of the *coordinatio perfectionum*, and why he was so careful to note that the first parts of each of the disjunctions were the *perfectiones simpliciter*, i.e., the attributes of God.[197] If Fernando had applied his *Artificium* to metaphysics, he would have taken each of these disjunctives and shown how they force us to acknowledge the attributes of God, arguing that if there is the *contingens*, then there must also be the *necessarium*, which is God; again, if there is the *diversum*, then also the *idem*, and so on, just as Duns Scotus had done, and even before Scotus, St. Bonaventure.[198] Quite in keeping with this Scotist orientation, Fernando ended the section on the transcendental perfections with a list of thirty-one "absolute perfections" which mimic the Scotist "pure perfections" and which therefore are all properly predicable of God.[199] Fernando specifically acknowledged that one whole sub-section of these

---

discussion of *perfectio* is much longer than that of any other of "the terms transcending being."

[194] Bonilla y San Martín, xv. lin. 1-4: "Perfectio simpliciter est quaecumque est melius ipsum quam non ipsum, id est, quodcumque sibi <in>compossibile, sicut intellectus et voluntas sunt meliora omnibus illis quae se non possunt compati cum eis" [the insertion of "in" in "incompossibile" is required by the sense of the subsequent clause]. Fernando then goes on to refute other definitions. Cf. Fernando's definition with Scotus's in Wolter, 163-64 nn. 3-5, quoting from the *De Primo Principio*, ed. Mueller, c. 4, p. 68: "Perfectio simpliciter dicitur quae in quolibet est melius ipsum quam non ipsum"; and p. 69: "Exponatur sic: melius quam non ipsum, id est, quam quodcumque positivum incompossibile, in quo includitur non ipsum"; and from *Quaestiones Quodlibetales*, q. 5, num. 13, in Duns Scotus, 25:216b: ". . . sed intelligitur ibi non ipsum pro quocumque sibi incompossibili etiam positive ut sit sensus: perfectio simpliciter est in quolibet melior quocumque sibi incompossibili."

[195] Cf. Fernando's list of eleven disjunctive transcendentals in Bonilla y San Martín, xviii–xix, with the list of fourteen disjunctive perfections which Wolter, 138, "culled from different passages of Scotus's works." Scotus has all but two of Fernando's disjunctives (nums. 3 and 10); and in the case of these two, we should keep in mind that Scotus explicitly did not name all the disjunctive perfections which he thought possible because "multa alia illimitata in entibus."

[196] Wolter, 130ff.

[197] Bonilla y San Martín, xix, lin. 12-13: "perfectiones simpliciter sunt omnes quae in dextra cadunt sub undecim divisionibus entis."

[198] Wolter, 132ff., effectively brings this out, quoting from St. Bonaventure's *Quaestio Disputata de Mysterio Trinitatis*.

[199] Cf. Bonilla y San Martín, xix–xx, with Wolter, 11 and 164. The items recorded by Wolter are merely by way of example since Scotus never bothered to give a full list of what in his view would have been virtually an unlimited number of such perfections.

termini equales enti were nothing other than the *modi intrinseci enti* taught by the Scotists.[200] Indeed, in this section Fernando endorsed as the principle of individuation perhaps the most characteristic and controversial of Scotist concepts, that of *haecceitas*.[201] Scotus is the most commonly named scholastic, and the Scotists the most frequently mentioned philosophical school in the *De Artificio*.[202] The only Latin author later than Scotus whom Fernando cited in the *De Artificio* was the Spanish Scotist Nicholas Bonet.[203] That he criticized Bonet only confirms the fact that Fernando had worked his way through more recent Scotist literature. Though we cannot label Fernando simply a Scotist—his eclecticism renders such an assertion hazardous—it is significant that in a dialogue on divine foreknowledge written by Georgius Benignus at Rome in 1471 Fernando was portrayed as especially adept in things Scotist.[204]

Although Fernando's own particular combination of Lullism and Scotist philosophy has escaped previous notice, the symbiosis of Lullism with the Augustinian-Franciscan philosophical tradition in general, and with Scotism in particular, has been recognized. As the brothers Carreras y Artau put it, "En el panorama de conjunto del pensamiento medieval, el lulismo se configura como una dirección singular dentro del franciscanismo."[205] Lull agreed with Duns Scotus on controversial theological issues such as the Immaculate Conception and whether the Second Person of the Trinity would have become man even if man had not fallen.[206] But it was actually the Scotist philosophical doctrine of the formal distinction *ex parte rei* which Lullists found most attractive. Since the Scotist formal distinction postulated formalities *ex parte rei* in God and creatures, it could be used to defend the nine *dignitates* which Lull posited in God and which were the basis of the Lullian universal *Ars*.[207] However, the first clear instances of this linkage of Lull and Scotus

---

[200] Bonilla y San Martín, xlii, lin. 15–16 and xliii, lin. 2.

[201] Bonilla y San Martín, xliii, lin. 13.

[202] Fernando cited Scotus at Bonilla y San Martín, xiv, lin. 2; xx, lin. 27; and xxiii, lin. 4; and the *Scotistae* at xxxiii, lin. 26; xlii, lin. 15; and xliii, lin. 3 and 12. He cited St. Thomas Aquinas at xi, lin. 32 and xiv, lin. 2; the *Thomistae* at xxxiii, lin. 25. Albert the Great is cited once (xiv.2), Augustine once (xxxiii.5), Averroes (xxxi.24, xxxix.2) and Avicenna (xiii.40, xxiv.11) twice.

[203] Bonilla y San Martín, xx.24. It is interesting that Fernando attacked Bonet for diverging from Scotus, who happened to agree with Aristotle on the issue at hand.

[204] *De Libertate et Immutabilitate Dei*, which according to one copy, BAV, MS Vat. lat. 1056, f. 2v, reports a colloquium in Bessarion's house of 1 June 1471. To be sure, the interlocutors of the dialogue reflect Benignus's own knowledge of Scotus; but it is reasonable to suppose that Benignus maintained a certain verisimilitude. On f. 7r, Benignus has Fernando correct Bessarion concerning Scotus, and, on 18v, pass judgment on Bessarion's analysis of Scotus. On f. 28v, Fernando is made to cite Scotus; on ff. 34v and 62v, he cites Nicholas Bonet.

[205] Carreras y Artau, 2:70.

[206] See, for instance, Platzeck (1963), 100; and the authorities cited below in n. 318, p. 51.

[207] This has already been pointed out by Victor, 517.

known to scholars are late, coming out of the school of Pere Deguí, the orthodoxy of whose Lullian *Ianua Artis* Fernando had been called upon to judge in 1484.[208] Deguí wrote two works *de formalitatibus* where he expounded Lullist metaphysics in Scotist terminology.[209] The *Ars Metaphysicalis* of Deguí's student, Jaime Janer, does the same thing[210]; and in the correspondence of still another disciple of Deguí, Arnaldo Descós, we have a clear affirmation of Scotus's exceptional agreement with Lull.[211] Also, Bernardo de Lavinheta, who was important in the spread of Lullism at Paris in the early sixteenth century, is said to have been trained as a Scotist.[212] But all these Spaniards were a generation or more younger than Fernando. So Fernando is our earliest evidence of the symbiosis of Scotism and Lullism in Spain. Significantly, the Roman commission of 1484–1485, half of whose members were Spanish, cleared Deguí of the most serious charges against him mainly by interpreting him as agreeing with John Duns Scotus.

Other than the *De Artificio*, Fernando wrote only one other extant philosophical work and, like the *De Artificio*, it involved Cardinal Bessarion. In early 1470 a controversy at the University of Louvain concerning the philosophic problem of future contingents attracted the attention of the Roman Curia. The controversy itself was several decades old; but its final, decisive phase began in December 1465 when, in a *quodlibet* disputation, Petrus de Rivo, a professor of rhetoric in the Arts faculty at Louvain, argued that Aristotle was right to have considered propositions concerning future contingents to be neither true nor false, but neutral.[213] An old foe of Petrus de Rivo at Louvain, the theologian Henricus de Zoemeren, attacked Petrus's position as heretical on the grounds that it threatened the validity of religious prophesy and the possibility of divine foreknowledge. Henricus de Zoemeren failed to win over the university to his view. So, in January or February 1470, he appealed to Rome. He may have written to other authorities in Rome, but we know for sure that he wrote Cardinal Bessarion, whom he had served during the cardinal's legation in Germany in 1460–1461.[214] He apparently had known Bes-

---

[208] See *infra*.

[209] That is, the *Opus de Formalitatibus, sive Metaphysica* (first edition: 1489; see Rogent and Durán, num. 9), and the *Tractatus Brevis Formalitatum* (first edition: 1489?; see ibid., 11, no. 12). While describing Deguí's metaphysical position, Carreras y Artau, 2:73ff., do not explicitly connect him to Scotus.

[210] Not seen; the only edition was published at Valencia in 1506 (Rogent and Durán, num. 36); see Carreras y Artau, 2:77ff.

[211] See Fita (*Descós*, 1891), 430–31, in a letter of 1488 to Pedro Vadell: ". . . vehementer gaudeo, quum presertim Scotum prae manibus habeas, tum quod ipse excellens doctor prae se fert nescio quid sublimitatis atque inauditae singularitatis, tum quia concordat mirum in modum cum nostro Divo Raymundo." Cf. Carreras y Artau, 2:78 n. 62.

[212] Hillgarth, 289.

[213] For all aspects of the controversy see Baudry. See also Dal Pra. For the general issue see Normore.

[214] See Appendix 9.

sarion since 1449.[215] We can also document his presence as a member of Bessarion's *familia* at Rome in 1458.[216] So when Henricus wrote to Bessarion, he could feel confident of receiving a sympathetic hearing. In response, Bessarion asked his protégé, the former Franciscan friar and future Pope Sixtus IV, then Cardinal of St. Peter in Chains, Francesco della Rovere, to write a critique of Petrus de Rivo's position as presented by Henricus de Zoemeren.[217] Bessarion also commissioned another theologian at Rome to examine Petrus de Rivo's assertions.[218] The anonymous author is doubtless to be indentified with one of the interlocutors of Georgius Benignus's previously mentioned dialogue on divine foreknowledge, which is set in Bessarion's house. Fernando of Cordova contributed two treatises to the controversy. The first, in which he treated the scriptural texts used by Petrus de Rivo, is lost.[219] The second, like the first, is probably to be dated between the second half of 1470 and the first half of 1471.[220] Like the other members of the Bessarion circle, Fernando opposed Petrus de Rivo, but he gives no indication, at least in the extant treatise, as to who commissioned him to write. In any case, after Francesco della Rovere became Pope Sixtus IV, he appointed Fernando to a commission charged with examining the accusations against Petrus de Rivo.[221] Towards the end of 1472 Petrus de Rivo himself came to Rome to plead his case. On 18 March 1473, Fernando and the other members of the commission signed a report condemning Petrus's arguments, but also certifying that the accused had abjured his errors in their pres-

---

[215] Ibid.

[216] See Capizzi, 213 and 240, for one Henricus de Zoemeren, clericus Leodicensis diocesis, as a witness to a document dated Rome, 17 September 1458, concerning Bessarion's purchase of some property at Rome.

[217] Edited by Baudry, 113–25. At the start and end of the treatise, della Rovere addressed his dedicatee as *reverendissime domine*, but he did not name him. However, in a marginal note in one of the two manuscripts used by Baudry, one reads: "Nota. Primo scribit cardinalis s. Petri ad vincula, ordinis minorum s. Francisci ad cardinalem Grecum, a quo recepit litteram m. Henrici Zoemeren continentem ut sibi respondeatur ad V puncta per eum proposita" (p. 113 n. 1).

[218] Edited in Baudry, 126–33. The author addressed the work to "domino meo metuendissimo domino Niceno, episcopo cardinali" (p. 126). A manuscript overlooked by Baudry is Florence, Riccard. 162, ff. 81r–85v (adespotic); cf. Kristeller (1963–1992), 1:189.

[219] Baudry, 170: "Quia vero nituntur solvere rationes ex divinis litteris acceptas [*by Petrus de Rivo*] iam in alio tractatu ostendimus eos aliter esse interpretatos quam spiritus efflagitat . . ."

[220] Discussed in Baudry, 35 and 64, and edited in 134–70. The two manuscripts of the treatise known to Baudry are Paris, Bibliothèque Nationale, lat. 3169, ff. 16r–25r, and lat. 4152, ff. 80r–88r, both of which contain other treatises in the controversy; see Baudry, 49–56.

[221] Baudry, 44; and Du Plessis D'Argentré, 1:278b–280a. Fernando signed himself "subdiaconus apostolicus." The other members of the commission were the Dominican bishop of Brescia and vicar of Rome, Domenico Dominici, the papal *Datarius* Francisco of Toledo, the theologians Ioachim de Lerma and Baptista Brenden, and the *Advocati consistoriales* Bartholomaeus de Stabia and Antonius Canacia. The document also refers to unspecified "other" witnesses.

ence. In his extant treatise, Fernando refuted Petrus de Rivo on narrow logical grounds. The treatise, therefore, tells us little about his general philosophical position except that he opposed the Ockhamist *opinio communis*,[222] and that he considered propositions of future contingents determinedly true or false.

In addition to these five philosophical treatises (the *De Laudibus Platonis*, the *De Duabus Philosophiis*, the *De Artificio*, and the two treatises on future contingents), Fernando apparently wrote for Bessarion a work in theology which is now lost, but which we know dealt with the Eucharist because of its description in the early inventories of the Biblioteca Marciana.[223] Between 1463 and 1469 Bessarion composed in Greek and then translated into Latin a treatise on the words of consecration.[224] Finding the cardinal's argument heretical, George of Trebizond attacked it in a work which, he later claimed, he suppressed out of deference to the cardinal's honor.[225] George also said that he had received Bessarion's treatise from Niccolò Palmieri, who, it would seem, had also been scandalized by it.[226] I suggest that Fernando's lost treatise on the Eucharist had something to do with this controversy. It probably is not a coincidence that, as we have seen, Palmieri was asked by Pope Paul II to examine Fernando's *De Laudibus Platonis*.

While Bessarion was still alive, Fernando wrote two other theological tracts. One, entitled *An Licita Sit cum Saracenis Pax*, was addressed to Pope Paul II (1464–1471).[227] It is lost,[228] but we are probably safe in believing that it was written in 1466 when Paul II was vigorously urging King Matthias Corvinus of Hungary and the Republic of Venice not to sign a

---

[222] For this phrase see Normore, 370 and 376. See also Baudry, 14ff.

[223] Labowsky, 119; 238, num. 903 (c) of the 1474 inventory: "quinque quinterniones Ferrandi de corpore Christi;" 289, num. 958 of the 1524 inventory: "Fernandi Cordubensis de sacratissimis verbis, in pergameno, in quinternionibus;" 305, num. 407 of the 1543 inventory: "Fernandi Cordubensis de sacris verbis sanguinis, in pergameno;" and 347 for the inventory of 1545/46: "Fernandi Cordubensis de eucharistia."

[224] The Greek and Latin texts are edited in Mohler, 3:24ff. For the Latin version and the date see Monfasani (1981), 171.

[225] Monfasani (1981), 171; and Monfasani (1984), 169; 185 n. to § 29; 485, f. 126r; and 757, num. CXCIII.

[226] Monfasani (1984), 169, § 29.

[227] Labowsky, 119; 236, num. 854 of the 1474 inventory: "Ferdinandi de pace, in papiro;" 305, num. 410 of the 1543 inventory: "Ferdinandi Cordubensis, An licita sit cum Saracenis pax, in papiro"; 347 for the 1545/46 inventory: "Fernandi Cordubensis an licita sit pax inita cum Saracenis, ad Paulum II pontificem maximum," a title which is repeated in the coeval index for this inventory (p. 394). I suspect that this work is also num. 962 of the 1524 inventory rather than the mysterious *De Differentiis* as suggested interrogatively by Labowsky (p. 289): "Ferdinandi Cordubensis opusculum quoddam, in papyro."

[228] J. Simler, who had access to the inventory of Bessarion's library in Venice, cited this work in his additions to Gesner (Gesner, 196). Bonilla y San Martín, 87, with no more than Simler's reference to go on, mistakenly suggested that the treatise was written for Pope Pius II.

peace treaty with the Ottomans.[229] In these circumstances, and especially since Bessarion owned the only known copy of the work, I would
further suggest that Fernando argued against the legitimacy of a peace
with the Moslems.

The other theological treatise was the *Adversus Hereticos Qui Fraterculi
dela Opinione Appellantur.*[230] Fernando addressed the work to Cardinal
Guillaume d'Estouteville, who, Fernando acknowledged in the preface,[231] had specifically commissioned it. The Fraticelli had been discovered near Rome in the summer of 1466.[232] Their trial continued on well
into the autumn, and the pope was still ordering measures against them
in 1467. The shock provoked a number of curialists, in addition to
Fernando, to write refutations.[233] An initial *terminus ante quem* for
Fernando's treatise would be d'Estouteville's death on 22 January 1483.
However, Fernando surely wrote it much earlier. Significant for the
dating is the fact that Fernando did not call himself a papal subdeacon.
He did not use this title in the *De Laudibus Platonis* of late 1466–January
1467; but in the *De Artificio* of late 1468–early 1469, he thanked Bessarion
for helping him acquire this office in a tone which suggests that he
received it only recently.[234] Thereafter Fernando regularly advertised
the title in the headings of his works. So he most probably finished the
Adversus Hereticos sometime in 1467 or 1468.

In refuting the Fraticelli, Fernando did more than defend the right of
the pope and of clerics to material possessions and temporal power.[235]
He also asserted the papal plenitude of power over all laymen in secular
affairs and the papal *dominium* over all the earth.[236] As Christ's vicar, the

---

[229] See Pastor, 2:84–85.

[230] The only copy I know is the dedication manuscript, BAV, Vat. lat. 1127. For
a description see the introduction to Appendix 7, page 83. For literature on
d'Estouteville see Esposito Aliano; and Darricau. For Vat. lat. 1127 as part of
d'Estouteville's library see Esposito Aliano, 323–24 and 327.

[231] Appendix 7, § 2, and esp. §§ 3–5.

[232] For literature on the episode see Monfasani (1991).

[233] Each is discussed in detail in Monfasani (1991).

[234] Bonilla y San Martín, ix, lin. 25–26: "Rem pro meritis meis difficiliorem
fortassis tu [*Bessarion*] feceris cum tuo aspirato favore atque beneficio sedis
apostolicae subdiaconus creatus sum."

[235] In addition to the discussion in Monfasani (1991), see Douie, 55–78.

[236] For example, Tractatus 1, cap. 4, handles the question, "utrum papa per
potestatem iuridicionis sibi datam a Christo in terra vere sit princeps regum
terre." To which he responded (ibid.): "affirmativam partem questionis huius
magnopere tueri cupio atque demonstrare." In Tract. 1, cap. 16 (f. 66r–68r) he
argued: "quod Christus non solum sacerdos fuerit secundum ordinem Mel-
chisedech, sed etiam secundum eundem ordinem rex." He dedicated all of the
second Tractatus to demonstrating the universal extent of papal power in worldly
matters. Cap. 8 has the thesis in the table of contents (f. 79r): "in bonis temporalibus magis debere atque teneri Christianos subici pape quam dominis propriis
secundum aliquem modum," which was modified to ". . . subici pape quam
imperatori" in the chapter itself (f. 85v). Cap. 14 (f. 88r) "probat papam in quolibet
regno posse regem de novo instituere." In several chapters he discussed the papal

pope was not only the supreme *sacerdos*, but also the universal *rex*.[237] Fernando was thus an apologist for the most extreme claims of papal political power. Like his fellow Spaniard in Rome and polemicist against the Fraticelli, Rodrigo Sánchez de Arévalo,[238] Fernando seems to have appropriated the ideas of the recently deceased papal apologist Agostino Favaroni (d. 1443), who based his case for Christ's human royalty on the hypostatic union of His natures.[239] In early 1468 Sánchez's extreme hierocratic views provoked still another Spaniard in Rome, the celebrated Cardinal Juan Torquemada to write a brief rebuttal.[240] As for Fernando, Torquemada either ignored him or died (26 September 1468) before he could respond. The latter possibility argues for a date in 1468 for the publication of Fernando's *Adversus Hereticos*.[241] In any event, the dedicatee of Fernando's work, Cardinal d'Estouteville, fully agreed with Fernando's hierocratic position against Torquemada since we know that in a consistory of 1473 he unequivocally asserted that the pope possessed worldly dominion over all laymen, including the emperor.[242] I suspect that Fernando did not dedicate the *Adversus Hereticos* to Bessarion because the Greek cardinal did not share Fernando's extreme opinion concerning papal power and, as patron of the Franciscan Order, probably did not like Fernando's zeal in defending ecclesiastical wealth against the Franciscan ideal of poverty.[243]

---

power of granting dispensations from the law (e.g., on f. 88v, cap. 16: "Utrum papa per plenitudinem potestatis in temporalibus usurarium absolvere possit absque hoc, quod usuras restituat." The answer is yes in some circumstances). In some of the last chapters (31-33 on f. 94r-v) of the Tractatus he justified the legality and finality of the Donation of Constantine.

[237] On the concept of Christ's royalty and, by extension, the pope's in the later Middle Ages, see J. Leclerq.

[238] See Trame, 141-42. Trame treats the dependency on Favaroni as a possibility rather than as a proven fact. For Sánchez's views on the papal world monarchy see also Jedin (1954).

[239] On Favaroni and his treatises *De Christo Capite Ecclesiae et Eius Inclito Principatu* and *De Principatu Papae* see J. Leclerq, 261-64, and the literature cited in Monfasani (1991), 187 n. 48. After proving Christ's temporal *principatus* from the hypostatic union in the first two chapters of the first Tractatus of the *Adversus Hereticos*, Fernando argued affirmatively in the third chapter (ff. 18v-19v) that "regnum et iurisdictionis potestatem quam Christus in quantum homo habet super angelos et homines possit committere pape ita ut possit esse papa vicarius Christi in celo et in terra, id est, super angelos et homines."

[240] See Jedin (1942); Trame, 156-59; Theeuws; and Izbecki, 28, 110-12.

[241] While he was finishing the *Adversus Hereticos* or shortly thereafter, Fernando must have become concerned that his discussion of Christ's hypostatic union and worldly dominion might cause him trouble since he added to the end a disclaimer, submitting his statements to the judgment of the Church (see the end of the introduction in Appendix 7).

[242] See Jedin (1942), 267; and Ammannati, 146.

[243] Bessarion took an interest in the theology and history of the debate on poverty; his library preserves a manuscript, Zan. lat. 142 (= 1669) of the Biblioteca Marciana, Venice, which contains the very large corpus of texts prepared for Pope John XXII in 1322 when he solicited the opinions of theologians before

Indeed, Fernando argued that cardinals and other Roman curialists should possess wealth proportionate to their lofty status.[244] He thus felt no qualms in defending the rich food, the large retinues, the luxurious clothing, and the worldly *iocus et risus* enjoyed by members of the Curia.[245]

One peculiarity of the treatise is that when Fernando turned to defending the Donation of Constantine, he completely ignored Lorenzo Valla's attack on its authenticity.[246] Although he knew Valla from 1444 onwards at Naples and Rome, I would not be surprised if Fernando never read Valla's *Declamatio.*

Early on in the *Adversus Hereticos* Fernando referred to a *tractatus*, which I have not found, "concerning the ways in which the church may be decapitated, amongst which we posited the deposing of ecclesiastical orders and the government of the world."[247] His position there, as in the *Adversus Hereticos*, seems to have been that the pope could depose any ecclesiastical or secular official as long as he provided for a successor. It is not clear when and under what circumstances Fernando wrote this lost treatise. Since it apparently had to do with the removal of the pope and prelates, it perhaps was an anti-conciliarist tract. The *Adversus Hereticos* probably absorbed some of its arguments.

---

deciding against the Franciscans concerning evangelical poverty; for a description of the manuscript see Zanetti, 81–83; for an analysis of the corpus and an edition of one of its texts see Sikes.

[244] Cap. 26 of Tractatus 4 (ff. 132v–134v) of the *Adversus Hereticos* argues: "quod falsso [*sic*] ippocrite Fraterculi obiciunt ecclesiasticis viris cum negant licere eis de bonis ecclesie delicatam ducere vitam pro semetip<s>is delicatos cibos vescentibus et utentibus preciosis vestibus atque equis et ornamentis equorum et cetera que per ippocrisim ecclesiasticis viris inpingere soliti sunt." Another contemporary curialist, Cardinal Jean Jouffroy, also strongly insisted upon the propriety of ecclesiastical wealth, especially of cardinals; see Miglio; and Monfasani (1991), 177–78, 187, 195.

[245] In addition to cap. 26 of Tr. 4, cited in the previous note see also cap. 39 of the same Tractatus (ff. 155r–160v), where Fernando cites Cicero in support of the value of joking.

[246] See the end of n. 236, page 39. Valla wrote his refutation at Naples in 1440 (see Valla [1978], 10–11).

[247] Tractatus 1, c. 35 (f. 95r): "[*Rubric*] Utrum auctoritate pape posset imperium ab ecclesia tolli; idem de papatu queri potest. / De hac difficultate et sequenti multa diximus in tractatu meo de modis quibus decol<l>aratur ecclesia, inter quos posuimus detrahere ordines ecclesiasticos et monarchiam orbis. Ibi autem diximus papam nec de ratione nec de iure posse tollere omnes episcopatus nisi succedant eis episcopis sublatis alii. Idem dicendum de principatibus et monarchiis et imperio." Cf. Douie, 65.

THE PONTIFICATE OF SIXTUS IV

Fernando did not suffer any great material loss when Cardinal Bessarion died on 18 November 1472. As we have seen and will see again, Fernando made it his business to cultivate the favor of other cardinals. More importantly, on 8 August 1471, a former member of the Bessarion circle, Francesco della Rovere, became Pope Sixtus IV.[248] As a Scotist theologian, Sixtus also had intellectual as well as personal ties to Fernando. Eventually Sixtus would even try to find a bishopric for Fernando in Spain.

However, the importance of these ties emerged only gradually during Sixtus's pontificate. In the meantime, Fernando sought other patrons. In the *Adversus Hereticos* written under Pope Paul II, Fernando had defended ecclesiastical temporal power and wealth in general. Now, in the pontificate of Sixtus IV, he decided to defend his own particular financial interests. In a work entitled *De Misterio Pallii, et An pro Eo Aliquod Temporale absque Simonie Labe Exigi Possit* and addressed to Cardinal Francesco Todeschini-Piccolomini (the future Pope Pius III), Fernando justified the financial privileges he himself enjoyed as papal subdeacon.[249] As we have seen, Fernando gained this office in 1467–1468 through the influence of his patron, Cardinal Bessarion.[250] In his *De Caeremoniis Curiae Romanae* of 1488, Agostino Patrizi-Piccolomini specified that in his time (*nostris temporibus*) the *subdiaconi participantes* (i.e., those sharing in the common revenues of the office) were five in number.[251] Papal subdeacons had various liturgical and household functions, such as holding the paten with the consecrated host at mass and reading edifying literature at table.[252] The pallium concerned papal subdeacons in a special way.[253] It was a liturgical garment of white wool meant exclusively for archbishops and patriarchs. By church law, they could not exercise their office until they received it. Papal subdeacons were responsible for the

---

[248] For literature and information on Sixtus and culture at Rome see Lee; and Miglio et al.

[249] I know of two fifteenth-century manuscripts, one of which is the dedication copy. It was never printed. See Appendix 8. The text is listed in Schulte, 2:370.

[250] See p. 38.

[251] Dykmans, 2:494.23–24.

[252] See Dykmans, 2:229, and under "sous-diacres apostoliques" in the index; Schimmelpfennig, 236–41, and 521 (index); Guillemain, 52 and 370.

[253] See H. Leclercq, *Enciclopedia cattolica*, 9 (1952):646–47; and especially A. Piccolomini in Dykmans, 1:173–74, 176, 177.14–21; and Dykmans's commentary in 1:141*–45* and 2:229*.

confection of the pallium, and also took part in the ceremony in which
the prior of the cardinal deacons presented it to the newly elected archbishop or patriarch or his procurator. However, the recipient did not
really gain possession of the garment until he had paid a fee to the papal
subdeacons, calculated as a certain percentage of the taxes on the recipient's new church. From 1471 onwards, Francesco Todeschini-Piccolomini,
the future Pius III, was the prior of the cardinal deacons, and therefore
in charge of presenting the pallium.[254] Fernando wrote the *De Misterio
Pallii* after 18 November 1472 since he refers to Cardinal Bessarion as
dead,[255] and before 1481 since he cites the *De Misterio Pallii* in the *De Iure
Medios Exigendi Fructus*, dedicated to Sixtus IV about 1481.[256]

The first part of the *De Misterio Pallii* is taken up with the question
posed in the second part of its title: *an pro eo aliquid temporale absque
simonie labe exigi possit.* Fernando denied that taking money for the pallium was simony mainly on the grounds that the pallium was not a *res
spiritualis.*[257] In the preface, he referred to the criticism of *Parisienses
quidam,*[258] but in the treatise proper he was more specific, refuting by
name the commentary on Genesis of the secular master of theology
Henry of Langenstein (or, of Hainbuch), who taught at Paris 1363–1383
before moving to the University of Vienna in 1384, where he remained
until his death in 1397,[259] the commentary on Peter Lombard's *Four Book*

---

[254] Dykmans, 1:143*. On his career see Strnad; on the dedication of the *De
Misterio Pallii*, see Strnad, 335–36.

[255] MS Florence, BN, Magl. XXXI, 17, f. 130v: ". . . auctoritate Eusebii Cesari-
ensis in sermone De Epifania a celeberrime memorie Bizarrione cardinali [*empty
space, enough for one word*] Greco in Latinum tradducto ita dicentis: 'nihil antiquius
veste illa sacerdotali archipresuli nostri que illi vesti de veteri testamento successit
effod. . . .'" Eusebius of Caesarea did not leave nor did Cardinal Bessarion translate any such sermon; see n. 152, page 27.

[256] Fernando of Cordova (c. 1481), f. 25r: "Sed plenius discernimus in tractatu
nostro de pal<l>io ea in parte, an liceat subdiacono pro eo exigere pecunias."

[257] This constitutes by far the larger part of the treatise, encompassing ff. 3v–
129v in MS Florence, BN, Magl. XXXI, 17 (henceforth cited as M). See M, f. 18v:
"Non ergo pallium enumerari inter res spirituales potest, ergo nec pro eo pecuni-
aria exactio redargui simonie cum sola exactio temporalis pro spirituali constituat
simoniam." Cf. *Corpus Iuris Canonici*, 2:749ff.: Lib. 5, tit. 3: *De simonia, et ne aliquid
pro spiritualibus exigatur vel promittatur.*

[258] See Appendix 8, § 4. In § 6, he referred to someone who was *praecipue* the
leader of the critics, but whom he would not name *honoris gratia.*

[259] See M, f. 4v: ". . . ut Iudas a Christo non est redemptus, qui vendidit
redemptorem, ita nec subdiaconus est glorificandus, qui spiritum sanctum
vendidit glorificatorem. Hanc argumentandi rationem, quamquam non tan [*sic;
see Appendix 8, § 1 n. 1*] expresam adversus exactores pecunie pro pallio attigit
Henrricus [*sic*] de Hasia, fundator universitatis Vienensis super Genesim super
litteram, cuius sententia paulo post a nobis exponetur." F. 7r: "Nam et Henrricum
de Hasia, quem apud Australes Vienensis universitatis fundatorem affirmant,
magne et doctrine et sanctitatis virum, ita in interpretatione [interpretratione *M*]
tertii capituli Geneseos loqutum accepimus super eo loco, 'in sudore vultus tui
vesceris pane tuo, homo [*Gen. 3:19*].' . . ." F. 14r: "Adhuc [aduch *M*] ut Henrricus
de Asia argumentatur. . . ." F. 45r: "Sunt tamen qui putent, et hii quidem viri

of Sentences of the Dominican Durand of Saint-Pourçain (d. 1334),[260] and arguments, which Fernando may have learned second-hand, of the Franciscans John of Rupella (d. 1245)[261] and John of Ripa, active at Paris in the mid-fourteenth century.[262] It is possible that Fernando also had in mind one or more contemporary opponents.[263] But otherwise it would seem he was answering critics of the practice of charging a fee for the pallium during the Avignon papacy. In the second part of the treatise, contrary to expectations raised by the title, Fernando did not initiate the reader into any arcane mysteries, but rather addressed in twenty-five distinctions, each further divided into a number of *problemata*, practical topics concerning the pallium, such as its origin, form, and purpose.[264] Showing off his supposed command of Hebrew, Fernando promised in the preface to clear up in the future the confusion among biblical commentators between the *ephod* and the *ephobad.*[265] As far as I can tell, he never wrote such a work.

Fernando wrote other works of special interest to Roman curialists. One is the treatise *De Consultandi Ratione*, which is presently lost. It was addressed to the Spanish Cardinal Auxias de Podio sometime between 12 December 1477, when Auxias became cardinal presbyter of S. Sabina, as Fernando referred to him, and 2-3 September 1483, when Auxias

---

auctoritatis non vulgaris, has differentias nulla ratione posse simonie convenire, inter quos est Henrricus de Hasia, fundator universitatis Vienensis in opere suo super Genesim et Durandus quarto Sententiarum, q. 25." On Henry of Langenstein see Lohr (1967–1974), 24:226; for his still unedited commentary on Genesis see Stegmüller, 2:31–34; and Steneck, who makes no mention of papal subdeacons or the pallium. The reference to Durandus a S. Porciano, O.P., is to Bk. 4, d. 25, q. 4, of his *In Petri Lombardi Sententias Commentaria*, which I consulted in Durandus, 1:ff. 364v–366v.

[260] See the last quotation in the previous note. The reference in this case is to Bk. 4, d. 25, q. 4 (Durandus, 1:f. 365v): "Utrum simonia committatur illis tribus modis consuetis assignari, scilicet, per munus a manu, per munus a lingua, et per munus ab obsequio." The editor of Durandus's commentary cites Thomas Aquinas, *Summa Theologiae*, 2.2, q. 100, ar. 5, who, in fact, asks a similar question and comes to the same affirmative decision.

[261] M, f. 11v: "Item obiiciunt quidam subdiaconis, inter quos fuit frater Iohannes de Rupella, quod subdiaconi antequam traddant pallium, volunt non solum exigere pecunias, sed cauti fieri de pecunia exacta, quod sine simoniaco crimine fieri non posse ex sententia omnium utriusque iuris consultorum perspicuum [perspicuam M] est." On this thirteenth-century Franciscan see Fabro (1938); and Gründel.

[262] M, f. 124v: "Ad tertiam rationem dicimus quod hec ratio fuit quondam cuiusdam magistri Parisiensis Iohannis de Riparia, cui [*scil., rationi*] magno opere innitebatur ut doceret exactionem pecunie pro pallio esse illicitam in genere viciossissimi criminis simonie." I am assuming Fernando means the Scotist Ioannes de Ripa, active at Paris in the middle of the fourteenth century; see Lohr (1974–1982), 27:275; and Appendix 6B, § 42 n. 103 of this volume.

[263] See n. 258, p. 42.

[264] Ff. 130r–155v in M.

[265] See Appendix 8, § 2.

died.[266] In the nineteenth century, the very ornate dedication copy, which was apparently the only copy extant, was owned by Cardinal Antonio Pallotta (d. 1834).[267] In 1851, Gaetano Moroni, the former secretary of Pope Gregory XVI, stated that Pallotta bequeathed the manuscript to Gregory XVI (d. 1846).[268] But I have not been able to find any reference to the manuscript after Moroni's allusion to it in 1851.[269] Though the manuscript may still exist, we are dependent for our knowledge of it and of the treatise it contained on two rather unsatisfactory early nineteenth-century descriptions. According to one of these accounts, the *De Consultandi Ratione* treated the responsibilities of a cardinal towards the pope, and in particular on when and how to advise, i.e., the "Gius practico cardinalizio."[270] Its first part offered fifteen *conclusiones* which were "altrettanto norme con che un degno Cardinale possa bellamente i

---

[266] See Cancellieri, p. xff.; and Della Campa, p. viiff. Della Campa's pamphlet is an invective correcting Cancellieri. Della Campa expressed the hope that Cardinal Pallotta would see to the publishing of the text (p. xxiii), but neither Della Campana nor Cancellieri published any part of the text apart from the title: "Ferdinandi [sic] Cordubensis apostolici subdiaconi de consultandi ratione ad reverendissimum in Christo patrem et dominum, dominum Ausiam, tituli sancti Sabine praesbiterum cardinalem, Montis Regalis vulgo appellatum, tractatus incipit foeliciter." The title page carried Auxias de Podio's coat of arms. The parchment manuscript consisted of 190 folios. For the dates of Auxias as cardinal see Eubel, 2:17, num. VII, 5. Cancellieri, p. xlviii, quoted the following ownership note of Cardinal Girolamo Verallo (d. 10 Oct. 1555; see the *Enciclopedia Cattolica*, 12:1244–45) at the end of the manuscript: "Hic liber pervenit ad manus meas cum essem simplex doctor, quod fuit quoddam praesagium fortunae meae quoniam postea fui constitutus Auditoratui Rotae Apostolicae, deinde factus Episcopus Brittonoriensis. . . ." This note is followed by another: "Postea pervenit ad manus Iosephi Gerponi." I have not been able to identify Gerponus.

[267] Both Cancellieri and Della Campa addressed their pamphlets to Pallotta, concerning whom see the *Enciclopedia Cattolica*, 9:647.

[268] Moroni, 51:66–67: "[*Cardinal Pallotta*] lasciò a Gregorio XVI . . . il codice membranaceo di Ferdinando [sic] Cordubense, *De consultandi ratione*, che Cancellieri avea illustrato con *Lettera al cardinal Ant. Pallotta*, Pesaro, 1826." Moroni knew Gregory XVI's private library very well not only because he was the pope's secretary, but also because he used it in compiling his famous *Dizionario*. See Bignami Odier-Ruysschaert, 216, 228 n. 98; and Croci.

[269] On Gregory XVI's private library see C. Frati, 268; and *Bibliofilia*, 28 (1926–1927):226–27, for a manuscript of 191 folios then possessed by the Marchese Benedetto Guglielmi di Vulci, which consisted of an "Indice de'libri e manoscritti esistenti nella particolare Biblioteca della Santità di Nostro Signore Papa Gregorio XVI Felicemente Regnante. 1833" with the colophon "Fatto e continuato da me stesso scrivente Gaetano Moroni, e proseguito dal medesimo Pontefice, di suo venerato pugno. . . . Giugno 1846." The last dated entry is of 1842. Moroni added the title and colophon after the Pope's death in 1846. The notice "I libri di Gregorio XVI," *Il Buonarotti*, ser. 2, 11 (1872):202–03, taken from Gregory XVI's testament does not mention any manuscripts. It does say that apart from books specifically given to Moroni and other institutions, Gregory XVI left his library to the Congregation of the Propagation of the Faith; but I could not find the manuscript in Kowalsky's inventory of the Congregation. See also Federico, 163–64.

[270] Della Campa, p. xii.

suoi doveri adempiendo diportarsi col Sommo Pontefice."[271] The second
part consisted of forty-five distinctions elaborating and illustrating the
first part.

Fernando aggressively served curialist interests in another work, the
*De Iure Medios Exigendi Fructus Quos Vulgo Annatos Dicunt et Romani
Pontificis in Temporalibus Potestate*, dedicated to Pope Sixtus IV and printed
at Rome about 1481.[272] The second part of the treatise, i.e., *de Romani
pontificis in temporalibus potestate*, never appeared.[273] I doubt Fernando
ever wrote it. But even without it we have abundant material in his other
writings to document Fernando's assertion of papal temporal sovereignty
over the world. Indeed, this claim is the central argument in Fernando's
preface to the *De Medios Exigendi Fructus*.[274] The preface itself was so
long that Fernando must have feared that Sixtus IV would not read it.
Thus in the dedication copy and in the edition itself the first thing the
reader encounters is a one-paragraph précis of the preface. At the end
of the treatise Fernando appended two bizarre lists. The first categorized
all the *genera personarum* who owed the pope *annates* as the universal

---

[271] Della Campa, p. xiv.

[272] The edition, attributed to Georgius Herolt, carries no notice of date, place,
or printer (*GW* 9797; Hain-Copinger 5719; Goff, F-103). The dedication copy is
MS Vatican, Vat. lat. 1128, which is an elaborately decorated parchment manuscript of 200 folios, described by Pelzer, 1:767-68. A second manuscript in the Vatican is Barb. lat. 1493 (formerly XXVI, 30), which is a sixteenth-century paper, folio-
size miscellany with unnumbered folios written in double columns. The *De Iure
Medios Exigendi Fructus* is the first work, occupying ff. 1r-67ra, lacking the summary of the preface found in the printed edition and the dedication copy, but containing the epilogue quoted in the next note (preface: ff. 1r-4v; treatise proper:
f. 5r sq.); see Kristeller (1963-1992), 2:447. A third Vatican manuscript, Vat. lat.
3495 (paper, s. XVI, miscellany of 92 unnumbered folios; see Kristeller
[1963-1992], 2:320), contains an excerpt on ff. 76r-77r, consisting of the title (the
author is called Ferdinandus Cordubensis) and the passage, "Concilii Constantiensis decretum de annatis ita habet . . . infra sex menses a die publicationis. Hec
in decreto Concilii Constantiensis," which occupies twenty lines on f. [25v] of the
printed edition. The text is listed in Schulte, 2:369. See also Bonilla y San Martín,
99-100.

[273] The printed edition and the two manuscripts of the treatise contain the following notice at the end: "Secundam huius operis partem de potestate pape in
temporalibus ob id in alterum transtulimus, quod altissima materia sit et speciale
desiderans opus, et quod principalior de mediis fructibus tractatus in maius volu-
men surrexit."

[274] See, for instance, f. [2v] of the printed edition: "Hac ratione inductos re-
ligiosissimos principes constat non medios fructus, non integros modo, sed ipsas
integras provincias, integra regna, integra imperia . . . Romanis non tam dedisse
quam reddidisse principibus ut unum in terris monarcham, unicum principem et
in spiritualibus et in temporalibus recognoscerent." Ibid., f. [4r]: ". . . vel donati-
onem Constantini, ut quidam putant, vel restitutionem, ut ego existimo. . . ." See
also f. 33v: "Preterea decimoquarto minor est potentia eius qui divino iure uni
preest populo quam eius qui eodem iure toti preest orbi. Sed pontifici summo
testamenti veteris date sunt decime decimarum totius populi, qui tantum Israel-
itico populo prefuit. Ergo pontifici novi testamenti, qui toti orbi preest, debe-
buntur non decime solum clericorum sed et laicorum totius orbis."

pastor.[275] Starting with Gentiles, Jews, and Moslems, he then listed forty-one professions, including prostitutes, pimps, thieves, and beggars.[276] The beggars, in turn, he subdivided into forty categories, which he described and to which he assigned their Italian names.[277] To defend the system of papal annates, Fernando used a large number of canonical and theological authorities.[278] He also resorted to secular sources, including Livy, Suetonius, Josephus, Pliny, Cicero, Seneca, Macrobius, Virgil, Servius, Priscian, Liutprand of Cremona, Euclid, and Aristotle. Turning the table on the humanists, he correctly refuted the view put forward by Flavio Biondo and Platina, that Pope Boniface IX (1389–1404) was the first to collect annates.[279] As Fernando showed, the practice was much older than this pope. But some of his most interesting citations either evaporate upon examination or prove to be other than what they seem. The Dardanus whom he cites as an authority "apud Graecos," he got straight out of Priscian.[280] His correction *secundum Hebraicam veritatem* of the Vulgate translation of Ex. 25:39 comes from Nicholas of Lyra.[281] He cites a sermon of Eusebius of Caesarea *de sacerdotali veste* that does not exist.[282] In an extraordinary display of erudition concerning the passage in the *Metaphysics* where Aristotle explains that mathematics originated in Egypt because the priests there had the leisure to pursue these studies, Fernando refers the reader to John Philoponus's commentary, Themistius' *Excerpta* on the Metaphysics, and Alexander of Aphrodisias' *De Syllogismis Hypotheticis.*[283] The commentary attributed to Philo-

---

[275] Fernando announced his working principle at the start of the list (Fernando of Cordova [c. 1481], f. [74r]): "Et quia pontifex maximus pascendus est temporaliter ab eis quos pascit spiritualiter, ut docet apostolus I Cor. IX, fieri necesse est ut quot sunt personarum genera quos [*recte* quas] pabulo celesti per orbem terrrarum pascit a tot terreno pabulo ipse pastor pasci debeat."

[276] Fernando of Cordova (c. 1481), ff. [74r–80r].

[277] Fernando of Cordova (c. 1481), ff. [74v, 81v–88r]. I quote the full list of beggars in Monfasani (1991), 189–90 n. 58; to the literature there cited must be added Camporesi, with a useful introduction and collection of texts.

[278] On annates see Pugliese; and Kirsch.

[279] Fernando of Cordova (c. 1481), f. [23v]; see Biondo, *Historiarum ab Inclinatione Romanorum Imperii Decades,* dec. 2, bk. 10 *ad finem* (Biondo, f. E 7r); and Platina, *Liber de Vita Christi ac Omnium Pontificum* (Platina, 3.1:291.34). Fernando also correctly noted that Platina derived his information from Biondo. On Pope Boniface IX's measures concerning annates see Pugliese, 126–28 and 132–33.

[280] Fernando of Cordova (c. 1481), f. [42r], repeating Priscian, *De Fig. Numer.* 10 (in Keil, 3:408.18–19); and f. [43v], repeating ibid. 14 (in Keil, 3:409.30–31).

[281] Fernando of Cordova (c. 1481), f. [42r]; see Appendix 8, n. 5, page 90.

[282] Fernando of Cordova (c. 1481), f. [41v]. In the *De Misterio Pallii* (M, f. 79r), he cited the sermon *de veste sacerdotali* of Maximus. But Maximus the Confessor left no sermons, and none of the extant sermons of Maximus of Turin carry this title or discuss this subject (see Maximus episcopus Taurinensis).

[283] Fernando of Cordova (c. 1481), f. [33r]: "Super quo, inquam, loco [*Metaph.* 1.981b17–25] ita Iohannes grammaticus habet: 'Egyptii primum deinde omnium gentium sacerdotes ommium hominum fuerunt locupletes, presertim maximus sacerdos. Nam inferiores sacerdotes in ingressu sacerdotii, id est, beneficii, mediam

ponus is of exceptional rarity.[284] It has never been edited, though Francesco Patrizi translated it into Latin in the sixteenth century. So the fact that Fernando knew of this commentary is a tribute to his erudition. However, the passage he cites is not to be found in Patrizi's translation[285]; and, if it does exist in the Greek, I very much doubt Fernando could have found it on his own. As for Themistius's *Excerpta*, the cited passage may exist, but it is not in the published scholia extracted from Themistius's lost commentary on the *Metaphysics*.[286] On the other hand, a passage in Asclepius's commentary on the *Metaphysics*, which Fernando does not mention, comes close to what Fernando attributed to Philoponus and Themistius, and may very well have been Fernando's source, supplied to him by a competent Greek scholar.[287] Finally, Alexander of Aphrodisias did not write a work entitled *De Syllogismis Hypotheticis*.[288] In other words, Fernando cited texts from the vast storehouse of his memory with no concern for accuracy (though he could be more or less correct), but with every intent of making the resulting jumble impressively erudite. In equally impressive fashion, Fernando cites Eustratius's commentary on Aristotle's *Nicomachean Ethics* as his source for Plato's views on taxation in the *Republic* and *Laws*.[289] Eustratius, translated by Robert Grosse-

---

partem reddituum summo sacerdoti ministrabant.' Idem dicit Themistius in excerptis super Methaphisicis Aristotelis. Idem Alexander Peripatheticus [Paripatheticus *correxi*] repetit in tractatu vulgari de silogismis ipotheticis.''

[284] Only two manuscripts are known (Vienna, Österreichische Nationalbibliothek, Phil gr. 189; and BAV, Urb. gr. 49 [anonymous commentary]); see Kristeller (1964), 176, n. 7.

[285] Another rare text, published in 1583, whose title specifies *Expositiones in Omnes XIIII Aristotelis Libros*; I consulted the copy at the Biblioteca Nazionale in Rome (shelf mark: 14. 12F. 26).

[286] The only *Excerpta* I have been able to find are from Themistius' paraphrase of Bk. Lambda, and not Bk. Alpha, where 981b is located. These *excerpta* have been edited by Brandis, 798–813. The paraphrase of Bk. Lambda has been edited by Landauer (see Themistius; for a concordance between Landauer and Brandis see Gigon, p. li). For Alexander see Alexander of Aphrodisias, 6–7 (= Brandis, 9; Gigon, 524–25).

[287] See Asclepius, 12.25–26 (this passage is not part of the excerpts edited by Brandis; see the concordance between the editions in Gigon, p. xliii): "οἱ ἱερεῖς τὰ ἀναγκαῖα εἶχον ἄλλοθεν αὐτοῖς παρεχόμενα καὶ ἐσχόλαζον μόνοις τοῖς μαθήμασιν.''

[288] No writings of the Aristotelian Alexander of Aigai are extant. For the *fortuna* of Alexander of Aphrodisias and pseudo-Alexander see Cranz.

[289] Fernando of Cordova (c. 1481), f. [71r-v]: "Instituendarum autem annatarum ratio originalis a philosophie fonte profecta est, que et accipi potest ex libris De republica atque legibus Platonis, et repetita ab Eustacio Aristotelicorum librorum in ethicis interprete. Nam constat et Platonem et Eustacium ita locutos: Consuevere quidam in bene institutis civitatibus, ubi necessitas urget alicuius comparande summe pecuniarie ingentis, eam quidem non extorquere a civibus ab eis exigentes. Nam id quidem gravissimum et intolerabile videretur. Sed potius inducunt in animo levissimas imponere exactiones eis in rebus sine quibus humana vita transigi nequit, ut exempli causa super pane, vino, carnibus; et quamquam quod imponitur unicuique libre vel panis vel carnium vel unicuique

teste, made no such reference; his anonymous continuator, also translated by Grosseteste, did once refer to the *Republic* and *Laws* together, but
in a passage which had nothing to do with taxation.[290]

Fernando's writings also reflect his scientific interests. While at Paris
in 1445 he claimed to have already written a commentary on Ptolemy's
Almagest.[291] But what is extant are two works from his later years in
Rome. The first is a medical text, the *De Secretis Humane Nature per Urinam
Cognoscendis*, dedicated to Fernando's fellow curialist and provost of the
cathedral chapter of Albi, Gui Barbut (Guido Barbutus).[292] In the *De
Artificio* Fernando mentions a witticism made at the expense of Lullism
by Barbut while hunting "with the cardinal" (d'Estouteville?), which
proves that despite his mocking attitude, Barbut, like Fernando, had
delved into the Lullian *Art*.[293] In the preface to the *De Secretis*, Fernando
explained that it was at Barbut's request that he was stepping "beyond
the bounds of my profession" of philosophy and theology and diverting
his attention from *res altissimae* to *haec stercora et urinae*.[294] As its title indicates, the treatise explores what urine can tell us about the physical con-
dition and temperament of a patient. In a second section, it was also supposed to discuss for the sheer fun of it (*delectationis gratia*) questions such
as: "in quo est maior delectatio, an in coeundo vel comedendo vel
egerendo," and: "in quo est in coeundo maior delectatio, an in mare an
in femina."[295] But as it stands in the sole extant manuscript, the treatise

---

mensure vini levissimum sit, nihil minus eius est ponderis ut collectum sit
magnum aliquid tum quoniam ab omnibus excepto nemine colligitur, tum quoniam in eis rebus imponitur quibus omnes utuntur, tum preterea quia usus
talium rerum quotidianus est. Atque ita fit ut sine ullius gravamine et quodam-
modo insensibiliter necessitati provideatur reipublice."

[290] See Eustratius, 585.13, concerning *Eth. Nic.*, 10.1177a34; the separate references to the *Laws* and *Republic* in the commentary are no more relevant. I also
consulted the Latin translation in Grosseteste (incomplete; only vols. 1–4 have
appeared).

[291] See n. 59, p. 12.

[292] The treatise is only known from a paper miscellany of different hands and
fascicles, MS BAV, Regin. lat. 1773, ff. 49r–61v (in a fifteenth-century Gothic cursive hand), which once belonged to Pier Leoni; see Kristeller (1963–1992), 2:484;
and Ruysschaert, 54–55, num. 10. The preface and the table of contents have been
published by Poupardin, 537–42, and by Bonilla y San Martín (from Poupardin),
93–96 (note that both omit a word and mistranscribe another at the end of the
preface; read "secunda *problemata tum* quadam varietate . . . tractat"). Fernando
simply called Barbut a *nobilis atque generosus vir* in the *De secretis*; but in the *De
Artificio* he referred to him in this way (Bonilla y San Martín, viii, lin. 29 sq.):
"unde est illud Guidonis Barbuti prepositi Albiensis facete dictum, qui cum
venatum cum cardinali proficisceretur. . . ."

[293] See the end of the previous note.

[294] Poupardin, 538; Bonilla y San Martín, 94: ". . . extra mee professionis terminos impulistis, quip<p>e qui licet nichil alienum a philosopho atque theologo
[theologum *cod.*] putem, tamen indignum videatur ingenium in rebus altissimis
atque ipsa divinitate versatum ad hec stercora et urinas revocare (revocat *cod.*)."

[295] These are questions num. 36 and num. 37 of the 47 questions listed in the
table for Part II.

ends with the thirteenth (and last) chapter of part 1. Given Fernando's writing habits, as seen in the *De Iure Medios Exigendi Fructus*, we should not assume that he ever wrote the second part. The *De Secretis* may be related to the lost *De Discretione Spirituum* which Fernando mentions in the *De Artificio.*[296] The *De Secretis* carries no indication of date; but I would think that he wrote it in the late 1460s–early 1470s, i.e., about the time he mentioned Barbut in the *De Artificio*. The personal physician of Lorenzo de' Medici, Pier Leoni, owned the sole extant manuscript of the *De Secretis.*[297] He also owned one of the two extant copies of Fernando's *De Misterio Pallii.*[298] Since Leoni lived for a while in Rome in the later fifteenth century,[299] he very well might have been an acquaintance of Fernando.

In 1478 at Rome, Fernando published his edition of Albert the Great's massive *De Animalibus.*[300] He appended to the start of the volume a series of tables which purport to give the correct (transliterated) spelling and meaning of the Greek and Arabic names of animals which Albert had either misspelled or left in meaningless transliterations because of his reliance on poor translations.[301] I cannot judge Fernando's Arabic, but his Greek certainly left something to be desired.[302] In the preface, Fernando strove mightily to defend Albert's Latinity against humanist critics.[303] I suspect that Fernando was especially thinking here of his former colleague in the Bessarion circle Theodore Gaza, who harshly

---

[296] Bonilla y San Martín, ix, lin. 2–3: "quod in tractatu nostro de discretione spirituum subtilius a nobis disertum est." See also ibid., 88–89.

[297] See n. 292, p. 48.

[298] See the introduction to Appendix 8, p. 89.

[299] See Guerra-Coppioli, 389–90.

[300] The edition was printed by Nicola Cardella with the date in the colophon, 2 April 1478 (*GW* 587; Hain-Copinger-Reichling 545; Goff, A-223). Some copies lack the first quire with Fernando's preface and glossary.

[301] The glossary is on ff. 1v–8v. In the preface Fernando explained the glossary in this way (Bonilla y San Martín, lxxx): "brevi tabella omnia animalium nomina vel Arabica vel Greca vel emendare corrupta vel reddere Latina que per immensum opus disseminata videntur."

[302] The glossary begins with names of fishes, from which I take these examples. What Fernando calls, "Ostra codermata, id est, pisces habentes duas carnes," must be *ostrakodermoi*, which simply means shell-fish, and certainly not a fish with "two fleshes." He correctly identifies *obstracta* (= *ostraka*, shell-fish) and *melachia*, but speaks of "ipopotanos Grece, id est piscis fluvialis," when the animal can only be the large mammal *hippopotamos*. Fernando's *trigottonus* simply is not a Greek name for fishes; and when he lists "hiccicos, pisces. Hiccis, idem," he must mean *ichthus*, "fish," though he asserts that in this section of the glossary he is listing names correctly transliterated in Albert. Fernando used the same names for genera of fishes in the *De Artificio* (Bonilla y San Martín, xlvi–xlviii).

[303] The whole preface is edited in Bonilla y San Martín, lxxvii–lxxx. Fernando's praise of Albert caught the attention of Grabmann, 108. See Bonilla y San Martín, lxxvii, lin. 18–20: "accedit et illud huic pene divino viro quod tanta sententiarum gravitate miro acumini coniuncta tanta eloquentia, licet quidam levisculi homines contra putent."

attacked medieval translators and deprecated the value of works dependent on medieval translations.[304] If Demosthenes's language is the standard for orators, Fernando argued, Albert's is the standard for philosophers.[305] Indeed, for Fernando, Albert was not merely a "defender
of Aristotelian philosophy," but also a rival of Aristotle for the leader-
ship of the *secta*.[306] And if Plato can be said to be Moses *Attice loquens*,
then Albert can be considered another Aristotle speaking in the Latin
tongue.[307]

Fernando dedicated the *De Animalibus* to Pope Sixtus IV. Since he also
dedicated to Sixtus IV the only other of his works to be printed, the *De
Iure Medios Exigendi Fructus*, I think it highly probable that Fernando's
former companion in the Bessarion circle subsidized both these publica-
tions. The editions of Albert's *De Animalibus* and the *De Iure Medios
Exigendi Fructus* have something else in common: an immodest title. In
the title of the former, Fernando is called an *in orbe famosissimus magister*,
and three years later, in the *De Iure Medios Exigendi Fructus*, the word
terrarum was added after *orbe* to eliminate any doubts about the extent
of his fame. The manuscript dedication copy of the *De Iure Medios Exigendi Fructus* has the same title.[308] So we cannot blame the *braggadocio* of
the titles on the printers, even if we were inclined to ignore the fact that
the volumes were published by different printers with the only common
denominators being Fernando's authorship and Sixtus IV's support.
Sixtus IV, in fact, proved to be a reasonably good patron to Fernando.
As we have seen, immediately after his election he gave Fernando rec-
ognition as a scholar by appointing him to the papal commission which
decided the case of Petrus de Riva and the controversy at Louvain on
future contingents.[309] He also tried to find a bishopric for Fernando in
Castile. Sixtus's recommendation to the royal court is lost, but in his
response of 6 July 1483, the powerful Cardinal of Toledo, Pedro González
de Mendoza, reported that he had passed on to Queen Isabella of Castile
the Pope's request in favor of Fernando.[310] Yet when Sixtus died a year
later, Fernando was still only an apostolic subdeacon.

Sixtus also played a role in the last notice we have of Fernando's activi-

---

[304] For example, see Schmitt, 267.

[305] Bonilla y San Martín, lxxix, lin. 24–26: ". . . ut quod laudi inter oratores
Demosteni, quod lex orandi fuerit, ita et viro huic quod phylosophandi lex fuerit
iure tribui potest."

[306] Ibid., p. lxxvii, lin. 8–12: ". . . ita Aristotelice philosophie non defensorem
modo, sed et usque ad minutissima verba acutissimasque sententias emulatorem
fuisse constat ut cuius phylosophiam sectaretur, dicendi quoque exprimeret
caracterem, facileque discernere nescias interpres ne sit Aristotelis an ipse sit
Aristoteles quem interpretetur."

[307] Ibid., p. lxxvii, lin. 14–16: "et illud vulgatum, 'quis enim Plato quam alter
Moyses Attice loquens?' Alberto nostro ad comparationem Aristotelis Perypathe-
tice discipline principis iure possit aptari."

[308] See n. 272, p. 45.

[309] See p. 36.

[310] See Batllori (1958).

ties in Rome. In February 1485, the Roman printer Eucharius Silber published the *Ars Brevis* of Ramon Lull. Probably that same month, as a companion piece to the Lullian *Ars*, Silber also printed the *Ianua Artis Magistri
Raymundi Lulli*, of Pere Deguí, a Catalan priest who was the first holder
of the chair in Lullism established on Majorca in 1481 and who before
his death in 1500 became the chaplain of Ferdinand and Isabella.[311] The
Roman edition of Deguí's *Ianua* carries a report of a theological commission addressed to an unidentified pope which certifies the orthodoxy
of Deguí's work.[312] One of the signers of the report was Fernando of
Cordova.

The background to the report is as follows. In a brief of 12 September
1483, Sixtus IV had ordered Pere Deguí to Rome to answer charges of
heresy stemming from the *Ianua*.[313] Deguí had written the *Ianua* in 1473,
but it was first printed in 1482 (in Barcelona).[314] On 11 September 1483,
the day before Sixtus's brief, a papal commission of cardinals, probably
the very same ones who advised him to bring Deguí to trial for
heresy,[315] had issued a bull prohibiting theological criticism of some
verses engraved on an altar in a Dominican church in Aragon.[316] The
verses expressed the Thomistic view that Christ would not have been
born if man had not sinned.[317] Following John Duns Scotus, Ramon Lull
rejected this view[318]; and it was apparently Lullists who had caused the

---

[311] None of the authorities on Deguí seems to have known Sixtus IV's brief
discussed below. So my account of the episode will differ somewhat from theirs.
See Pérez Martínez; Batllori (1944), 493–99; Fita (*Boyl*, 1891), 288–323 passim;
Fita, (*Descós*, 1891), 381–96 and passim thereafter; Custerer, 297–301; and
Carreras y Artau, 2:72–76.

[312] See Rogent and Durán, num. 7; and Fava, 190. I edit the report in Appendix 10.

[313] See Fontana. The addressee of the papal brief (unnamed in the copy preserved in ASV, Armadio XXXIX, 16, f. 20r, though he probably was Diego de Avellaneda, Bishop of Palma on Majorca) was charged with the responsibility of
informing Deguí of the papal command. The brief explains that Deguí was
accused of attempting in the *Ianua* to "quodam novo modo tradere productionem
rerum omnium extenditque vires suas adusque productionem personarum divinarum." Furthermore, a group of cardinals had already made a preliminary
examination of the work at Sixtus's request and found it to contain "propositiones
. . . falsas et erroneas, aliquas vero integritati fidei suspectas, quibus iam a pluribus annis apud Maioricas animos infecit plurimorum."

[314] See Fita (*Descós*, 1891), 382–83; Rogent and Durán, num. 4.

[315] The four, as listed in the bull cited in the next note, were Oliverio Carafa
(cardinal of Sta. Sabina), Giovanni Arcimboldi (cardinal of S. Prassedi), Jorge de
Costa, O. Cister. (cardinal of Ss. Marcellino e Pietro), and Gabriele Rangone,
O. F. M. (cardinal of Ss. Sergio e Baccho).

[316] The bull is printed in Diago, ff. 60v–61r (= Bk. 1, c. 33).

[317] The verses, inscribed on an altar dedicated to the Virgin Mary, run:
"Non abhorres peccatores, / sine quibus nunquam fores / tanto digna filio." On
Thomas Aquinas's position see his *Sum. Theol.* 3, qu. 1, art. 3; and *Comm. in
Sent.* 3, dist. 1, qu. 1, art. 3; see also Bonnefoy.

[318] See Minges, 2:368–70; Eijo Garay; Haubst; Nicolau; and Platzeck (1962),
103–04.

controversy in Aragon which provoked the Dominican Inquisitor of
Majorca, Guillem Caselles, to come to Rome and secure the approbation
of the verses and, implicitly, of St. Thomas's opinion on the issue.[319]
Caselles was so successful in Rome that he turned the tables on his Lullist opponents and persuaded the cardinals to place Deguí under suspi-
cion of heresy. According to a petition of 18 June 1483 sent from Majorca
to the Aragonese royal court, Caselles had accused Deguí and his followers of maintaining eight heretical conclusions.[320] However, according
to the Roman *approbatio* signed by Fernando, the number of questionable
propositions were reduced to three.[321]

Deguí arrived in Rome at the end of 1483 or in early 1484.[322] By then,
or soon after Sixtus IV, a Scotist theologian, probably became suspicious
that the charges against Deguí reflected Dominican prejudice against
Scotist theology and philosophy. Consequently, he appointed a theological commission to judge Deguí which by its very composition could only
return a favorable decision. Two of its members, Guillermus Bodivit[323]
and Bishop Dominicus Antonius de Pignerolio of Fano,[324] were, like the
pope himself, Franciscan theologians; a third was Jaume Conil, whom
later developments prove to have been a Lullist[325]; a fourth was Fernando, whose sympathy with Scotism and familiarity with Lullism were
certainly among the reasons why Sixtus assigned him to the commission; and the last two, Ioannes, Abbot of St. Bernard in Valencia[326] and
Bishop Franciscus de Noya of Cefalù,[327] were scholars whose loyalties I
cannot determine from other evidence, but who were not, in any case,
Dominicans. Pointedly, the commission exonerated Deguí mainly by
interpreting him as agreeing with Scotus.[328]

Though in the rubric of later printings of the *Ianua* the commission's

---

[319] The cardinals were quite specific about his presence (Diago, f. 60va): "Cum
nuper ad Romanam curiam venisset venerabilis magister Guillermus Caselles,
s. theologiae professor ordinis Praedicatorum et inquisitor haereticae pravitatis
in regno Maioricarum. . . ."

[320] Pérez Martínez, 303: "dient lo dit Mestre Dagui e sos dexebles tenir e
affirmar vuyt conclusions hereticals."

[321] See Appendix 10. Menéndez y Pelayo, 1:556, has misled later historians by
describing the text he found in MS Milan, Bibl. Ambros., N 240 sup., as the in-
quisitorial *censura* against Deguí, when, in fact, it is the *approbatio* edited in
Appendix 8.

[322] See Fita (*Boyl*, 1891), 298 and 301-02, for letters of Deguí's followers discussing his absence in Rome datable to February and April 1484.

[323] On Bodivit, who was a Breton, see Sbaraglia, 1:335b, num. 1667 bis;
Levot, 1:114; O'Malley, 246 and passim, on some sermons of Bodivit: one before
Sixtus IV for the feast of the Annunciation on 25 March 1484 and another before
Innocent VIII for the feast of the Holy Trinity on 29 May 1485.

[324] Eubel, 2:152; Ughelli, 1:667, who calls him "Pedemontanus."

[325] See Janer (= Rogent and Durán, 34-35, num. 36), which contains on ff.
276r-277v a postscript of Conil and others approving the work.

[326] I have no information concerning him.

[327] See Eubel, 2:125.

[328] See Appendix 10.

report is addressed to Sixtus IV, we have the explicit assertion of one of
its members, Jaume Conil, that the commission finished its work in the
first year of the pontificate of Innocent VIII (elected 29 August 1484).[329]
Moreover, Franciscus de Noya, who signed himself as the bishop of
Cefalù, did not receive this title until 26 November 1484, three months
after the death of Sixtus IV.[330] Deguí returned to Majorca after seeing to
the printing of Lull's *Ars Brevis* and his own *Ianua Artis* at Rome in early
1485.[331] He was back in Rome at the end of 1486.[332] But by then Fernando was probably dead.

Fernando died in 1486 according to the inscription on his sepulchral
monument. The monument itself is surprisingly large, rising about six
meters and consisting of a full-length statue of Fernando resting upon
his bier, under which there is a large plaque containing his epitaph. The
Cardinal of Portugal, Jorge de Costa, erected the monument in the church
of S. Giacomo degli Spagnuoli, but it is now to be found in the cloister
of S. Maria di Montserrat opposite the entrance to the cloister on the via
Giulia.[333]

---

[329] See n. 325, p. 52. See also Custerer, 297 and 348, where a bull of 20 January 1500 of Alexander VI to Ferdinand of Aragon is quoted which referred to Innocent VIII's approval of Lull's orthodoxy: ". . . est approbata per Francorum regem,
per cancellarium universitatis studii Pariensiensis, et per legatum summi pontificis et pontificem Innocentium."

[330] Eubel 2:125.

[331] See Rogent and Durán, num. 6 and num. 7; for his return to Majorca see
the colophon of his *Metaphysica*: "Composuit magister Petrus Dagui hoc opus in
regno Maioricarum in Podio Rande, vigesimo die Septembris anno domini millesimo octuagesimo quinto CCCC" (Deguí, f. bb 9v [= Hain-Reichling 8547;
Rogent and Durán, num. 26; Goff, G-549], which I consulted in the Pierpont
Morgan Library). See Fita (*Descós*, 1891), 390–91. There was a real need to reprint
the *Ianua* because in his brief of 12 September 1483, Sixtus had ordered the confis-
cation of all copies of the *editio princeps*. As Fontana, 472, points out, this order
is doubtless reponsible at least in part for the exceptional rarity of the first edition.
The only copy cited in the literature is that of the Biblioteca Nacional in Madrid.

[332] The colophon of his treatise *Formalitates Breves* has this colophon: "Com-
posuit magister Petrus Dagui presentes breves distinctiones Rome anno domini
MCCCC octuagesimo sexto, die vero decima Decembris." (I used the printing
Daguí [c. 1500], f. a 6v [Goff, G-545; not in Hain-Copinger-Reichling nor in
Rogent and Durán; seen at the Huntington Library]).

[333] See Appendix 11.

APPENDIX 1

A List of Authentic, Doubtful, and Misattributed Works of Fernando of Cordova

Virtually all the bibliographical information I have concerning these texts can be read in the monograph proper and in the appendices. Consequently, in most cases, this list serves as an index of the main discussions of these works.

AUTHENTIC WORKS
(in Approximate Chronological Order)

Propositiones Defended at Vienna in September 1448
See pp. 19-21 and Appendix 6.
De Laudibus Platonis ex Testimoniis Tum Sacrorum Interpretum, Tum Ethnicorum adversus Quosdam Doctrinam Eius et Vitam Carpere Solitos
See p. 24-25.
De Duabus Philosophiis et Praestantia Philosophiae Platonis supra Aristotelis
Lost; see pp. 25-26.
De Discretione Spirituum
Lost; see p. 49.
De Artificio Omnis et Investigandi et Inveniendi Natura Scibilis
See pp. 26-35.
Dialectica
Lost; see p. 31.
De Eucharistia
Lost; see p. 37.
An Licita Sit cum Saracenis Pax
Lost. See pp. 37-38.
Tractatus de Modis Quibus Decollaratur Ecclesia
Lost. See p. 40.
Adversus Hereticos Qui Fraterculi Dela Opinione Apellantur
See pp. 38-40 and Appendix 7.
First Treatise on Future Contingents
Lost; see p. 36.
Second Treatise on Future Contingents
See pp. 36-37.
De Misterio Pallii, et An pro Eo Aliquod Temporale absque Simonie Labe Exigi Possit
See pp. 41-43 and Appendix 8.
De Secretis Humane Nature per Urinam Cognoscendis
See pp. 48-49.
De Iure Medios Exigendi Fructus Quos Vulgo Annatos Dicunt et Romani Pontificis in Temporalibus Potestate
See pp. 45-48.

De Consultandi Ratione
Lost; see pp. 43–45.
Edition of Albert the Great's *De Animalibus*
See pp. 49–50.
Approbatio Libelli Petri Dagui
See pp. 51–53.

Doubtful Works

Commentary on Ptolemy's *Almagest*
See pp. 12 and 48.
Commentary on the *Apocalypse* and Other Books of the Bible
See p. 12; and Stegmüller, 2:309, num. 2270.
Letter to the King of France Urging Peace
See n. 44, page 10.
Practica
See p. 31.
De Differentiis Quibus Plato ab Aristotile Discidet
See nn. 142 and 227, pages 26 and 37.
Treatise on the Biblical *Ephod*
See p. 43.

Misattributed Works

De Haereticis et Damnatis
Bonilla y San Martín, 102, cited this work from Montfaucon, 1:102; but the manuscript which Montfaucon cited, BAV, Vat. lat. 1127 is that of the authentic *Adversus Hereticos Qui Fraterculi dela Opinione Appellantur.*
Sermo de S. Augustino
Redlich, 48 n. 193, attributes this work to Fernando on the basis of MS Munich, Bayerische Staatsbibliothek, Clm. 18223, ff. 233v–239v, which I have seen in photographs. However, the rubric on f. 233r carries the date "In Avenione, presentibus cardinalibus, anno domini MCCCLII." The "Fernandus de Hyspania" who wrote this sermon is therefore not our Fernando.

APPENDIX 2

Papal Documents Concerning Fernando of Cordova

Beltrán de Heredia has published six of these nine documents. However, he also seems to refer to a document which I believe to be a ghost. At 1:137, he states concerning Fernando: "Ocupó desde 1454 la escolastría de Burgos." But he reports no document to this effect. What he does report (3:76–77, num. 1152) is that on 4 April 1454 Pope Nicholas V authorized the establishment of a teaching post (*scholastria*) for the education of poor clerics at the cathedral of Burgos and conferred this office on Alfonso López (Alfonsus Lupi). Beltrán de Heredia further reports (3:79, num. 1155) that on 13 July 1454 the occupier of the Burgos *scholastria*, Alfonso López, resigned to the papacy his personal share of the income of the cathedral (*portio*) so that it would be united to the *scholastria* in perpetuity. The next notice on the *scholastria* at Burgos is dated 14 February 1517, when Pope Leo X reestablished the *scholastria*, which obviously had disappeared some time earlier (3:226–27, num. 1304). As far as the *Bulario* is concerned, Alfonso López was the only holder of this *scholastria* in 1454. I suspect that because of some inadvertency Beltrán de Heredia confused Fernando with Alfonso López. Moreover, it is hard to believe that Fernando would go off to teach in a small school in Burgos when before and after 1454 we find him at Rome busily collecting benefices and cultivating important patrons.

1

1 FEBRUARY 1448, VATICAN ("Romae, apud Sanctum Petrum, Kalendas Februarii, anno primo")

Source: ASV, Suppl. 423, f. 93r-v.

Literature: Denifle and Chatelain, 2:632 n. 4, first called attention to this document, citing it as "Suppl. Nicol. V, n° 416, fol. 93." Beltrán de Heredia, 3:19–20, num. 1088, edits it.

Summary: Fernandus de Cordoba (written as "Cordoa" in the register), papal ambassador and doctor of theology ("oratori vestro . . . magistro in sacra theologia"), supplicates Pope Nicholas V and is granted the power to claim in the papal court of the *Litterae Contradictoriae* during his absence from the Curia in the service of Cardinal Juan Carvajal, papal legate in Germany, a canonry or benefice which corresponds to the expectative previously granted him by Pope Nicholas V, but from which the chicanery of others had blocked him in this court.

2

22 SEPTEMBER 1449, FABRIANO

Source: ASV, Reg. Vat. 410, ff. 225r–226r.

Literature: First reported by Sassi, 178. I thank Dr. Concetta Bianca for calling Sassi's work to my attention.

Summary: Pope Nicholas V grants Fernandus de Corduba, doctor of theology and canon of Seville, the same legal standing and perogatives as a member of the papal household in the pursuit of a canonry in the diocese of Seville and a canonry in the diocese of Cordova for which the pope had granted him expectives dated 14 June 1447. Fernandus had been having difficulty implementing these expectives.

Text: Nicolaus etc. Dilecto filio Fernando de Corduba, canonico Ispalenensi, magistro in theologio [*sic*], salutem etc. Litterarum sciencia, vite ac morum honestas, aliaque laudabilia probitatis et virtutum merita, super quibus apud nos fidedigno commendaris testimonio, nos inducunt ut te specialibus favoribus et graciis prosequamur, dudum siquidem, videlicet, sub datum decimo octavo Kalendas Iulii pontificatus nostri anno primo, tibi de uno Ispalensis et alio Cordubensis ecclesiarum canonicatibus cum reservatione totidem inibi prebendarum ac dignitatis, personatus, administrationis, vel officii alterius earumdem ecclesiarum, etiam si ad illam, illum, vel illud consuevisset quis per electionem assumi eique cura immineret animarum, necnon prestimoniorum, prestimonialium portionum, et simplicium beneficiorum in Ispalensi ac Cordubensi civitatibus et diocesibus unius, duorum, trium seu plurimum ipsarum ecclesiarum canonici seu canonicorum aut in illis seu civitatibus et diocesibus predicitis beneficati vel beneficatorum, quorum quidem prestimoniorum, portionium, et beneficiorum fructus, redditus, et proventus certe tunc expresse librarum Turonensium parvarum summe valorem annuum non excederent, vacancium tunc aut simul vel successive vacaturorum per alias nostras litteras gratiose duximus providendum, prout in eisdem litteris plenius continetur. Cum autem, sicut exhibita nobis nuper pro parte tua peticio continebat, nos postmodum quam plura<s> diversis personis expectivas et aliasque gratias nominandi seu conferendi beneficia, facultates et de primo vacaturis seu alias speciales reservationes ac de sic reservatis, cum vacabunt, conferendi mandata, antelationes, quoque prerogativas, declarationes, exceptiones, suspensiones, indulta, et litteras concessimus, per que tibi in assecutione prebendarum, dignitatis, personatus, administrationis vel officii, necnon prestimoniorum, portionum, et beneficiorum predictorum preiudicium seu impedimentum aliquod afferri potest et dictum affertur, nos, qui dudum nonnullis familiaribus nostris continuis commensalibus in certo libro Cancellarie apostolice descriptis quasdam in assecutione beneficiorum vigore gratiarum /f. 225v/ eis per nos concessarum facienda prerogativas et antelationes concessimus ac deinde declaravimus nostre intentionis fuisse et esse quod per quascumque expectivas nominandi seu conferendi de primo vacaturis facultates vel alias speciales reservationes et de sic reservatis conferendi mandata, suppressiones, uniones, annexiones, et reductiones ad ius commune, gratias, concessiones, et indulta cum quibusvis prerogativarum favoribus, antelationibus, declarationibus, etiam motu proprio, sub quibusvis verborum formis et aliis clausulis derogatoriis et insolitis quibuscumque personis, cuiuscumque gradus, dignitatis, conditionis, et ordinis existerent, ecclesiis, monasteriis, eorumque mensis etiam capitularibus concessa et in antea concedenda non intendebamus [intendebat *correxi*] fieri preiudicium aliquod sive veris famililiaribus continuis commensalibus in libro Cancellarie apostolice descriptis huiusmodi, qm [*sic*] ipsi familiares essent potiores in assecutione beneficiorum vigore gratiarum eis concessarum, omnibus premissis et aliis quibuscumque, etiam si eis derogaretur expresse, ut litterarum tibi concessarum predictarum effectum quantocius consequaris, proinde ac te premissorum meritorum tuorum intuitu gratioso favore prosequi volentes, necnon omnia et singula beneficia ecclesiastica cum cura et sine cura, que etiam ex quibusvis apostolicis dispensationibus obtines et expectas, ac in quibus et ad quevis tibi quomodolibet competit, quecunque, quot-cumque, et qualiacumque sint eorumque fructuum, reddituum, et proventuum veros valores annuos [*recte*, veri valores annui], necnon litterarum, dispensationum, prerogativarum, antelationum, et declarationis predicatorum tenores presentibus pro expressis habentes, tuis in hac parte supplicationibus inclinati, volumus et apostolica tibi auctoritate concedemus pariter et decrevimus quod in predictis ac quibusvis aliis prerogativis, antelationibus, declarationibus, exceptionibus, ac suspensionibus graciis et indultis prefatis descriptis familiaribus per nos hactenus concessis et imposterum forsitan concedendis uti et gaudere possis et debeas in omnibus et per omnia pari modo absque aliqua differencia perinde ac si unus ex veris ex dictis descriptis familiaribus et descriptus esses nosque etiam specialiter et expresse et tibi huiusmodi prerogativas, antelationes, declarationes, suspensiones et exceptiones, gratias et indulta vere concessisse<mus>. Que omnia et singula etiam, in quantum opus sit, de verbo ad verbum concedimus et pro te /*f. 226r*/ facimus per presentes, declarantes nostre intentionis esse te in assecutione predicta non ad similitudinem habentium prerogativas, antelationes, declarationes, exceptiones, et suppositiones predictas ad instar nostrorum familiarum descriptorum, sed ad similitudinem ipsorum familiarum descriptorum in iudicio extra ubilibet absque alia differencia ac si unus et verus ex descriptis predictis esses, ut profertur, censeri et reputari omnibusque aliis etiam auctoritate nostra expectantibus ac etiam ad instar familiarum descriptorum huiusmodi prerogativas, antelationes, declarationes, exceptiones, suspensiones, gratias, et indulta huiusmodi habentibus pro tempore in assecutione prefata omnino anteferri deberi, non obstantibus. . . . Datum Fabriani, Camerinensi diocesi, anno etc. millesimo quadringentesimo quadragesimo nono, decimo Kalendas Octobris, pontificatus nostri anno tercio.

3

30 SEPTEMBER 1449, FABRIANO

Source: ASV, Reg. Vat. 390, ff. 179v–182r.

Literature: First reported by Sassi, 147, and called to my attention by Dr. Concetta Bianca.

Summary: Pope Nicholas V orders the bishop of Spoleto (Berardus Eruli, doctor of both laws and papal *Referendarius*) as well as the dean of the church of Burgos and the dean of the church of Seguenza to install Fernandus de Corduba, cleric of Cordova and doctor of theology, in all the benefices in the diocese of Cuenca once held by Petrus Dalmatii, the recently deceased papal chaplain and apostolic abbreviator; and they are to substitute Fernandus in the place of Petrus in all court cases concerning these benefices and to see to it that Fernandus receives these contested benefices if the claims of others rest on expectatives and reservations.

Text: Nicolaus etc. venerabili fratri, episcopo Spolitano, et dilectis filiis, Burgensis et Seguntane ecclesiarum decanis, salutem etc. Litterarum scientia, vite ac morum honestas, aliaque laudabilia probitatis et virtutum merita, super quibus apud nos dilectus filius Fernandus de Corduba, clericus Cordubensis, magister in theologia, fidedigno commendatur testimonio, nos inducunt ut sibi reddamur ad gratiam liberales cum itaque, sicut accepimus, postquam quondam Petrus Dalmatii, noster et apostolice sedis capellanus, nonnulla prestimonia, prestimoniales portiones, et simplicia etiam servitoria beneficia in ecclesia, civitate, et diocesi Conchensi consistentia alias tunc certo modo seu diversis modis vacantia canonice sibi collata aliquam diu pacifice tenuerat et possederat et non-nulli se pro clericis seu alias ecclesiasticis personis gerentes dictum Petrum prestimoniis, portionibus, et beneficiis huiusmodi seu illorum possessione spoliaverant et in illis se intrudentes ea ex tunc per aliquot annos detinuerant, prout etiam tunc detinebant ac detinent, indebi<te> occupata huiusmodi prestimonia, portiones, et beneficia predicta per obitum eiusdem Petri . . . /f. 180r/ . . . Si que inter dictum Petrum ac eosdem detentores et quoscumque alios super ipsis vacantibus prestimoniis, potionibus, et beneficiis apostolica vel alia quavis auctoritate in prima, secunda, seu tercia instanciis in dicta curia vel extra eam tempore obitus Petri huiusmodi lites pendebant et adhuc pendent indecise status et quarumcunque /f. 180v/ sentenciarum etiam diffinitivarum pro vel contra eundem Petrum promulaturum . . . Motu proprio non ad ipsius Fernandi vel alterius pro eo nobis super hoc oblate petitionis instanciam, sed nostra mera liberalitate discretioni vestre per apostolica scripta mandamus quatenus vos vel duo aut unus vestrum eundem Fernandum in omni iure et ad omne ius siquod ipsi Petro tempore obitus sui huiusmodi in dictis prestimoniis, portionibus, et beneficiis seu ad ea ac illorum possessionem, quomodolibet competiit seu competere potuit, surrogetis, dictum ius sibi conferatis, et provideatis etiam de eodem necnon ipsum Fernandum ad ius, id est, ap<p>pontes [?] litium ac causarum huiusmodi, si que sunt persecutionem et defensionem in eo statu in quo dictus Petrus tempore premisso erat, si viveret, posset et deberet admitti, necnon ad possessionem eorumdem in qua forsan dictus Dalmatius /f. 181r/ tempore predicto existebat admittatis et admitti faciatis, ut est moris, et insuper vocatis litigantibus ac detentoribus huiusmodi, si qui sunt, et aliis qui fuerint evocandi [evocande *correxi*], omnes et singulas causas predictas in statu debito reassumentes, eas ulterius etiam in Romana curia audiatis et debito fine decidatis, facientes quod decreveritis per censuram ecclesiasticam firmiter observari. Testes autem qui fuerunt nominati, si se gratia odio vel timore subtraxerunt, censura simili appellatione cessante compellatis veritati testimonium perhibere. Et nichilminus si per eventum litis aut alias inveneritis nullum eorumdem litigantium et detentorum ante obitum huiusmodi seu ex post alias quam pretextu expectativarum, nominationum, et reservationum predicatarum in prestimoniis, portionibus, et beneficiis vacantibus predictis vel eorum aliquo ius habuisse et habere . . . Volumus pro expresso in prefata curia vel extra eam pendeat indecisa cum omnibus iuribus et pertinenciis suis prefato Fernando conferre et assignare eadem auctoritate curetis, inducentes per vos vel alium seu alios eundem Fernandum vel procuratorem suum eius nomine in corporalem possessionem prestimoniorum, portionum, et beneficiorum iuriumque pertinentiarum predictorum et defendentes inductum a motis predictis et quibuslibet aliis illicitis detentoribus . . . /f. 181v/ . . . /f. 182r/ . . . Datum Fabriani, Camerinensi diocesi, anno etc. millesimo quadringentesimo quadringesimo nono, pridie Kalendas Octobris, pontificatus nostri anno tercio.

4

6 MARCH 1460, SIENA ("Senis, pridie nonas Martii anno secundo")

Source: ASV, Suppl. 528, f. 32v.

Literature: Partially edited by Beltrán de Heredia, 3:98, num. 1180, though he gives no indication that he omitted about a third of the text, consisting mainly of *formulae*.

Summary: Fernandus de Cordoba, *magister in theologia* and *archidiaconus de Moya in ecclesia Conchensi*, supplicates Pope Pius II and is granted the right to hold imcompatible benefices, including any incompatible with his archdeaconry.

5

27 October 1460, Rome ("Romae, sexto Kalendas Novembris anno tertio")
  Source: ASV, Reg. Vat. 508, ff. 323r–324r, with an *epistola exsecutoria* on f. 324r–v.
  Literature: Partially edited by Beltrán de Heredia, 3:102–03, num. 1187.
  Summary: Pope Pius II reserves to Fernandus de Corduba, "tibi, qui in studio Urbis facultatem theologiae publice legis," a praestimonial portion in the church of Sierra de Yeguas in the diocese of Seville vacated by Alfonsus de Fonses (= de Fonseca, bishop of Seville from 3 Dec. 1460 to his death in 1473; see Eubel, 2:165) who has been appointed administrator of the diocese pending his thirtieth birthday when he will be made archbishop. Fernandus's appointment will be voided if Alfonsus dies before he is thirty. The *epistola exsecutoria* of the same date, not mentioned by Beltrán de Heredia, is addressed to the "episcopo Ortano [Niccolò Palmieri] et dilectis filiis [*sic*] Antonio Santri, canonico Cordubensi ac officiali Ispalensi."

6

16 December 1460, Vatican
  Source: ASV, Suppl. 540, f. 148v–149v.
  Literature: Partially edited by Beltrán de Heredia, 3:103–04, num. 1189, who gives no indication that he has omitted about half the relevant text and who is not consistently accurate in what he does edit.
  Summary: Fernandus de Cordoba, *sacrae theologiae professor*, supplicates Pope Pius II and is allowed to cede to Gundisalvus de Saavedra, cleric of Seville, a canonry and a prebend in Seville vacated by the death of Gundisalvus Fernandi de Poria (Beltrán de Heredia: Gundisalvus Alejava) which he, Fernandus, had received by papal authority, but which Gundisalvus de Saavedra was contesting in court at Rome before Sancius Rovicrus (Beltrán de Heredia: Sancius Frovicius), *auditor sacri palatii causarum*. In compensation, Gundisalvus de Saavedra commits himself and any successor in said benefice to pay an annual pension of 12,000 meravedís plus the proceeds of the church of S. Ioannes de Astigia in the diocese of Seville worth up to 10,000 meravedís annually, and, finally, another annual pension of 1,700 meravedís.
  Text: Beatissime pater, vacantibus alias quibusdam canonicatibus et prebendis ecclesie Ispalensis per obitum quondam Gundisalvi Fernandi de Poria, clerici ultimi possessoris earumdem extra Romana Curia defuncti, . . . *As in Beltrán de Heredia with some minor omissions until p. 104.10–13, where Beltrán de Heredia silently omits some formulae; however just before the date on line 14, he omits a full page of text, beginning:* Dudum, ut accepimus, utentibus lite coram dilecto filio Sancio Roviero, capellano et sacri palatii apostolici causarum auditore . . .; *and continuing at a certain point:* . . . inter partes huiusmodi fuit iusta concordia quod idem Gundisalvus in recompensam iuris eidem Fernando competentis inter alia dare et assignare debet prestimonia sive prestimoniales portiones usque ad sumam duodecim milium morapetivorum monete illis partibus cussato, que ad sumam sexaginta librarum Turonensium parvarum valent, annuatimque de facto prefactus Gundisalvus eidem Fernando dedit et assignavit prestimonialem portionem sancti Iohannis de Astigia Ispalensis diocesis cuius fructus etc. solum ascendunt annuatim ad sumam decem milium et trecentorum morapetivorum similium prout insuperne [?] desuper signata plenius continetur. Quare prefactus Fernandus in totum modum per dictum Gundisalvum extitit recompensatus, et ut concordia inter partes huiusmodi iusta servetur motu proprio etc. eidem Fernando super fructibus etc. dictorum canonicatim et prebendarum pensionem

annuam mile septingentorum morapetivorum similium per ipsum Gundisalvum et eius successorem predictos canonicatos et prebendas pro tempore obtinentes annis singulis in certis festivitatibus et loco ac sub penis in talibus i<m>poni solitis prefacto Fernando, quoad vixerat, persolvendam reservavimus, constituimus, et assignavimus . . . Datum Rome apud Sanctum Petrum decimoseptimo Kal. Ianuarii, anno tertio.

7

31 JANUARY 1461, VATICAN ("Romae, apud Sanctum Petrum, pridie Kalendas Februarii anno tertio")
   Source: ASV, Suppl. 536, ff. 43v–44r.
   Literature: Edited by Beltrán de Heredia, 3:105, num. 1191.
   Summary: Ferdinandus de Corduba, *archidiaconus de Moya in ecclesia Conchensi,* and *in sacra theologia magister,* supplicates Pope Pius II and is granted the parish of S. Martha de Ferezinos (Beltrán de Heredia: Serecinos), in the diocese of Leon vacated by Sancius Didaci de Burgos, who failed to become a priest in a year's time; Fernandus is further allowed to hold concomitantly the archdeaconry of Moya.

8

18 AUGUST 1461, TIVOLI ("Tibure, quintodecimo Kalendas Septembris anno tertio")
   Source: ASV, Suppl. 542, ff. 215v–216v.
   Literature: Edited by Beltrán de Heredia, 3:112–113, num. 1197.
   Summary: Fernandus de Corduba, archdeacon of Moya in the diocese of Cuenca, supplicates Pope Pius II and is granted expectatives on the next vacant canonries and prebends in the dioceses of Cuenca and Cordova, even against the nominatees of the King of Castile. Furthermore, the papal letter will be for two canonries and it will be valid as if it were dated 24 November 1458 ("ac si sub data octavo Kalendas Decembris anno primo concessae forent").

9

14 JULY 1463, TIVOLI
   Source: ASV, Reg. Vat. 492, ff. 198v–200r.
   Summary: Pope Pius II grants to Fernandus de Corduba, canon of Cuenca and doctor of theology, the prebends in the diocese of Cuenca of Garsias Alvari, the newly elected bishop of Astorga (see "Alvarez de Toledo, [Garcia]" in DHGE, 2 [1914]:886–87), and commands Fernandus to cede to Bernardus Petri the prebends of the deceased Fernandus Yanes over which he, Ioannes Morvecus, and Bernardus has been litigating at the papal court.
   Text: Pius etc. dilecto filio Fernando de Corduba, canonico Conchensi, magistro in theologia, salutem etc. Litterarum scientia, vite ac morum honestas, aliaque laudabilia probitatis et virtutum merita, super quibus apud nos fidedigno commendatur testimonio nos inducunt ut tibi reddamur ad gratiam liberales . . . Dudum de persona dilecti filii Garsie Alvari, electi Astoricensis . . . ecclesie Astoricensi tunc pastore carenti . . . providimus . . . ac volumus prout quod ipse Garsias electus canonicatum et prebendam ecclesie Conchensis quos tempore provisionis et prefectionis predictarum obtinebat et quos ex tunc vacare decrevimus . . . Cum itaque propterea canonicatus et prebenda predicti per voluntatem et decretum huiusmodi apud sedem ipsam vacaverint et vacent ad presens, . . . nos tibi, qui, ut accepimus, contra dilectos filios Bernardum Petri, clericum Tolentani diocesis, familiarem nostrum, et Iohannem Morveco, qui se gerit pro clerico,

super quibusdam aliis canonicatu et prebenda dicte ecclesie quos olim tunc per obitum quondam Fernandi Yanes, ipsius ecclesie canonici extra Romanam curiam defuncti, vacantes tam tu quam idem Bernardus vigore quarundam per nos unicuique vestrum gratiose concessarum litterarum vigore infra tempus legittimum acceptastis et de illis vobis provideri obtinuistis tam tu <quam Bernardus> et quos quilibet vestrum ad se de iure spectare asserit coram dilecto filio magistro Sancio Romero, cappellano nostro et causarum palacii apostolici auditore in prima instancia, . . . de nostra mera liberalitate primo dictos canonicatum et prebendam . . . /f. 199r/ . . . apostolica tibi auctoritate conferimus. . . . /f. 199v/ . . . Volumus autem quod ex nunc prefatum Bernardum super aliis canonicatu et prebenda predictis, super quibus contra eum litigas, ut prefertur, in pace dimittas. . . . /f. 200r/ . . . Datum Tibure, anno etc. millesimo CCCCLXIII, pridie Idus Iulii, pontificatus nostri anno quinto.

APPENDIX 3

Calendar of Documents on "Fernandus de Medina Diocesis Cordubensis" and "Fernandus de Corduba" at the Spanish College in Bologna, 1442–1446

I first encountered these documents in Piana (1966), 363–70; and Piana (1976), 2:91. Six documents are involved, of which I have consulted all but the first in microfilm.

Piana believed that the documents referred to two different individuals (cf. Piana [1966], 364 n. 1, and the index, p. 589: "Ferdinandus de Metina [Medina]" and "Ferdinandus de Corduba"), but they obviously refer to the same person. First, the statutes of the College allowed for *only one* student to be sent from the diocese of Cordova, and he was supposed to read theology; see Marti, 134.24: "De Cordubensi [i.e., diocesi] unus qui audiat theologiam." Doc. 2a–b in 1443 clearly treats Fernandus de Medina and Fernandus de Corduba as the same person. The bishop or his vicars was supposed to visit the college early every September. In listing the members of the college present at the visitation of 1445, doc. 3 refers to Fernandus de Corduba and doc. 4, dated the next day, refers to Fernandus de Medina. Doc. 5 and doc. 6, dated a few days apart in 1446, do exactly the same thing. Either name was applicable to the Fernandus de Corduba who had come to the Spanish College as a student of theology by 1442 and had then transferred to medicine in violation of the college statutes. It was this Fernandus de Corduba who would seemed to have taught medicine at the University of Bologna in 1447–1448; see n. 25, p. 6.

1

30 DECEMBER 1442 (the document reads "1443" because in the Nativity style of Bologna the year began on 25 December)

Source: Bologna, Archivio Arcivescovile, Ricuperi vari, num. 56 (not seen; quoted by Piana [1976], 2:91).

Summary: Fernandus de Medina, *scholaris* and *consiliarius* of the Spanish College, is named as a witness.

2

3–6 SEPTEMBER 1443

Source: Bologna, Archivio di Stato, Rogati di Filippo Formaglini, Busta 6, num. 185 (cf. Piana [1966], 363–65, num. 58).

Summary: In a very large file of material accumulated during the visitation of 1443, two statements are relevant.

a) The student Petrus Marinus alleges that the student Iacobus de Portugallia falsely claimed a place in the college as a representative of the clergy of Toledo and then of Cordova. However, he and Fernandus de Medina claim the same one place in the college allotted to the clergy of Cordova, as is clear from the register of the notary Tomasinus de Cimeriis. Furthermore, Fernandus de Medina is supposed to be studying theology, but is actually following lectures in medicine, as fellow student Iohannes de Salas confirms: "Erant ipsemet [Iacobus] et dominus Fernandus in civitate Cordubensi et concurrebant in petendo istud titulum et ambo habuerunt. Item dominus Fernandus de Medina de Corduba. . . . Dominus Iacobus de Portugallia [dixit quod] dominus Fernandus de Medina non habet titulum bonum ex actis Tomasini de Cimeriis . . . Item dominus Fernandus est in cauda canonistarum et est in cauda medicorum. . . . Dominus Iohannes de Salas . . . Item dixit quod dominus Fernandus est transmutatus ad lecturam medicine; debuit legere theologiam."

b) In another statement, which is probably the final version of the statement found in *a*, Petrus Marinus, who signed the statement as Petrus Marigenero [Marigñō], repeated his charges against Iacobus de Portugallia and Fernandus de Corduba: "Quarto. Circa Iachobum de Portugalia dico [i.e., ego, Petrus Marinus] quod ipse a principio sui ingressus in ista domo fuit admissus cum uno titulo ecclesie Tolletane, in quo se nominavit de Saria de Galicia, essendo de Portugalia . . . Presentavit quasdam litteras ecclesie Cordubensis ut eum admitterent [i.e., the rector and counselors of the College] . . . quod facere non potuerunt rector et consilliarii istis rationibus. Nam quando ille titulus secundus fuit sibi datus, ipse et dominus Fernandus de Corduba concur<r>ebant in petendo [petetendo *cod.*] eumdem titulum ibi, in illa civitate Cordubenssi, et ambo habuerunt illum titulum et venerunt in hiis partibus. Sed primo venit dictus dominus Fernandus quam dictus Iachobus.

Quinto. Circa Fernandum de Corduba dico quod ipse est unus de conventiculatoribus et insidiatoribus camerarum nocte et [nocte et: nocteque *cod.*] die. Item quod iste fuit admissus ad theologiam per titulum ecclesie Cordubensis [Cordubenssi *cod.*], non essendo fundatus prout statuta mandabant et mandant. Et cum semper ipse fuisset in hac intentione nunquam audiendi theologiam, ymo pocius medicinam, habuit alium titulum ecclesie Yspalensis ad audiendum medicinam. Et fuit translatus de theologia ad medicinam, quod fieri non poterat qualicumque dispensatione cum hoc expresse prohibeant statuta. [He is quoting the words of the statutes; see Marti, 128.16-19: "et ad alteram predictarum scienciarum a principio admissus, aliam audire non possit nec aliqualiter se transferre *qualicumque eciam dispensacione* munitus." (my emphasis)] Idcirco ipsum tamquam non habentem [habentes *cod.*] ius pronuncietis, quod poteritis videre per Tomasinum notarium supra dictum. Et ego lacius ostendam quando volueritis videre et examinare. Ideo hoc dico testificando."

3

6 SEPTEMBER 1445

Source: Ibid., Rogiti di Rolando Castellano, busta 23, num. 32 (cf. Piana [1966], 367-68, num. 59).

Summary: Fernandus de Corduba is recorded among the six students of the Spanish College present at the episcopal visitation. "pro parte iterum sex scolarium dicti collegii, videlicet, dominorum Luppi Ochon, Antonii de Portugallia, Johannis Martini de Aragonia, Iacobi de Sarina, Bartolomei de Corduba, et Fernandi de Corduba."

4

7 SEPTEMBER 1445

Source: Ibid., num. 38 (cf. Piana [1966], 366-67).

Summary: The visitation finds five students present. ". . . presentibus ibidem ad hec . . . scolaribus dicti colegii, videlicet, domino Lippo Ochon, domino Ptolomeo de Corduba, domino Iacobo de Sarris, et domino Fernando de Medina."

5

2 SEPTEMBER 1446

Source: Ibid., num. 33 (cf. Piana [1966], 368–69, num. 60, who mistakenly cites, at 369 n. 2, busta 25, num. 27).

Summary: The episcopal visitors list the members of the Spanish College present. "Nomina vero presentium sunt ista, videlicet: dominus Sanctius de Sanzano in canonico studens, vicerector; dominus Luppus de Ochon in canonico; consilarii dominus Bartolomeus de Corduba in medicina, dominus Antonius de Portugalia in canonico, Fernandus de Corduba in medicina, dominus Iohannes de Ageza in canonico; capellani sunt dominus Johannes de Sales, dominus Thimodeus, dominus Iohannes de Francia, dominus Antonius de Pina servens pro domino Petro de Sancto Sebastiano."

6

13 SEPTEMBER 1446

Source: Ibid., num. 27 (cf. Piana [1966], 368–69, num. 60, who mistakenly cites, at 369 n. 3, busta 25, num. 33–34).

Summary: The episcopal visitors mention Fernandus de Medina as a counselor of the Spanish College. "Ideo nos Sancius de Sansano, vicerector, et conciliarius Lupus de Ocon, etiam consciliarius [*sic*] Fernandus de Medina, scolares sacri collegii domini Sabinensis Bononensis, Yspanorum vulgariter nuncupati, clerici Calagurritanae dyocesis et Cordubensis."

APPENDIX 4

A Report on Fernando of Cordova in Siena, July 1446

The report is found on f. Iv of MS Bologna, Biblioteca Universitaria, 1885 (henceforth = B). B is a paper miscellany containing medical texts and completely written and owned by one Leonardus, active at Siena from the 1440s to the 1460s (see *infra*). It is cursorily described by L. Frati, 16:407, num. 997, who gives the dimensions as 215 × 150 mm, but does not identify any of the texts. There are about 40 blank folios at the beginning, after which follow: ffs. I–II, 1r-v: miscellaneous notes (f. IIr-v: is a palimpsest); ff. 2r-53v: [Arnaldus de Villanova] *De egritudine a capite usque ad pedes* (2r-5v: table of chapters; 6r-53v: treatise); f. 54: blank; f. 55r: brief of Pope Calixtus III to the Signoria of Siena, dated Rome, 18 Sept. 1455; f. 55v: blank; ff. 56r-144v: [Ioannes de Rupescissa, *De quinta essentia*]; ff. 145-156: blank; ff. 157-202v: medical recipes; ff. 203-226, I: blank.

I have not been able to identify Leonardus, the author of the report, in the literature on Siena, including Zdekauer; Garosi, who gives on pp. 356-98 a list of 550 Sienese doctors from 774 to 1555; and Fioravanti (1981). I would like to thank, however, Prof. William Bowsky for his bibliographical suggestions.

In addition to the report edited below, B contains notes of chronological interest. On f. Iv, before the report on Fernando: "Die Lune quarta Iulii 1446 maxima tempestas et turbo ventorum advenit Senas . . ." (four more lines on the storm; similar report in the *Cronaca Senese di Tommaso Fecini* in Lisini and Iacometti, 857.36); and in a different hand: "Sed die XII Novembris 1517 maior advenit ventus, qui duravit fere per spatium unius diei . . ." (four more lines); on f. IIr: "Die 19 Septembris 1440;" f. IIv: "Die XI Martii 1449 ego Leonardus ex aborsu [*sic; lege* abortu] facto a venerabili muliere domina Iacoba, uxore egregii artium et medicine doctoris magistri Iohannis a Dominici, vidi . . ." (five more lines); on f. 1r: "A di 6 di settembre 1455 in sabato a le 21 hora fu morto in nel [*sic; in delendum est*] palagio di Siena nela sala del papa el magnifico signore [*post* signore *supra lin.* miser *manus recentior add.*] Giberto da Correggio, capitano generale del comune di Siena . . ." (eight more lines); f. 40r, marg.: "1463. 7 Septembris;" on f. 110r, marg.: "Frater Bernardinus Senensis sic vocatus in vita . . . mortuus est die 20 Maii 1449 . . . canonizatus fuit Rome a papa Nicolao Quinto die 24 Maii 1450 . . ." (one line more); f. 157r, marg.: "D. Fernandi [*post* Fernandi *supra lin.* Lu..iani (?) filis [!] *manus recentior add.*] Cordubensis die 24 Iulii 1446;" f. 159r, marg.: "Fernandus;" f. 161r: "F<ernandus?> Rome [?] die [*spatium*] Aprili<s> 1447;" f. 162r, marg.: "die 20 Septembris 1447, Senis."

The report on f. Iv is as follows:

Die Martis XVIIII Iulii 1446 vir doctissimus, in pluribus scientiis clarissimus Fernandus Cordubensis in cathedrali ecclesia Senensi, adstantibus excellentibus et doctissimis viris et doctoribus et multitudine civium, disputavit quolibetice offerens se in omnibus scientiis responsurum; et sic omnibus arguentibus et interogantibus optime, elegantissime, et facundissime respondit[1] et ostendit profecto deum illi contulisse mirabile ingenium, stupendam memoriam, exuberantem facundiam, gratissimamque humanitatem.[2] Et ita et talem se gessit cum esset annorum XXI, quod mirabilis, stupendus, et supra naturam reputatus fuit ab omnibus et presertim in memoria. Nam fere omnes libros philosophicos, theologicos, sacros, contenta, testus, tractatus, et dicta, medicinales etiam scripturas et testus ita videbantur illi esse omnia cognita et memorie commendata, ac si omnes[3] libros cuiuscunque scientie apertos ante oculos habuisset, adeo quod ab omnibus iudicatum est neminem vidisse nec audivisse nec in scripturis divinis et humanis aliquem fuisse qui talis memoria esset sicut iste.

Vir iste mirabilis in decimo anno sue etatis doctoratus fuit in artibus, in XIII doctoratus in sacra pagina, in XV doctoratus in medicina, in XX a rege Anglie insignitus fuit militia.

Die Veneris 22 recessit ut iret ad ci<vita>tem Neapolitanam ad Alfonsum regem Aragonum. Hospitatus est illo sero in Cuna, fortillatio hospitalis de la Scala.[4] Sequenti sero hospitatus est in abbatia Montis Oliveti[5] et illinc sequenti domenica versus Romam iter suum arripuit. Ego[6] Leonardus continuo fui[7] secum per aliquot dies et miranda cognovi de viro isto, quo nullum fere diebus meis cognovi esse ita humilem, humanum, et gratiosum.

Rediit idem Fernandus Senas cum reverendissimo domino sancti Angeli die 20 Settembris 1447. Discessit die 21 de mane et hospitatus est mecum, cum iam mensibus octo [?] effectus esset conceptus [?] . . . [tria verba] felix [?] . . . [unum verbum] quem suo nunc / . . . [duo verba]-sit a domino Christo [?] . . . [unum verbum].

---

[1] respondidit B.

[2] u ante humanitatem del. B.

[3] ea ante omnes del. B.

[4] For the village of Cuna, south of Siena, where the Ospedale di Santa Maria della Scala of Siena had many holdings, see Epstein, 30 and passim (v. indicem). I thank Professor William M. Bowsky for calling this book to my attention.

[5] That is, the Abbazia Monte Oliveto Maggiore.

[6] etiam ante ego del. B.

[7] ass ante fui del. B.

APPENDIX 5

Letter of the Sienese Government to King Alfonso V of Aragon, 21 July 1446, Concerning Fernando of Cordova*

Die XXI Iulii[1]

Regi Aragonum scriptum est hac forma, videlicet:[2]

Serenissime pater etc., Fernandus Hispanensis, vir sume [sic][3] excellentie omniumque artium peritissimus, cum hiter[4] per hanc urbem haberet, tam mirificie [sic], pene divine quadam in eius disputatione se gessit ut nostrarum partium esse duxserimus eius virtutis [sic][5] haud quaquam[6] reticere. Quocircha cum sumopere cupiat ad serenitatem maiestatis vestre adcedere, a qua, ut plerique omnes virtuosi, dignia [sic] virtutis sue premia spettat,[7] eum pro viribus eidem inpensissime commendare constatuimus. Cernimus nanque in hoc viro tantam rerum fere omnium scientiam ut divine potius numine aliquo aflatum quam humanis operibus institutum[8] putaverimus; matematiceque scientie, naturales,[9] morales, medicine, sacre scripture, quorum singulis excellere[10] preclarissimum[11] munus esset, usque adeo in eo eminent ut non modo cultos nostri temporis anteiret, sed cum omni vestustate conferri posse videatur. Preterea tante memorie est ut nequaquam inferior Ciro, quem numerosissimi exercitus sui nomina sigilatim tenere vetustas peribet,[12] ullo pacto habendus sit, nec inferior Cinea, Pirrhi leggato, qui post meridiem eius diei qua Romam ingressus est, senatores singulos equestrumque omnem ordinem propriis nominibus salutavit, nec inferior Mitridati, qui duabus viginti diversis[13] gentibus quibus inperabat ius sine interprete[14] ullo eorum vernacula lingnue [sic] dicere consueverat. Set ne eius virtutis [sic][15] potius laudibus efferre quam veritatem

---

* S = Siena, Archivio di Stato, Fondo Concistorio, filza 1667, f. 8r (I have retained the idiosyncratic spelling of the document).

[1] *ex* Iunii *corr.* S.

[2] *In marg.* S: Gratis per mandata dominorum.

[3] *recte* summe.

[4] That is, iter.

[5] *recte*, virtutes.

[6] ante *ante* haud quaquam *del.* S.

[7] *pro* exspectat.

[8] *ex* institutus *corrigere videtur* S.

[9] nihil (?) *ante* naturales *del.* S.

[10] *ex* excelleret *corr.* S.

[11] The scribe got confused here, first writing *precarissimum*, then changing *pr-* to *pl-*, and never correcting the spelling of the word.

[12] See Pliny *HN* 7.24 for the memory feats of Cyrus the Great, Pyrrhus' emissary Cineas, and Mithridates, King of Persia.

[13] duob (?) *ante* diversis *del.* S.

[14] *ex* interpretre *corr.* S.

[15] *v. n.* 5 *supra.*

ipsam[16] sponere[17] videamur, breviter eam perstringemus, hocque uno erimus contenti, ut nostro testimonio huius viri ingenium serenitati vestre clare liqueat, quod quidem, cum se esibuerit, optime verbis nostris responsurum et laudes omnes superaturum fore putamus. Eum igitur, tametsi nequaquam opus sit, maiestati vestre plurimum comendamus; gratissimumque nobis, tamquam si in civem nostrum proferretur, quicquid[18] dignitatis sue ac s(erenitatis) m(aiestatis) v(estre) eidem exabebitur.[19] Datum Senis, die dicta etc.

---

[16] ef (?) *ante* ipsam *del. S.*
[17] *pro* exponere.
[18] quiduid *ante* quidquid *del. S.*
[19] *pro* exhibebitur.

APPENDIX 6

Fernando of Cordova at the University of Vienna, September 1448

M = Mainz, Stadtbibliothek, I 121; s. XV, paper, miscellany; seen in partial microfilm; ff. 125r-136v are in one northern gothic cursive. See Kristeller (1963-1992), 3:605b. Ff. 125r-127v: Fernando's *propositiones*; 127v-128r: unidentified *acta* concerning Fernando and Cardinal Juan Carvajal at the University of Vienna; 128r-136v: Georgius Tudel of Gingen's rebuttal of Fernando's *propositiones*.

W = Wien, Schottenkloster, 407 (*olim* 320); s. XV, paper, miscellany of 229 ff., in four hands; seen in partial prints from microfilm; ff. 2v-16r are in one northern gothic cursive. See Hübl, 349-52, num. 320. Ff. 2v-8r: Fernando's *propositiones*; 8v-16r: Georgius Tudel of Gingen's rebuttal of Fernando's *propositiones*.

6A. Fragment of University *Acta* Concerning Fernando of Cordova

Only M contains the entry concerning Fernando. I could not identify the exact source of the entry. It does not come from the presently preserved acts of the arts faculty of the University of Vienna. I consulted in photocopies from the Universitätsarchiv of the University of Vienna ff. 178r-180r of Liber II and ff. Ir-IIv, 1r-25r of Liber III of the acts of the Arts Faculty, which cover the period from April 1447 to October 1449, and found nothing on Fernando. The acts of the theological faculty of the University of Vienna do discuss Fernando (Uiblein, 1:228-31), but offer a different text than that in M.

The copyist or editor who inserted the extract in M was careless. The sequence of paragraphs is a jumble, perhaps based on improperly ordered loose sheets. Fernando's *propositiones* immediately precede the extract in M; yet the extract refers to them as "Subscriptas conclusiones" (§ 1). This means that § 1 belongs at the start, not at the end of the *propositiones*. I suspect that § 1 derives from Fernando's published announcement of his forthcoming disputation, where he listed his *propositiones*. Furthermore, § 4 reports events which precede in time those reported in §§ 2-3, while §§ 5-7, which speak of how the university would receive the Cardinal Legate Juan Carvajal, should, in turn, precede § 4 and §§ 2-3, which refer to Cardinal Carvajal as being present at Fernando's disputation at the University. Thus, the proper sequence in M should be: §§ 5-7, then § 1, then Fernando's *propositiones*, then § 4, then §§ 2-3, and then §§ 8 sq. (i.e., Georgius Tudel of Gingen's rebuttal, of which I have transcribed only the opening and closing lines).

For an interpretation of the entry in M see pp. 19-20. I have transcribed completely all of the entry pertaining to Fernando (= §§ 1-4) and the first line of the subsequent paragraphs (= §§ 5-8).

/M 127v/

[Fragmenta Actorum Universitatis Wienensis]

(1) Subscriptas conclusiones in hac clarissima universitatum Fernandus de Carduba [sic] disputabit sub assignandis loco et die.

(2) Anno ab incarnatione domini nostri Ihesu Christi 1448 proxima feria quinta ante festum Mathei apostoli et ewangeliste, Fernandus de Carduba [sic], artium ac sacre theologie doctor, questionem suprascriptam cum conclusionibus ac propositonibus annexis in aula universitatis studii Wienensis et ad eam opponentibus respondet etc.

(3) Deinde, feria sexta seu altera Sappati, magister Georgius Tudel de Gingen, sacre theologie bacchalarius formatus, prefati domini Fernandi questionis per eum publicate collationis gratia opposita<m> sustenuit positionem et audivit opponentes, videlicet, dominum legatum et dominum Fernandum, cui precedenti die contradixisse debuit. Sed quia ad desiderium et instanciam seriosam legati ac cardinalis nominati Sancti Angeli etc., ita illud negocium dilatum fuit.

(4) Et feria secunda ante festum Mathei Fernandus debuit respondere etc. Fecit ex causa sua. Post hoc supplicavit universitati in hunc modum: quia exquisitis causis precepto michi, Fernando de Carduba [sic], iniunctum est ut iam publicate [puplicate M] conclusiones ac hodie disputande ad diem Iovis, feriam quintam proxime [feriam quintam proxime feriam M], differrentur, sicut [sicut: iam M] huius universitatis Wien<en>sis essent canones, efficio me dicta die Iovis feria quinta proxime futura hora septima easdem disputaturum; rogoque humiliter prefatam universitatem compacare ad decorem actus et excusationem disputationis etc.

(5) Anno 1448 mandatum rectoris circa adventum legati ad universitatem Wiennam etc.

(6) Rector universitatis studii Wienensis mandat omnibus doctoribus, /M 128r/ nobilibus magistris, licentiatis, bacchalariis, et scolaribus . . .

(7) Decanus facultatis arcium mandit omnibus magistris, licentiatis, bacchalariis, et scolaribus . . .

(8) Sequitur nunc positio magistri Georgii de Gingen. In nomine domini nostri Ihesu Christi.   Amen.

(9) "Deus in terram respexit et implevit illam bonis suis." Ecclesiastici 16 [v. 5]. Si deus implere dignatus est bonis significanter suis terram humani [humanam M] generis, inter que bona sunt et iam intellectus, sapientia, et scientia, dona spiritus sancti, hominum salutariter directoria . . . /M 128v–M 136v/ . . .   (10) [desinit] ut merea<n>tur perhennem contemplacionem summe veritatis, que est Ihesus Christus, patris sapientia et virtus, cum eodem patre et spiritu sancto, in seculorum secula benedictus.   Amen.

6B. The *Propositiones* Argued by Fernando of Cordova

In both M and W, Fernando's *propositiones* appear with Georgius Tudel of Gingen's rebuttal. This leads me to think that it was Tudel who combined the two and published them together. I give the *incipit-desinit* of the Tudel's text at the end of Appendix 6A.

To clarify the structure of Fernando's *propositiones*, I have numbered their six parts (Part I, Theology; Part II, Metaphysics; Part III, Physics; Part IV, Ethics; Part V, Logic; Part VI, Sophistic) and the three articles in Part I.

/M 125r, W 2v/

[Propositiones Magistri Fernandi de Corduba]

I

[Propositiones theologicae]

(1) Utrum Christum, sive ut patris verbum sive ut humanam naturam supponitantem, summum bene essendi gradum per caritatem consequi potuisse sit affirmandum.[1]

I.1

(2) Ad articulum primum, ubi esse verbi[1] in quantum tale supponitur de intrinsico[2] eius[3] constitutivo, infrascriptas et conclusiones[4] et propositiones veras affirmo.[5]

(3) Prima conclusio.[6] Quemadmodum[7] nullum producere potissima atque prima est[8] ratio essendi patri, sic nullum vel produci vel dici est prima ratio essendi verbo.   (4) Probatur ex sententia Salomonis libro Parabulorum, ubi tres questiones in dubium movet.[9] Prima quidem "quod nomen eius," hoc est, patris. Secunda, "quod nomen filii eius, si nosti." Extrema vero est spiritus quem "obtinuit[10] in manibus eius."   (5) Hec Salomonis verba superiorem conclusionem inferunt. Et probo illationem. Nam aput Aristotelem nono Methaphisice: "questio aliud supponitur et aliud querit."[11]   (6) Sed in conclusione secunda et prima Salomon filium patremque esse supposuit,[12] qui relationem[13] nominat, ut notat forma sue questionis. Ergo aliud supposuit, sed non nisi personale. (7) Aliquid ergo est suppositum abstractum in personis divinis ante omnem

---

[1] verbum W.
[2] *sic* W; intrinssico M.
[3] eius *om.* W.
[4] et conclusiones *om.* M.
[5] etc. *post* affirmo *add.* M.
[6] prima conclusio *in marg.* W; *om.* M.
[7] quemadmodum *om.* M.
[8] quemadmodum *ante* est *add.* M.
[9] Cf. Prov. 30:4.
[10] obtinet *ante* obtinuit *del.* M.
[11] Cf. Arist. *Metaph.* 9, 1049a15–17, which is only vaguely close.
[12] supponit M.
[13] relatione M.

relationem[14] ac notionalem actum. Exinde efficitur ut nullo actu notionali[15] constituatur persona aliqua in esse tali. Secunda ratio: omne[16] suppositum preintelligitur sue actioni aut relationi active et passive.   (8) Textus est expressus quinto Methaphisice, 18, 19, 17, 48, 47 commentis;[17] et septimo Methaphisice, commento 10,[18] 37, penultimo;[19] et 10 Methaphisice, commento 38;[20] et 11 Methaphisice, commento 4;[21] et primo De anima, commento 2;[22] et 2 De anima commento, 25;[23] et 3 De anima, commento 29.[24]   (9) Suppositum ergo divinum preintelligitur sue productioni. Non ergo per ipsam[25] constituitur, quod voluit conclusio.[26] /W 3r/

(10) Prima propositio.[27] Filii produci formaliter dici est, probo auctoritate Augustini 8 De trinitate, capitulo 10.[28] Item aput Anselmum hec questio est formalis: filius est verbum; ergo dici est produci, sed non aliter quam per formalem rationem.[29]

(11) Secunda propositio.[30] Cum illis non sentio qui[31] aut primum intelligendi actum aut abstracte aliquod[32] divini verbi productum affirmant.   (12) Probatur quia in aliquo priori originis est verbum, in quo non intelligitur actus intellectus. Ergo propositio vera itaque quia nunquam prius productum est origine ratione producente.[33]

---

[14] ante omnem relationem *om. W.*

[15] notionale *M.*

[16] omnino *M.*

[17] I find all the references in this section to Aristotle and Averroes's commentary dubious, because none of the texts cited seem relevant; sometimes the specific comment seems not even to exist. We cannot excuse Fernando on the grounds that his manuscript copy employed a different numbering system than the sixteenth-century edition which I cite because in the case of the *De anima* we have a modern critical edition of Averroes's commentary based on the manuscripts (edited by F. S. Crawford, Cambridge, Mass., 1953) and for every reference given by Fernando the numbering of the comment in the sixteenth edition agrees with the critical edition. Thus according to the Aristotle *Opera Omnia* of Venice, 1562–74, vol. 8, there are only 35 comments of Averroes in Bk. 5 of the *Metaph* though Fernando cites comments 47 and 48; comments 17–19 are ibid., ff. 123r–127r.

[18] 1° *M.*

[19] Cf. ibid., ff. 160v–161r, 189r-v, and 207r-v (comment 59 is the penultimate comment of Averroes).

[20] The highest numbered comment in Bk. 10 in 26.

[21] The Venetian *op. om.* has no comments for this book.

[22] 22 *M.* Cf. ibid., vol. Suppl. 2, ff. 1v–2r (= ed. Crawford, 4–5).

[23] Ibid., f. 61v (= ed. Crawford, 165–66).

[24] Cf. ibid., f. 170v (= ed. Crawford, 467–68).

[25] ipsum (ip̅m̅) *MW.*

[26] etc. *post* conclusio *add M.*

[27] prima propositio *in marg. W, in textu M.*

[28] Cf. Augustine, *De Trinitate*, ed. Mountain-Glorie, 1:290–91, which is not relevant; but see § 32 n. 74.

[29] I am not sure what text he means; cf. *Monologion*, cc. 33–36 (in Anselm, 1:51–55); and *De Fide Trinitatis*, cc. 3 and 8, in *PL* 158:265–72, 280–82.

[30] secunda propositio *in marg. W, in textu M.*

[31] que [q̅] *MW.*

[32] aliquam *MW.*

[33] etc. *post* producente *add. M.*

(13) Tertia propositio.[34] Priorem origine patrem in se cognoscere essenciam quam intelligat. Eam in verbo producto cum Salomone concedo. Probitur propositio.[35] (14) Nam pater in aliquo priori /M 125v/ est beatus, in quo non producit filium. Ergo consequentia nota est quia non est beatus nisi essenciam cognoscens aut ut in se ipsa est aut in patre. (15) Antecedens probo quia nullam perfectionem sibi intrinsicam habet pater a persona producta et[36] beatitudo est perfectio intrinsica persone beate. (16) Sed in illo priori sit pater perfecte beatus. In isto ergo priori habet obiectum perfecte beatificans. (17) Non autem videtur in isto priori habere essentiam communicatam tribus ut obiectum, sed vel essentiam abstracte vel essentiam ut est in una persona. Tum ergo antecedens verum. (18) Ceterum hec conclusio elici potest ex Augustino, Enchiridio 44,[37] De origine anime 7,[38] De trinitate 5,[39] et pluribus aliis locis.

(19) Quarta propositio.[40] Non sequitur hoc: se dicit ad intra in divinis; simile ergo in natura sibi generat. Probo quia spiritus sanctus et filius dicunt se; non tamen simile sibi generantur.[41]

(20) Secunda conclusio.[42] Propriissimam patris artem esse verbum fide ac ratione tenendum est, atque multo propriorem quam sibi ipse pater.[43] (21) Probatur: secunde persone ex vi[44] sue productionis convenit quod est noticia declarativa quia est producta per actum memorie exprimentis talem noticiam et ideo non pro parte dicuntur de ea que pertinent ad /W 3v/ perfectionem cognitionis active.

(22) Prima propositio.[45] Prius origine[46] filium a patre cognitum quam in esse productum ratione necessaria convinci[47] potest. Hec[48] propositio est probata ex tertia superiori.

(23) Secunda propositio.[49] Quedam in divinis relacio haberi potest que nulli suppositorum sit ratio incommunicabiliter existendi. (24) Probo.[50] Omnis ratio incommunicabiliter existendi[51] est incommunicabilis. Sed aliqua[52] relatio in divinis est communicabilis. Ergo minor probatur cum maior per se sit nota quia aliqua relatione duo supposita divina referuntur ad unum. Ergo duo illa supposita habunt communem relacionem.[53]

---

[34] tertia propositio *in marg. W, in textu M.*
[35] probitur propositio: probo *W.*
[36] et *om. W.*
[37] I found nothing relevant in this chapter (CCSL, 46:74–75).
[38] 7: septimo 7 *M.* There are four books in the *De origine animae* (*PL* 44, 475–548), and I do not know to what passage Fernando is referring.
[39] Cf. Augustine, *De Trinitate*, ed. Mountain-Gloire, 1:206–27, perhaps c. 6 (pp. 211–12).
[40] quarta propositio *in marg. W, in textu M.*
[41] etc. *post* generantur *add. M.*
[42] secunda conclusio *in marg. W, in textu M.*
[43] patri *W.* See § 39 n. 86.
[44] vi: in *M.*
[45] prima propositio *in marg. W, in textu M.*
[46] priorem originem *MW.*
[47] convina [?] *M.*
[48] illa *M.*
[49] secunda propositio *in marg. W, in textu M.*
[50] probo *W:* illa propositio probatur *M.*
[51] existendi *om. W.*
[52] aliqua<n>tus [?] *M.*
[53] etc. *post* relationem *add. M.*

(25) Tertia propositio.[54] Eam quidem[55] sententiam illorum non tollerandam[56] existimo qui[57] posse esse deum priorem veritatem affirmant quam deum esse. (26) Hec[58] est <probata ab> Augustino[59] De heresibus[60] in libro Retractionum.[61] Probatur ratione quia deum esse est simpliciter[62] prima veritas, sicut deus est. (27) Nam deus est deum esse, quod probo quia nichil est tam bonum sicut deus. Sed quam bonus est deus tam bonum est deum esse.[63] Ergo est deus.[64]

(28) Quarta propositio.[65] Quod pater preter ceteras personas sui actioni non[66] preintelligitur, id est, causatur,[67] quod[68] prima incommunicabilis entitas nullam[69] alteram aut originem aut natura<m> supponere possit. (29) Illa propositio nota est quia oppositum predicati infert oppositum subiecti quia si sui actioni preintelligetur pater, ergo sua actio non esset prima incommunicabilis entitas.[70] (30) Et hoc est satis /M 126r/ ad veritatem illius causalis que est quarta propositio predicta.[71]

(31) Tertia conclusio.[72] Verbum divinum intelligibilem speciem patris aut intelligendi actum aut dicendi potentiam vel rectam rationem factibilium apud ingenitam personam aut posse dici eius formaliter esse nego. (32) Probatur hec conclusio[73] pro qualibet sui parte. Primo per Augustinum 8 De trinitate, capitulo 10, ubi dicit fantasiam sartaginis esse verbum eius.[74] Sed fantasia sartaginis, dicit, formaliter aliud a specie. Ergo verbum non est formaliter species. (33) Secunda pars probatur quia nichil formaliter est prius se ipso origine. Sed verbum originis prioritate est post omnem actum intelligendi. In divinis verbum ergo non est formaliter actus intelligendi.[75] (34) Minor est sententia Augustini 5 De trinitate[76] et 7[77] et[78] multis locis. (35) Per eandem concludo tertiam[79] partem conclu-

---

[54] tertia propositio *in marg. W, in textu M.*
[55] quid *M.*
[56] tollerando *M.*
[57] quod *M.*
[58] hec *W* : illa propositio probatur et *M.*
[59] probata ab Augustino : Augustinus *MW.*
[60] I do not know what passage he is referring to; I consulted the *De Heresibus* in CCSL 46:283–345.
[61] Again the reference is too vague; I consulted the *Retractiones* in *PL* 1:583–656.
[62] simpliciter: simer [*sic*] *M.*
[63] deum esse *bis M.*
[64] etc. *post* deus *add M.*
[65] quarta propositio *in marg. W, in textu M.*
[66] non *om. M.*
[67] causa *W.*
[68] quoque *M.*
[69] nullam . . . entitas [§ 29.1 n. 70] *om. W.*
[70] V. § 28.5 n. 69.
[71] etc. *post* predicta *add. M.*
[72] tertia conclusio *in marg. W, in textu M.*
[73] probatur hec conclusio *W* : illa conclusio probatur *M.*
[74] eius *om. M.* Fernando is actually referring to the *phantasia Carthaginis* in Bk. 8, c. 6 and Bk. 9, c. 6 of the *De Trinitate* (ed. Mountain-Glorie, 1:281, 302–03).
[75] in divinis verbum . . . intelligendi *om. W.*
[76] See § 18 n. 39.
[77] Perhaps Bk. 7, c. 3 of the *De Trinitate* (ed. Mountain-Glorie, 1:249–50).
[78] et *om. M.*
[79] etiam *W.*

sionis, quod nec dicendi potentiam, et quartam, quod nec rectam rationem factibilium, et quintam, quod nec posse dici eius.[80] /W 4r/

(36) Quarta conclusio.[81] Quamquam nullius obiecti a potentia simplex apprehensio sit verbum respectu eiusdem obiecti, possibile tamen est[82] prius de aliquo obiecto formari verbum quam idipsum a formante potentia apprehendi. Hec ex precedenti patet.[83]

(37) Quinta conclusio.[84] Nichil formalius esse verbo potest quam esse patris sapientiam.   (38) Probatur auctoritate apostoli Ad Hebraeos 1 [v.3?], Ad Corinthios 1 [1 Cor. 1:25?], ubi agit de constitutivo[85] verbi et dicit esse sapientiam. (39) Ceterum est ars patris (8 De trinitate, capitulo 7),[86] sed non respectu factibilium. Ergo respectu eternorum.   (40) Et hoc est sapientia 1 Methaphisice[87] et 6 Ethicorum[88] et 2 De generatione[89] ac[90] commentatore commento 56 et 64,[91] et 5 Methaphisice commento 31[92] et 8 Phisicorum commento 21[93] et Avicenna in tractatu 5 <in> secundo Methaphisice[94] et Augustinus 15 De trinitate, capitulo 6;[95] 8 De trinitate, capitulo 2.[96]

(41) Corollarium.[97] Necesse est per absoluta, non per relativa personas[98] constitui, licet oppositum istius[99] conclusionis fere ab omnibus teneatur.   (42) Tamen cum Salomone ubi supra predictam sententiam teneo. Multos[100] tamen[101] atque magne auctoritatis vestros sic opinatos fuisse vidimus, ut Bonaventuram Senensem,[102]

---

[80] etc. *post* eius *add. M.*

[81] quarta conclusio *in marg. W, in textu M.*

[82] est *om. W.*

[83] hec ex precedenti patet W : illa conclusio probatur ex precedenti etc. *M.*

[84] quinta conclusio *in marg. W, in textu M.*

[85] constitutione *M.*

[86] See *De Trinitate* Bk. 6, c. 10 (ed. Mountain-Glorie, 1:241.21–22).

[87] *Metaph.* 1.981b25–983a23.

[88] *Eth. Nicom.* 6.1141a9–b8.

[89] I could not find a relevant passage in the *De gen. et corr.*

[90] et *W.*

[91] Cf. Aristotle, *Op. Om.*, vol. 5, ff. 385v and 387v, neither of which are relevant.

[92] Cf. ibid., vol. 8, f. 138r-v.

[93] Cf. ibid., vol. 4, ff. 355v–356v.

[94] Cf. Avicenna, *Liber de Philosophia Prima*, 1, c. 2 (= Avicenna, 16.91 ff.).

[95] This is ed. Mountain-Glorie, 2:471–74, but Bk. 7, c. 3 (ibid., 1:251–54) would be better.

[96] Cf. ibid. Bk. 7, c. 3 (ed. Mountain-Glorie, 1:251–54).

[97] -em *in marg. scr. W; verbum est excisum in mea photographa, sed forte non in manuscr.*

[98] per absoluta et not per relationem personas W : personas per absoluta et non per relationem *M.*

[99] istius W : illius idei sive *M.*

[100] vel *ante* multos *del. M.*

[101] tamen W : quoque *M.*

[102] Senensem Bonaventure, : Crucum *M.* Cf. Bonaventura, *Comm. in Sentent.* 1, d. 26, a. 1, q. 3 (Bonaventura, 1:423–26), which has the theme "cum personae distinguantur, aut distinguuntur per aliquod absolutum aut respectivum; per absolutum non . . . igitur necesse est quod differant per aliquod respectivum;" concerning which see Stohr, 109–24; and Michel, 1736.

Iohannem de Rippa,[103] Halinton Anglicum.[104]   (43) Eam tamen probo ratione
dupliciter. Primo, unumquodque enim suppositum preintelligitur sue[105] actioni.
In eo ergo priori, in quo pater preintelligitur generationi, vel pater est ad se vel
ad alterum.   (44) Si ad se, propositum habeo personam, scilicet patris, per absolutum[106] constitui. Si ad alterum, scilicet per filium. Ergo filius intelligitur ante
suam productionem. Ergo non est terminus formalis generationis, et hoc non est
[srathodum].[107] /M 126v/   (45) Secundo, omnis relatio realis presupponit duo
extrema realiter distincta. Hanc probo per Aristotelem 5 Methaphisice, capitulo
de eodem,[108] ubi negat idem esse relationem realem ex hoc, quod[109] extrema distincta realiter non habet.[110]   (46) Relatio ergo realis in divinis supponit duo
extrema distincta. Sed nullum supponens constituit quod supponit, sed est
tantum ipsum vel re vel /W 4v/ ratione.   (47) Ergo ante omnem relationem est
suppositum patris in esse personali constitutum. Non ergo per relationem constituitur, quod probandum acceptaveram.[111]

I.2

(48) Ad secundum questionis articulum, ubi supponitur verbum habere
rationem terminandi unionem nature humane ad ipsum.[112]

(49) Prima conclusio.[113] Quod unionem duplicis nature in uno supposito ter-
minat proprietas relativa.[114] Patet[115] quod nullum abstractum est ratione terminandi unionem neque est reale terminatum ex se. Alioquando non verbum magis
quam pater est. Incarnatum igitur aliquid relativum.

(50) Prima propositio.[116] Si per possibile Christum naturam assumptam
atque viventem dimisisse constaret, verbum quid[117] non esset. Eam naturam
dimissam fuisse Christum.   (51) Probo illam:[118] quidquam[119] est deus, semper
est et fuit deus. Sed iste homo dimissus non est deus. Iste ergo non fuit deus.
(52) Secundo, hec humanitas sic derelicta nunquam fuit deus. Sed hic homo est
hec humanitas. Igitur hic homo nunquam fuit deus.

---

[103] John of Ripa's trinitarian teaching is complex and difficult; but cf. Borchert, 1:468, 488, 490–94, for his resistance to accepting fully Duns Scotus's doctrine on the absolute basis of the distinction between the divine Persons.

[104] Presumably Robert de Alyngdon, chancellor of the University of Oxford
1393–1395, opponent of John Wyclif, and author of a lost work *De Christi Humani-
tate*, to which Fernando may be referring; see Emden, 1:30–31; and Lohr
(1967–1974), 29:96–97.

[105] sua *M*.

[106] absoluta *M*.

[107] srathodum [?] *W* : sathecum [?] necessarium etc. *M*.

[108] eadem *M*.

[109] quod *om. M*.

[110] Cf. *Metaph.* 5.1020b35–1021a1.

[111] acceptaveram: accepa^r [= accepatur (*sic*)] *M*; acceperãm *W*.

[112] etc. *post* ipsum *add. M*.

[113] prima conclusio *in marg. W* : sit prima conclusio, licet secundi articuli; est
relativa proprietas *in textu M*.

[114] relativa proprietas *om. M*.

[115] patet *W* : illa conclusio probatur *M*.

[116] prima propositio *in marg. W, in textu M*.

[117] quod *M*.

[118] *Sc.*, propositionem. probo illam *W* : illa propositio probatur *M*.

[119] quamquam *M*.

(53) Corollarium.[120] Tempore quo verbum nulli creature supponitaliter est unitum, cum tamen future creature[121] vivendum[122] esset, que[123] vocetur Christus,[124] falsum est dicere "filius dei erit filius" si[125] hec conclusio correcte infertur ex precedenti.[126]

(54) Secunda conclusio.[127] Aliquis homo fuit ab eterno cuius humanitas incepit esse.

(55) Tertia[128] conclusio.[129] Etiam si Christus humanam naturam assumptam dimisisset, verbum esset. Istum fuisse virginis filium probo[130] tamen quia aliquando esset homo, nullius hominis filius.

(56) Corollarium.[131] Per hoc infero correcte quod non sequitur: hec mulier peperit istum quando peperit Christum. Ergo[132] ista fuit mater istius vel incepit esse mater.[133]

(57) Corollarium.[134] Non sequitur: hec[135] nunquam fuit vera; hic[136] homo nascitur de muliere; ergo hic nunquam nascebatur de muliere. Patet corollarium /W 5r/ apud Sapientem ex precedenti.

(58) Corollarium.[137] Stante ydiomatum[138] communicatione, hec non se inferunt: Petrus traxit originem secundum carnem ex semine deciso de substantia et carne Iohannis; ergo hic Petrus est filius Iohannis. Hoc[139] est facile probatum[140] in casu corollarii precedentis.

I.3

(59) Articulus tertius est[141] titulo[142] questionis responsivus.

(60) Prima conclusio.[143] Quamvis omnem cartitatem in[144] infinitum augeri posse affirmem, tamen[145] Christum summum et bene essendi ac caritatem gradum attigisse huic sententie non contradicit. (61) Primam[146] conclusionem

---

[120] corollarium in marg. W, in textu M.
[121] creature om. M.
[122] vivendi W.
[123] qui M; quod ante que del. W.
[124] Christus : a [=?] MW.
[125] si : a M.
[126] etc. post precedente add. M.
[127] secunda conclusio : c. W; secunda conclusio seu corollarium M.
[128] tertia W : secunda M (v. § 54. 1 supra).
[129] tertia [secunda] conclusio in marg. W, in textu M.
[130] probo W : probatur illa conclusio M.
[131] corollarium om. M, in marg. W.
[132] igitur M.
[133] materem post mater add.M.
[134] corollarium in marg. W, in textu M.
[135] That is, propositio.
[136] hic om. M.
[137] corollarium in marg. W, in textu M.
[138] ideomatum W.
[139] et ante hoc add. M.
[140] probationem W; facile [probatum] W : probatum facile M.
[141] et ante est add. M.
[142] titulus M.
[143] prima conclusio in marg. W : de illa sit prima conclusio ista in textu M.
[144] in om. M.
[145] tantum W.
[146] illam M.

ad titulum non probo ideo quod nota sit unicuiquam intelligenti pro qualibet parte.[147] /M 127r/

(62) Prima propositio.[148] Dilectionem que producta caritas est intrinsice dilectionem esse nego. Probo:[149] nulla ratio competit alicui intrinsice cui non competit, circumscripto aliquo alio quod non est sibi intrinsicum, sed circumscriptis potentia et obiecto, talis qualitas. (63) Que dilectio non remaneret dilectio. Ergo illa caritas non est formaliter dilectio.

(64) Secunda propositio.[150] Cum magistro teneo, qui caritatem qua accepti sumus deo spiritum sanctum affirmavit atque satis esse sine aliquo habitu nove dilectionis animam informante.[151]

(65) Ultima propositio.[152] Ultimam conclusionem[153] teneo venerabili cum magistro per auctoritates suas et aliquas alias quas non posuit.[154] In littera de rationibus pro nunc supersedeo. (66) Et hoc satis gratia brevitatis sit. Conclusiones theologicas pro parvitate mei ingenii, utrum sit, decidere,[155] emendare, corrigere pro[156] vestra sapientia.[157]

II

(67) Propositiones methaphisicales[158] iuxta primum articulum theologicorum.[159]

(68) Prima.[160] Sicut suppositum divinum et sua essentia inter se formaliter differunt, sic necesse est in creaturis essentiam ab esse[161] formaliter distare. /W 5v/

(69) [Secunda.] Primam propositionem[162] non sufficienter[163] terministe diviserunt. Tum ad refellendi[164] proxime condicionis sententiam dicunt aut essentiam priorem[165] esse est aut posteriorem.[166]

---

[147] primam . . . parte *in medio paginae tanquam rubricam scr. W.*

[148] prima propositio *in marg. W, in textu M.*

[149] probo *W* : illa proposito probatur *M.*

[150] secunda propositio *in marg. W* : ultimam conclusionem *M.*

[151] etc. *post* informante *add. M.* The reference would seem to be to Peter Lombard (*Sent.*, 4, d. 27, a. 3), who did not expound this doctrine as much as simply allude to St. Augustine. More appropriate would be William of Ockham, *Scriptum* 1, dist. 17, q. 1: "Utrum praeter spiritum sanctum necesse sit ponere caritatem absolutam creatam, animam formaliter informantem" (= *Op. Th.* 3:440–66). Perhaps the scribe or by Fernando himself *per lapsum* omitted the adjective *venerabili* before *magistro.*

[152] ultima propositio *in marg. W, om. M.*

[153] ultimam conclusionem *W* : illa conclusio *M* (*v.* § *64 n. 150*). Fernando never states the conclusion, unless he means the prior proposition.

[154] That is, William of Ockham; see § 64 n. 151.

[155] dicĭdere [?] *MW.*

[156] per *M.*

[157] etc. etc. (*sic*) *post* sapientia *add. M.*

[158] propositiones metaphisicales : methaphisicas *W.*

[159] theoloycorum *MW.*

[160] prima *om. W.*

[161] et sua essentia . . . essentiam ab esse : a sua essentia inter se *M.*

[162] prima proposito *M; om. W.*

[163] sufficienter : sufficient te *M.*

[164] revellendi *W.*

[165] prior *W.*

[166] posterior *W.*

(70) Tertia propositio.[167] In solo deo idem est esse et quod est.[168] Corollarium.[169] Nulla creatura est que est.[170]

(71) Quarta propositio.[171] Necesse est universale haberi[172] preter opus intellectus.[173]

III

(72) Propositiones naturales ad articulum[174] questionis.

(73) [Prima.] Impossibile est intensionem aut remissionem qualitatis attendi penes propinquitatem ad summum gradum aut[175] distanciam a non gradu.

(74) [Secunda.] Intensionem fieri per addicionem gradus ad gradum, utraque remanente,[176] affirmo.

(75) [Tertia.] Ex ratione intensionis qualitatum sensibilium demonstrative concludi[177] potest[178] falsam esse Platonis sententiam de immortalitate anime per compares stellas.[179]

(76) [Quarta.] Omne mixtum est ita intensum precipue sicut excessus[180] precipue acceptus per quem intensior qualitas excedit suum contrarium.

(77) [Quinta.] Necesse est omnem latitudinem motus ad quietum terminatam esse uniformiter acquisitam si omnis latitudo gradualis suo medio gradui correspondet.

IV

(78) Morales

(79) [Prima.] In politico[181] regimine peccatorum[182] optimus rex est quam optima lex.

(80) [Secunda.] Possible est virtutem moralem eodem actu et generari et[183] augeri.

---

[167] tertia propositio *om. W.*

[168] etc. *post* est *add. M.*

[169] corollarium *om. W.*

[170] etc. *post* est *add. M.*

[171] quarta propositio *om. W.*

[172] habere *M.*

[173] etc. *post* intellectus *add. M.*

[174] articulum : titulum *M.*

[175] ad *M.*

[176] est *ante* remanente *add. M.*

[177] usque *ante* concludi *add. W.*

[178] possunt *W.*

[179] Cf. Calcidius's translation of Plato's *Tim.* 42B4: "Et victricibus quidem ad comparis stellae contubernium sedemque reditum patere acturis . . ." (Calcidius, 37.9-10); but Fernando may have gotten this information secondhand, e.g., from Thomas Aquinas, *Quaestiones Disputatae de Veritate*, q. 18.7 (Thomas Aquinas, 556.107-08): "Platonici dicebant animas fuisse ante corpora et post corpus redire ad compares stellas;" or from Albert the Great, *Summa de Creaturis*, Pars 2, q.5, a. 3 : "Utrum omnes animae ante corpus fuerunt creatae in comparibus stellis?" (Albertus Magnus [1890-1899], 35:73-82).

[180] precipue sicut excessus *om. M.*

[181] pollicito *MW* (polli^to *W*).

[182] pecōr *MW.*

[183] et *om. M.*

(81) [Tertia.] Propositis voluntati duobus bonis imparibus, potest voluntas velle minus bonum, obmisso magis bono.[184]

(82) [Quarta.] Falsam esse Platonis sententiam affirmo, qui poetas posse esse cives optime civitatis negavit.[185] /M 127v/

V

(83) Logicas[186] demonstrativas

(84) [Prima.] In demonstratione potissima concluditur propria passio de subiecto, /W 6r/ mediante diffinitione passionis et non subiecti.[187]

(85) [Secunda.] Necesse est de passione non modo cognosci quid dicitur, sed quia est.

VI

(86) Sophisticas

(87) [Prima.] Impossibile est aliquam propositionem dicere [?] se esse veram et se esse falsam.[188]

(88) [Secunda.] Aliqua[189] propositio est vera affirmativa non habens verbum reflexionis sui supra se, cuius subiectum pro nullo quod est supponit.[190]

(89) [Tertia.] Non sequitur hoc: est tibi positum sub forma positi propositum non repugnans, posito[191] a te admisso; ergo est a te concedendum.[192]

---

[184] etc. *post* bono *add.* M.

[185] posse . . . negavit : optime civitatis cives esse negavit posse negavit etc. M. See Plat. *Rep.* 8.568B, 10.595A and 607B, though Fernando doubtless derived this knowledge from a secondary source.

[186] loycas W.

[187] etc. *post* subiecti *add.* M.

[188] impossibile . . . falsam *om.* W.

[189] quod [?] *ante* aliqua *add.* M.

[190] etc. *post* supponit *add.* M.

[191] posito *om.* M.

[192] etc. *post* concedendum *add.* M; hec dominus Fernandus de Corduba *add.* W.

APPENDIX 7

Preface of Fernando of Cordova to Cardinal Guillaume d'Estouteville for the *Adversus Hereticos Qui Fraterculi dela Opinione Appellantur* and the Table of the Sections (*tractatus*) in the Treatise

I know no editions and only one manuscript: BAV, Vat. lat. 1127, mbr., s. XV, 235 × 168 mm., II + 168 ff. (ff. I–II, 4v, 103v, 167–168 are blank), in two hands (ff. 1–4: semi-hum. round; 5–166: gothic cursive), with the coat of arms of Cardinal d'Estouteville, elaborate initial and border on f. 1r, well described by Pelzer, 1:766–77. See also Esposito Aliano. Douie is inaccurate when discussing the manuscript; e.g., on p. 56 n. 228, she says that the treatise begins on f. 72r; and on p. 65 n. 259, that ff. 83–94 are missing.

The peculiar orthography of the manuscript is Fernando's, not the scribe's since the same peculiarities (e.g., confusion as when to redupli-cate the letter *s*) appear in his other writings. So, as a rule, I have pre-served the spelling of the manuscript except where sense and grammar dictate otherwise.

The preface runs from f. 1r to f. 4r, the treatise proper from f. 5r to f. 166r. On f. 166v there is this isolated disclaimer: "Que in primo huius operis capitulo diximus magis scolasticorum more protulimus quam obstinate pro veris tueri cupiamus, reliqua vero ecclesie sacrosancte deter-minacioni subicimus." The title of chapter 1 of Bk. 1, to which the dis-claimer refers, runs as follows (f. 6v): "De Christi inclito principatu, in quo dubitatur in quos sensus [*sic, instar* quo sensu] accipi debeat Christum esse regem in quantum homo, ut ex singulo sensu Christum sub ratione mortalis hominis fuisse principem regum terre per ipsam uni-onis ippostatice rationem facile convincamus."

I assign the siglum *H* to Vat. lat. 1127.

Fernandi Cordubensis adversus hereticos qui Fraterculi dela opinione vulgo appellantur ad reverendissimum in Christo patrem et illustrissimum dominum G. episcopum Hostienssem, sancte Romane ecclesie cardinalem, Rotomagens-sem vulgo appellatum, tractatus incipit foeliciter.

(1) Non ignoro fore nostra hec cum hominibus hereticis aggres<s>uros certa-mina in varias hominum reprehensiones incidere, partim admirancium post tot ab eruditissimis viris de hostibus fidei reportatos triunfos, post tanta certamina superata, post tot extintas /H1v/ lites sopitasque contenciones me novissime cum hostibus reintegrasse bellum et eos fractos iam viribus atque diuturna pugna defessos et ab ingeniis superatos acerrimis rurssum ad nova revocasse certamina, partim mea studia susceptosque pro ortodoxa fide labores temeritatis arguen-cium, quod putare videar non satis hucusque fidem ab aliis esse defenssam, sed meum pocius clipeum meamque tutelam desiderasse. (2) Sed nec ad id nos operis sponte nostra ing<r>essimus, et officii esse arbitramur non litterati hominis modo, sed experti omnino literarum sine ullo discrimine vel sapientie vel insipientie vel sexus vel etatis vel conditionis ingenue vel servilis, dum modo ille Catholicam fidem fuerit professus, vel revocare ab errore fratres, qui Christi

sanguine redempti sunt, seu, ubi obstinatos videant, vel evangelico atque apostolico rigore iugulare, vel, ubi id quidem per inpericiam non possint, saltem lignorum acervos ad cremandos eos instruere.

(3) Deinde tua nos iussa inpulerunt ut ad id operis inperiti quidem ac pene literarum expertes descenderemus, non quidem quod in me tantum ingenii atque erudictionis situm arbitrareris, sed, tanquam in omnium hominum genus clementissimus atque diligentissimus in filios pater, ut vires meas hac in re experireris et, ne per ocium torpescerent, exerceres. (4) Itaque iussibus tuis magis parentes quam confidentes nobis reffellere hereticos sumus aggressi, eos quidem qui principatui Christi atque eius vices gerenti<bu>s in terris ore sa- /H2r/ crilego detrahunt clericorumque criminantur possesas[1] divicias et cardineos principes submurmurant sibi non esse similimos, scilicet, obtorta cervice, oculis in terram deiectis, fronte subtristi, et crebris suspiriis sordidos atque discalciatos incedere, ut execrandi esse criminis putent (quorum sententiam, quoad vires suppetant ingenii, nos pollicemur exterminaturos) in principibus ecclesie atque cardinibus si risus misceant, si iocos, si tristiciam in fronte non simulent, si longa famulorum caterva stipati sint, si splendidiore. (5) Quod negocium preter tua, quibus obstringimur, iussa, eo libencius suscepimus quod Christiani hominis officium esse arbitremur, nihilque dignius, nihil acceptius deo esse putemus quam eniti ortodoxum hominem, quoad vires atque ingenia suppetant, ovem a Christo redemptam per heresum tenebras aberrantem ad rectam viam revocare atque conciliatam suo reddere redemptori. Quid melius, quid iocundius iuxta celitus aspiratum prophetam quam fratres unos atque unico patre Christo regenitos in unum fidei convenire culmen?[2] (6) Nam qui apostolice sedi colla submit<t>unt prosperari[3] usque ad dignam agni celestis intuicionem prospicimus. Qui vero per scisuram ab ea discedunt, per abrrupta gradientes animadvertimus, devios anfractus esse secutos et in profundum scelerum mergi atque in heresum profundissimos gurgites precipitari. Quibus magno opere eniti debemus /H2v/ ferre opem, iter veritatis patefacere, devios ad rectam viam revocare quo agno celesti eos nitidissimos atque purissimos offeramus. (7) Quid deo hac oblacione suavius? Quid[4] hoc acceptius sacrificio? Socratica illa est apud Platonem sentencia, cui sacre littere uno ore consentiunt:[5] qui succurrere perituro potest, si non succurrit, occidit.[6] Quod si divine voces tanto consenssu id fieri iubeant, cur dicere non[7] ausim mihi esse faciendum? Pasciemur, quantum in nobis situm est, figuram ac figmentum dei[8] feris ac volucribus, ut littere sacre locuntur,[9] in

---

[1] This is the normal spelling of the word in the treatise.
[2] Cf. Is. 27:12.
[3] propsperari *cod.*
[4] quod *H.*
[5] consenciunt *H.*
[6] I could not find this in Plato; but cf. Lact. *Div. Inst.* 6:11.19 (Lactantius, *Op. Om.*, 2:11.19), where there is no mention of Plato: "Qui succurrere perituro potest, si non succurrerit, occidit;" which seems the source of the same saying in Vincent of Beauvais, *Speculum Doctrinale*, 4:67, and the very similar saying in Pseudo-Publilius Syrus, *Proverbia*, 66 (Friedrich, 93 and 277). Cf. also Sen., *Apocol.* 14, 3:6: "Erant qui dicerent Sisyphum iam diu laturam fecisse, Tantalum siti periturum nisi illi succurreretur."
[7] non ausim mihi : ausim mihi non *H.*
[8] Gen. 1:26.
[9] Cf. Ez. 29:5 and Ier. 7:33.

predam iacere? (8) Quin pocius ubicumque homo etiam nobis incognitus ab invisibilis hostis faucibus impetitus est, ibi exigi officium nostrum putabimus? In quo enim magis iusticie ratio consistit quam in eo ut quod prestamus nostris per affectum, prestemus alienis per humanitatem, que est multo cercior iustiorque cum iam non homini prestatur solum, set deo, cui carissimum sacrificium est agnum immaculatum "in odorem suavitatis"[10] offerri.

(9) Et quamquam nobis quidem exorsso huic operi bona voluntas sit, perdifficili tamen operi innitimur remque nostros humeros supergressam aggredimur. Nam preter id, quod nobis satis cogniti sumus [*sic*],[11] quam parum nostra sciencia hereticorum tendiculas atque hostium fidei machinamenta precipitare possimus, arduum est homines in perfida vetustate obstinatos et a teneris annis in execranda obstinatione inveteratos ad ortodoxam revocare veritatem lucemque splendidis- /H3r/ simam Catholice fidei. Est enim eis natura insitum ut que ab adulescencia perceperunt, obstinate defendant; et id quidem faciunt non tan[12] rerum sciencia inducti quam inveterata quadam existimatione. (10) Nam magna quidem in hac mea etate afficior admiratione de conpluribus nostra et maiorum nostrum tempestate obduratissimis hostibus fidei, qui quanto annis magis in senectutem vergentibus apropincare[13] cernunt illum diem[14] quo sit eis ex hac vita demigrandum, cum[14] cogitare deberent quam puri abscedant, quam innocentes ad iudicium veniant, contra faciant hii nescio quem passi letargum, qui iam deficientibus corporis viribus in hoc admonentur[15] instantis ultime necesitatis, ut cupidius et ardentius hauriendis libidinibus intendant, vehemencius suas hereses tueantur adeo ut eis conterranei nostri Senece Cordubensis verba comode aptari possint, deridentis stultos senes: "non inquid bis pueri sumus, ut vulgo dicitur, set senper," a qua quidem voragine.[16] (11) Magni meriti apud deum esset, eciam si aggressi frustra nitamur, si eos persuasos efficere curaverimus ut liberet se quisque, dum licet, dum facultas adest, seseque ad deum tota mente convertat ut diem illum securus expectet, quo preses dominusque mundi deus de singulorum factis et cogitationibus iudicabit. (12) Nihil nobiscum ferre possumus nisi vitam bene atque in<n>ocenter actam. Ille ad deum copiosus, ille oppulentus adveniet, cui in primis astabunt ortodoxa fides, /H3v/ fida ad vicarium Christi subiectio (sine qua recta fides esse non potest), misericordia, pascientia [*sic*], caritas. Hec enim hereditas nostra que nec eripi cuiquam nec transferri ad alterum potest. (13) Quis est qui hec bona parare et adquirere sibi nolit? Venient qui esuriunt ut celesti cibo saturati sempiternam famem ponant. Venient qui siciunt ut aquam salutarem de perenni[17] fonte plenissimis faucibus trahant. Quo cibatu ac potu ceci nunc heretici, si fidem agnoverint, vide-

---

[10] Common Old Testament phrase; e.g., Ex. 29:18 and 25.

[11] An author's error, I believe, for "cognitum est."

[12] tam *H, sed v. (18) n. 25 infra.*

[13] That is, "appropinquare."

[14] Assuming a scribal error, I have transposed "cum" from its position before "illum deum"; but even so, the structure of this long sentence remains a hopeless muddle.

[15] admonemur *H.*

[16] Sen., *Frag.* 121 (*Opera,* ed. Haase) = Lact. *Div. Inst.* 2:4.14 (Lactantius, *Op. Om.,* 1:110.5–6): "Merito igitur senum stultitiam Seneca deridet: non, inquit, bis pueri sumus, ut vulgo dicitur, sed semper; verum hoc interest, quod maiora ludimus."

[17] perenipni *H.*

bunt; surdi audient; muti loquentur; claudi anbulabunt; stulti sapient; et egroti valebunt et mortui reviviscent. (14) Nos interim enitemur, quantum in nobis erit, eos de veritate erudire, non qui scientiam, sed qui fidem veram profitemur, magni esse meriti arbitrati, per quos iacentem fidem et, ut pene dixerim, dormientem censura celestis erexit. Satque erit[18] nobis vires attigisse veritatem ac pene tenuissime, nisi hereticos retrorssus infucata pravis opinionibus consuetudo rupuisset. Adhibebimus ad id quod attullerimus adverssus hereticos auctoritatibus de utroque instrumento[19] adiunctas rationes, quamquam maioribus nostris, etiam nulla ratione reddita, rationis sit credere, sed ne eis fidei suspiciende recusationis causas relinquamus.

(15) Tu, qui insita tibi ingenuitate ex illustrissima Francorum principum stirpe originem ducens in augenda religione Christiana Christianissimorum tuorum maiorum opera magnifica refers, huic exorsso operi pro tuenda fide sus- /H4r/ cepto aspira favores. Qui erigis templa in tan[20] splendidissimos cultus, qui litteris, qui hominibus cultui divino deditis faves, erige quoque a plausu tuo mentem meam quo acucior fiat aspirata favore tuo ad ipsos cultus celestis adversarios revincendos. Idque ab intemerata virgine inpetra, cuius templum ad eius gloriam regali munificentia extruxisti,[21] ut exorsso tanto operi prosperos successus aspiret.

Finit prologus. /H4v–5r/

(16) Fernandi Cordubenssis adverssus quorundam errores qui fratricheli dela opinione vulgo appellantur, in quibus cum orthodoxis hominibus magna dissensione concertant, liber incipit feliciter, qui iuxta horum decem hereses tractatus quoque decem conplexus est.

Primus tractatus de Christi loquitur in assumpta natura inclito principatu [= *ff. 5v–78v, in 20 chapters, the first of which, ff. 6v–16r, has the rubric*: De Christi inclito principatu, in quo dubitatur in quos sensus accipi debeat Christum esse regem in quantum homo, ut ex singulo sensu Christum sub ratione mortalis hominis fuisse principem regum terre per ipsam unionis ippostatice rationem facile convincamus;[22] *and the last of which, ff. 72r–78v, has the rubric (the table,*

---

[18] demonstrasse *post* erit *del.* H.

[19] That is, the Old and New Testaments.

[20] The scribe wrote "ta" with a line above the "a"; but see n. 25 below.

[21] That is, S. Maria Maggiore. From at least 1450 onward, until his death in 1483, D'Estouteville was a great benefactor of the church; see Marx; and Buchowiecki, 1:241.

[22] This first chapter, and therefore the treatise proper, begins (f. 6v): "Exploratum esse constat Christum sub racione assumpti hominis regem fuisse et iuxta Apocalipsim Iohannis [19:16] principem regum terre. In qua quidem sentencia non modo inter sacros doctores nulla lis est omnisque est sopita contencio, sed utrunque sacrarum litterarum testamentum tanta consensione testatur ut non satis admirari possim ridiculos hereticos, qui vulgo fraterculi dela opinione vocitantur, presertim eos qui maximam sibi erudicionem policentur, in tantam perductos esse cecitatem ut, pretermissis tan dilucidis de litteris divinis testimoniis sentenciisque sacratissimorum doctorum tan concorditer de Christi, in quantum homo, principatu senciencium, ad quasdam ridiculas confugerint raciones attullerintque et de evangeliis et de ecclesiasticis doctoribus ad sue hereseos confirmacionem, non modo que nichil virium habere possunt ad id quod probare pergunt, sed que ad suos evertendos errores possint retorqueri."

f. 6v): Capitulum 20, in quo argumenta et auctoritates fraterculorum dela opinione adversus Christi inclitum regnum adducuntur, et singula obiecta ex ordine reffelluntur.[23]].

(17) Secundus tractatus agit de principatu pape et summi pontificis potestate, quam Christus in quantum homo Petro reliquit et successoribus eius [= *ff. 78v–95r, in 35 chapters, though the table on f. 79r–v lists 37 chapters*].

Tercius tractatus illam abssolvit contraverssiam qua in ecclesie principes et inferioris ordinis possesas[24] divicias criminantur, querentes (ut eorum questionis formula utar) utrum Christus in quantum homo mortalis dicendus sit dominus habens proprietatem et dominium omnium rerum temporalium, et in quantum talis possit per temporis successus sibi dominia rerum conquirere que prius essent a se aliena [= *ff. 95r–103r, in 13 chapters*].

(18) Quartus tractatus disputat utrum appostoli, postquam fuerunt ad appostolatum assumpti, habuerint in speciali et sigilatim, non solum in comuni proprietatem et dominium multarum rerum, sed ut nunquam ab se abdicaverint, videlicet, proprietatem et dominium omnium rerum temporalium tan[25] mobilium quam immobilium, neque votum abdicacionis proprietatis et dominii emiserint, sed etiam post mis<s>ionem spiritus sancti super eos factam habuerint (ut eorum verbis utar) in speciali et sigilatim proprietatem et dominium proprium vestimentorum et calciamentorum et alimentorum; et utrum aliquando Christus eis consuluerit abdicationem[26] proprietatis et dominii omnium rerum.[26] [= *ff. 104r–161v, in 40 chapters*]. /H5v/

(19) Quintus tractatus: utrum Christus imposuerit aliam legem vivendi appostolis quam quibuscumque aliis discipulis, ut Lazaro, Marie, Marte, Ioseph ab Arimathia, et Dorcas etc. [= *ff. 162r–163r, in 2 chapters*].

Sextus tractatus: utrum litigare in iudicio pro rebus temporalibus diminuat de perfectione evangelica, licueritquene appostolis et evangelicis viris in speciali et sigilatim, etiam in comuni pro rebus temporalibus tanquam pro propriis in iudicio contendere [= *ff. 163r–165r, in 2 chapters*].

(20) Septimus tractatus: utrum dominus noster Ihesus Christus interdixit simpliciter et absolute appostolis ne possiderent aurum et argentum neque pecuniam in zonis vel solum pro tempore vie, cum irent ad predicandum, itaque (?) ut post redditum a predicacione libere possidere et portare potuissent [= *f. 165r–v, in one chapter*].

Octavus tractatus: utrum bona primitive ecclesie seu multitudinis credencium, de quibus Actuum secundo et quarto, ne quisquam eorum que possidebat aliquid suum esse dicebat, sed erant illis omnia comunia; essent quoque eis comunia post distribucionem vel quilibet post distribucionem dominus efficeretur et proprietarius sibi asignate porcionis; et an votum religiosorum necessario eget vita humana [= *f. 165v, consisting of a reference back to Tractatus 4*].

---

[23] This last chapter begins (f. 72r): "Iam tractationem istam de Christi, in quantum homo, inclito principatu tun comodissime claudere poterimus si ridicula fraterculorum absolverimus deliramenta, quibus probasse putant heresim esse afermare Christum sub ratione hominis assumpti regem esse. Argumentorum autem genera, quibus superiorem conclusionem reffellere pergunt, in tres constat esse rationes distributa. Nam quedam ex litteris sacris sumpta sunt, alia vero ex sacris earum interpretibus [interpetribus H]; presertim vero colligunt ex sanctorum patrum doctrinis per consequenciam quandam."

[24] See § 4 n. 1.

[25] "tan" is Fernando's spelling; see Appendix 8, § 1 n. 1.

[26] abdicationem . . . rerum: *add. in marg. inferiore* H.

(21) Nonus tractatus: utrum in rebus usu consumptibilibus usus vel iuris vel facti licite posit a proprietate et dominio separari et an in temporalibus rebus ius utendi, separata proprietate rei seu dominio, possit constitui vel haberi [= *ibid., consisting of a reference back to Tractatus 4*].

Decimus tractatus: utrum sint Ioh<ann>is vigessimi secundi excusaciones ad-mit<t>ende circa obiectas sibi hereses [= *ff. 165v–166r, consisting of a reference to the* De Planctu ecclesiae *of Alvaro Pelayo, O.F.M.*].

APPENDIX 8

Preface of Fernando of Cordova to
Cardinal Francesco Todeschini-Piccolomini
for the *De Misterio Pallii*

The two manuscripts known to me are:

1) Florence, BN, Magl. XXXI, 17. Membr., s. XV, consisting of IV + 155 + III ff., in one Ital. hum. round hand (the scribe signed himself on f. 155v: Petrus de Iaen), with frequent initials, decorated borders, marginalia in gold foil, and the coat of arms of Cardinal Todeschini-Piccolomini on f. 1r. This is obviously the dedication copy. Ff. 1r–3v contain the preface; ff. 3v–155v, the treatise proper. See Kristeller (1963–1992), 1:122.

2) BAV, Vat. lat. 5739. Chart., s. XV, miscellany, 211 ff., in one gothic cursive hand, with occasional marginal notes in the same hand. Ff. 1r–111r: Fernando of Cordova, *De Misterio Pallii* to Cardinal Francesco Todeschini-Piccolomini. Ff. 111v–114v: blank. Ff. 115r–211r: Nicolaus Cusanus, *De Concordantia Catholica* to Cardinal Giuliano Cesarini. Once owned by Pier Leoni. See Kristeller (1963–1992), 2:325; Haubst (*Studien*, 1955), 6–7; and Ruysschaert, 54–55, num. 10.

Since a collation of the Vatican manuscript produced only errors, I have based the text below exclusively on the dedication copy now in Florence (= M).

I have maintained the same orthographical policy as in Appendix 7.

Fernandi Cordubensis, apostolici subdiaconi, de pontificii pallii misterio, et an pro eo aliquid temporale absque simonie labe exigi possit ad reverendissimum in Christo patrem et dominum, dominum Franciscum Picholomineum, sancte Romane ecclesie diaconum cardinalem sancti Eustachii, Senensem vulgo appellatum, tractatus incipit foeliciter.

(1) Pallii, quo in argumentum extremi fastigii pontificie dignitatis amiciri solitos constat novi testamenti pontifices maximos, tanta maiestas est ut inter sacras vestes nihil vel concipi sacratius possit et inter spirituales res tan[1] ipsa spiritualitate prestare videatur ut vel unicum inter omnia ec<c>lesiastica ornamenta plenitudi- /M1v/ nis spiritualis potestatis signum sit institutum, quod et veteris instrumenti pallium prefigurare videtur. (2) Nam ante salvatoris adventum ephod superius pallium erat, quo tota sacerdotalis protegebatur ambitio, cum sacerdos maximus solus haberet licenciam ephod non lineo vestiendi, verum, ut scriptura comemorat, auro, iacinto,[2] purpura, coccino, bissoque contexto,[3] ut ridendos putem quosdam sacrarum litterarum interpretes,[4] quos paulo post in

---

[1] This is also the spelling in the *Adv. hereticos* written by a different scribe; see Appendix 7, nn. 12, 20, 25.

[2] That is, "hyacintho."

[3] Cf. Ex. 28:6.

[4] interpetres *M*. "Interpetres" is not Fernando's spelling; in the *De laud. Plat.* the word is spelled *interpres, -etis.*

palestram annuente deo citabimus, qui existiment, invecti adversus sedis apostolice subdiaconos, ephod hanc esse vestem omnibus veteris instrumenti sacerdotibus comunem, cum facile de sacris litteris redargui falsitatis possint, quod
illud pallium ephod sacerdotibus comune lineum sit, ob quod non ephod, sed
ephobad, id est, lineum vocitetur.[5] Hoc peculiare pontifici maximo non lineum,
sed superiore varietate distinctum et ex duodecim lapidibus ornatum, qui in
humero utroque residebant (cum comune sacerdotibus pallium lineum esset et
simplex et toto candore purissimum).   (3) Ob tantam pallii per significationem
spiritualitatem quidam tun[6] in vulgus homines, tun sacrarum et pontificiarum
litterarum interpretes[7] nos sedis apostolice subdiaconos in crimen vocant et
simoniace labis redarguunt quod pro re tan spirituali pecunias exigamus. Succur-
rendum his erroribus credidi et viros hos inpericie redarguendos, quos perspicuum est multa adversus nos de sacris voluminibus memori- /M2r/ ter copiose
dicere solitos, multa in nostram offensionem Romanorum pontificum atullisse
iura.   (4) Sed de clementia Christi diffidimus nihil ut, cum totum circuerint,
saltem quin nostris cassibus[8] claudantur. Quorum omnium propositionum
calles ad unum compitum confluunt, et pavidorum more cervorum, dum varios
evitant volatus,[9] spinarum fortissimis retibus inplicantur. Inter multos sunt Parisienses quidam, qui ad omnia argumentantur et missa ab ortodoxis spicula scuto
orationis eludunt. Illud adversus eos enitar, ut vel unica asta iaciatur que umbram
tegminis eorum et verba crepitantia vi sua penetret, nec diucius pasciatur [sic]
arte superari <eorum> qui, dum nesciunt, proprio capiuntur laqueo.   (5) Inter
hos sunt qui, ut vulgo scolasticorum dici solet, punctum in quo tota contro-
versia[10] disputationis vertitur fugiant et magno circuitu quod non querimus elo-
quntur ut, cum manum petantur, pedem porrigant, et dum argumenta argumentis connectunt ac per scripturarum latissimos campos infrenis equi libertate
bacantur, illud eis iure possit aptari quod vetus narrat historia: quidam cum
diserte diceret ferreturque impetu ac volubilitate verborum causamque omnino
non tangeret, prudens auditor et iudex bene inquit: "Et bene. Sed quo istud tan
bene?"   (6) Horum est precipue unus, cuius nomen honoris gracia reticeo.
Credatur experto. Novi hominem: quantus in clipeum asurgat, quo /M2v/ tur-
bine torqueat hastam. Sunt inter hos qui retoricentur et, ut Iheronimus
loquitur,[11] disputationum spinetis ad campos libere declamationis excurrant et,
cum ad compendium certationis tribuas quod postulant, tandem suis tellis se ipsi
conficiant, licet tergiversentur et in eodem luto semper hesitent.   (7) Neque

---

[5] Fernando seems to be referring to polemical commentators such as Henry
of Langenstein (see n. 259, p. 42), rather than a standard commentator such
as Nicholas of Lyra, who actually agrees with Fernando; see Nicholas's *Postilla
super totam bibliam*, Pars 1 (Rome, C. Sweynheim and A. Pannartz, 1471; Hain
num. 5231), unnum. fol. at I Reg. 2: "Ephod lineum non est tale vestimentum
sicut ephod summi sacerdotis." In the generation after Fernando, Antonio
Nebrija made the same distinction between the *ephod* and the *ephod bad*
("amictus lineus"): Nebrija, 80 and 759. See *Dictionnaire de la Bible*, 2 (Paris, 1910):
1865–69.
[6] An orthographical experiment of Fernando?
[7] See n. 4 above.
[8] That is, the plural of "cassa" in Italian ("box").
[9] That is, the plural of "volatus, -us" of medieval Latin: "spear."
[10] contraversia *M*.
[11] I suspect that this is a fictive reference, but cf. St. Jerome, *Contra Rufinum*
3:22 *ad finem* (*PL*, 23:495B–C).

cum contentiosis contentiosi esse cupimus. Non enim de adversario victoriam, sed contra mendacium querimus veritatem (quin potius libenter sileremus), ne illud evangelicum vel in enigmate pretergressi videamur ut <ei> qui iudicio velit nobiscum contendere et per lites aut iurgia auferre tunicam, eciam pallium, de quo in hac pallestra disceptaturi sumus, esse<t> cedendum.

(8) Huius autem contexte litis quem potissimum deligam arbitrum quam tuam paternitatem eruditissimam atque sapientissimam, que non in me modo minus peritum hominem, sed in omnes eruditissimos viros censoriam accipere possis virgulam? Cui[12] sum<m>a sapientia et doctrina singularis, qui Pio pontifici maximo non modo nepos, sed et excellentium et admirabilium eius principis virtutum successisti heres, illi Enee divino pene viro, cuius ingenium atque eloquentiam semper obstupui et, ut in sacris litteris, actiones apostolice loqu<u>ntur, illi iterum Enee, quem Petrus apostolorum princeps invenit, quem incolumitati pristine donavit,[13] cuius gratiam intuiti Lidenses, Saronii, Arabes ad fidem Christi, deserta gentilitate, conversi sunt,[14] et, ut Origenes loquitur,[15] cui claves comiserit regni celorum.   (9) Nam quanto /M3r/ splendore Romanum solium, admirabili illa sua eloquentia, et heroicis divinisque virtutibus illustraverit, vix cohibere me per singulos tractatus possum, ut pro virili silentio preteream quod tamen omnibus notum et fama clarissima celebratum est. Qui apostolicam sedem in pristinam dignitatem gloriamque restituit; et iam eo sedente Damasos illos, Gregorios, Leones magno opere non desideraremus. Certe per quamcumque datam occasionem illius laudes minime silentio preterire possum, quem Christus optimus maximus, cuius vices gerebat in terris, tanto spiritu sapiencie replevit ut in contione loquens, quemadmodum ipsi sepenumero audivimus, omnes non modo in admirationem, verum eciam in excessum quendam mentis ac stuporem converterit.   (10) Eam ingenii vim bone deus! Eam dicendi vehementiam, sentenciarum acumina, verborum ornatum, copiam, facilitatem, gravitatem, elegantiam, maiestatemque orationis quis satis admirari potuit? Tun ille nitor, ille candor, ille splendor Latine lingue quem nostrum

---

[12] cuius M.

[13] This clause, like the prior clause, is peculiar; Fernando can only mean here that St. Peter was in some way responsible for restoring Pius II to an original state of grace, which, without the benefit of any gloss, is an assertion difficult to square with Catholic theology.

[14] Fernando probably is referring to one or both of the legations Pius received from Eastern potentates, though I do not know who the Saronians were supposed to be nor the Lidians (inhabitants of Lydia in Asia Minor?). In April 1460, Pius was visited by Moses Gilbet, who claimed to represent the Eastern Patriarchs as well as Ibramhimbeg, the Prince of Caramania, and others. In December, envoys of the Emperor of Trebizond, of the *rex Persarum et maioris Armenie ac minoris Hiberie* (Georgia), of the Duke of Greater Georgia, and of the Lord of Greater Armenia came to Rome. The result, Pius claimed in his *Commentarii*, was an alliance with (note the mention of Arabia) "Bendias, Magrelie et Arabie rex, et Pancratius Hiberorum, qui nunc Georgiani vocantur, et Mania, marchio Gorye, et Hismahel, Synopi dominus et Casatimene, cui pater fuit Sediar, et Fabia, dux Anogasie, et Caramanus, Cilicie dominus" (Pius II, 1:322.36–323.3); see also ibid., 269; Campano, 82; Pastor, 3:245–49; Fallmerayer, 264–69 (text of two letters of Pius II); and Voigt, 3:644–50.

[15] This is probably a fictive reference since it merely asserts that Origen quoted Scripture; but cf. Origen, *In Matth.*, 14, *ad finem* concerning Mt. 16:19 (*PG*, 13: 1179–82, for the *vetus interpretatio*).

audientem non ad se totum convertit atque mirum in modum allexit? Cumque singuli oratores singulis pene dotibus et ornamentis sive nature sive industrie claruerint, gravitatem Isocrates, suavitatem Lisias, acumen Pericles, sonitum Eschines, vim Demostenes habuerit, itemque alii alia, ipsa omnia in uno Pio Enea cumulata esse nobis visa sunt. Quid de virtutibus, que voluntatem ipsam perficiunt atque deo illi, cuius vicem gerebat /M3v/ in terris, simillimum reddunt, clementia, facilitate, gravitate, constantia, pietate, iusticia, animique magnitudine? (11) Huic cum successeris, reverendissime pater, tantarum virtutum heres,[16] [tuus a me fit][17] ut te suplex orem ut huius tractatuli censorium iudicium digneris accipere ut ex tuo pendeam iudicio, et quod a tan sapientissimo domino vel probatum vel improbatum fuerit, id mihi pro lege sumendum putem.

(12) Quid, ne questionem principalem diutius morer, de re dicere incipiemus, sed si illud primum monuerimus, hanc controversie[18] rationem tun comodissime tractari posse si in partes tris distributam effecerimus, id est si primo loco quid in utramque partem obiici possit litteris consequemur, secundo loco, si decisionem questionis subiecerimus, extremo, si singula pallii misteria per diversa probleumata [sic] et ea quidem pro maiori parte solutu [sic] difficilima prosequamur.

[THE TREATISE]

(13) Itaque primum omnium hanc questionis formulam subiicimus, utrum liceat subdiacono preter simonie labem pro pallio exigere pecunias vel Romane curie consuetudinem pretendenti vel pontificis maximi ex certa sciencia tollerantiam; et argumentamur in primis pro parte negativa non rationibus eis modo quas constat adversario afferre solitos, sed et omnibus argumentandi generibus que ab eis afferri possint ut eorum argumentis nostra adiunxerimus argumenta multo quam illorum solutu difficiliora; et ea /M4r/ ipsa que ab illis inducuntur fortiora reddiderim quo facile perspici possit quantarum sint virium arma quibus subdiaconos vel[19] oppugnare possint vel nitantur.

(14) [des.] . . . /M155v/ . . . Quintum probleuma: utrum stipendium exactum relatum ad subdiaconum habentem oculum ad spiritualitatem pallii sit simoniacum. Dico quod sic. Idem enim est quemadmodum de canonico servienti matutinis[20] habente oculum ad fructuum perceptionem. Sed hec a nobis in theoriis sive generalibus sive specialibus subtilius diserta sunt.

---

[16] heres *in marg. add.* M.
[17] I cannot construe this passage; something is garbled here.
[18] contraversie M.
[19] vel *in marg. add.* M.
[20] That is, the liturgical office of Matins.

APPENDIX 9

Henricus de Zoemeren, Cardinal Bessarion,
and the University of Louvain

Baudry, 34, points out that Henricus de Zoemeren probably first made some contacts in Rome when he traveled there in 1449 on a mission for the university. Henricus dedicated to Cardinal Bessarion his epitome of the first part of William of Ockham's *Dialogus*. But citing only Molanus, 1:506, Baudry did not note that the dedication itself adds information, namely, that Henricus calls Bessarion "Apostolic Legate *per Alemaniam atque Germaniam*" and himself "eiusdem reverendissime dominationis devotissimus servulus et indignus capellanus." In the preface Henricus explains that Bessarion commissioned the work (he used phrases such as *iussit benignitas tua, desiderio tuo,* and *imponere dignaberis*). In the rubric of the *Epitome*, he specifies that he wrote the *Epitome* "in Wienna Austrie ad instantiam reverendissimi in Christo patris domini Bissarionis." I thank Mr. John Dooley of the Bryn Mawr College Library for photocopies of f. a 2r-v of the Louvain, 1481 edition of the *Epitome* (Hain 8435; Goff, H-53). In the colophon to the possible dedication copy, MS Cremona, B. Governativa, 132, Zoemeren further specifies that the work was "abbreviatum et in 16 dies scriptum;" see Mazzatinti-Sorbelli, 70:100-01; and Bianca, 42 n. 106. Another manuscript is Florence, Bibl. Laurenziana 20, 40 (see Bandini, 1:650-51). Bessarion arrived in Germany in mid-February 1460. After traveling to Nuremberg and the Rhineland, where perhaps Henricus joined up with his party, the cardinal remained in Vienna from 4 May 1460 to September 1461; see Meuthen.

According to Meuthen, Bessarion never traveled to Louvain; but according to Molanus, 1:793, Bessarion gave a manuscript of the bible to the "collegium theologorum" of the university (i.e., the Collegium Sancti Spiritus or Heilige Geestcollege). A bible containing the *ex-libris* of Giuliano Cesarini and of Bessarion once belonged to the college, and in a note in the manuscript Bessarion noted that Cesarini gave it to him at the Council of Florence (see Dequekker). This was probably the bible Henricus de Zoemeren gave the college in 1462 (ibid.). Unfortunately, as Prof. Jozef IJsewijn explained to me in communications of 2 February 1983 and 27 August 1986, the bible remained at the college until the abolition of the university in the French Revolution. The codex was in private possession until returned to the university after World War I (shelf mark D 565), only to perish in the burning of the university library in World War II. R. X. Ram, in a note to Molanus, 2:793, mistakenly identified this manuscript with the magnificently decorated Angevin bible then in the library of the seminary in Mechelen and now in the Katholieke Universiteit, Faculteit der Godgeleerdheid, Louvain (MS Seminarie Mechelen 1). The error was repeated by De Clercq, 25-26, cod. 1. But now see Dequekker, 122-34; Avril, 314-28; and Labowsky, 510-11. A description of the destroyed Bessarion bible is found in Le Clercq, 551 n. 5 from the previous page: "Elle est du XIVe siècle, sur vélin, de 393 feuillets, en petit format de 165 × 113 mm. Les gardes de son ancienne reliure portent l'ex-libris manuscrit de Julianus Cesarini, cardinal de S. Ange, son premier possesseur, la signature de Bessarion qui la reçut de lui et enfin une note d' Henri de Zomeren relatant la dernière donation. Elle devint la pro-priété de J. Fr. Van de Velde, dont la famille l'offrit récemment à Université."

Molanus, 2:862, also reports that in September 1470 Bessarion sent Henricus a copy of his *In Calumniatorem Platonis*. In his letter of 1983, Prof. IJsewijn told me that the volume is no longer at Louvain and that "it is hard to say whether it still exists or not." If it was returned to the university before World War I, "it certainly was burned in 1914, when the library was destroyed for the first time. At the time of that fire, work had begun to make a catalogue of the more than a thousand incunables of our library, but hardly a hundred were described before all were burnt. Bessarion's book is not in that partial list." The incunabulum is not men-tioned in Moreau.

APPENDIX 10

Verdict of the Papal Commission on Pere Deguí (Petrus Dagui)'s
Ianua Artis Magistri Raymundi Lull, **Rome, 1484**

I know of only one manuscript of the *Ianua Artis*: MS VIII b 9 (paper, miscellany, s. XV–XVI), ff. 95r–100v, of the Biblioteca della Collegiata (Kapitelbibliothek) of S. Candido-Innichen, which comes from the library of Nicolaus Pol (d. 1532); see Kristeller, (1963–1992), 2:140–41; Rubió y Balaguer (1917), 312, 315–17; Rubió y Balaguer (1913–1914), 743; Fisch-Schullian, 191, num. 260. This manuscript lacks the *approbatio* (seen in photocopy).

The only manuscript of the *approbatio* I have discovered is that in MS Milano, B. Ambrosiana, N 250 sup., ff. 88r–89v, where, strangely enough, it is appended not to a manuscript text of the *Ianua Artis*, but rather to the Seville, 1491 edition of Deguí's *Libellus Formalitatum*; see Kristeller (1963–1992), 1:303; Ceruti, 4:241. I have collated the manuscript from photographs and assigned it the siglum "M."

There were eight editions of the *Ianua*, namely:

1) Barcelona, Petrus Posa, 25 February 1482 (Rogent and Durán, num. 4; Copinger 3684). Seen in Madrid, Biblioteca Nacional.

2) Rome, (Eucharius Silber), 1485 (Rogent and Durán, num. 8; Reichling 606; Goff, G-543), to which I assign the siglum "R." Seen in a microfilm from the University of Illinois, Urbana-Champaign.

3) Barcelona, Petrus Posa, 1488 (Rogent and Durán, num. 8; Hain-Reichling 10323). Seen at BAV (shelf mark: Stamp. Incun. V. 53 [1]).

4) Seville, (Paulus de Colonia et socii), 1 March 1491 (Rogent and Durán, num. 13; Hain-Copinger-Reichling 8150). Seen at BAV (shelf mark: Stamp. Ross. 803).

5) Valencia, printer unknown, 1497 (Rogent and Durán, num. 23). Not seen.

6) Seville, (Stanislaus Polonus), 26 June 1500 (Rogent and Durán, num. 27; Goff, G-543), to which I assign the siglum "S." Seen at the Pierpont Morgan Library, New York.

7) Paris, (Petrus Levet?), ca. 1500 (Rogent and Durán, num. 23; Pellechet 4087). Seen in Paris, Bibliothèque Nationale. This edition probably has something to do with the *approbatio* of the University of Paris to which King Ferdinand of Aragon referred in a privilege dated 20 January 1500; see Custurer, 298 n. 5, and p. 348.

8) Cologne, *ingenui liberi* of Peter Quentell, May 1516 (Rogent and Durán, num. 61). Not seen. Rogent and Durán cite a copy in the Bibliothèque Municipale of Lyon. Library of Congress, *The National Union Catalog. Pre-1956 Imprints* (London, 1961–1978), 137:85, col. 1, reports a copy at Holy Name College in Silver Spring, Maryland; but the copy is now lost. As Mr. Paul J. Spaeth, Librarian at The Franciscan Institute, St. Bonaventure, New York, explained to me in a letter of 13 January 1987, the rare book holdings of Holy Name College have been transferred to the Institute, but not all items arrived and for those that did, the cataloging is poor.

The first edition to carry the verdict was that of Rome, 1485 (= R, ff. [16]r–[18]v). I have based the edition below on R. As controls I also collated the manuscript M and the edition of Seville, 1500 (= S, ff. b⁷ᵛ⁻⁹ᵛ). Editions 3, 4, and 7 include the verdict, and perhaps also editions 5 and 8, but I have not been able to verify this. The first paragraph and the list of commissioners at the end were reproduced from S by Custurer, 300.

Thus the sources collated for the text are:

M MS Ambros. N 250 sup.
R Edition num. 2 above.
S Edition num. 6 above.

The title preceding the verdict is not found in MR, and is doubtless a later gloss, probably Deguí's.

[Approbatio libelli Rome per iudices infra a beatissimo Sixto assignatos.]¹

(1) Beatissime pater, post pedum oscula beatorum. Sepius² fuimus cum magistro Petro Dagui ut videremus³ intellectum quem dat tractatui edito in doctrinam Raymundi Lull⁴ et signatis particulis in eodem tractatu, in quibus videtur oriri prima facie suspicio propter inusitatum modum loquendi et accipiendi terminos sicut in doctrina eiusdem Raymundi ita ut ignorantibus⁵ materiam subiectam magis videatur quedam obumbratio intus quam cognitio alicuius artis. (2) Dimissis⁶ que in logica, physica, et methaphisica⁷ dicuntur, solum ad⁸ tria aspeximus que in fide possunt generare suspitionem, que etiam secundum intelligere magistri Petri et aliquorum doctorum non male sonare videntur etc.

(3) Primum est quod omnis bonitas universaliter loquendo constituitur de hac absolutione et inclinatione seu fecunditate quadam ad habendum finem. Hoc videtur non intelligentibus materiam subiectam habere intellectum, quod essentia⁹ divina¹⁰ sicut essentia¹¹ creata sit constituta vel composita, que caret omni compositione, et ex his et cum his, ut volunt theologi et philosophi, cum ipsa sit non solum simpliciter simplex,¹² sed summe simplex. (4) Istud tamen salvatur tripliciter: primo quia Raymundus, quem sequitur magister Petrus, utitur suis¹³ propriis vocabulis, sicut et Damascenus utitur vocabulo compositione in tertio Sententiarum,¹⁴ ubi habet compositio ineffabilis Iesu,¹⁵ sic et Atha-

---

¹ MR om., S add. The first edition to carry this rubric identifying the pontiff as Sixtus IV was that of Barcelona, 1488.
² sepe S.
³ viderimus S.
⁴ Luyll M.
⁵ inorantibus MR.
⁶ dimimissis R.
⁷ methafisica R.
⁸ a S.
⁹ esse M.
¹⁰ diviva R.
¹¹ esse M.
¹² simplex om. S.
¹³ suis om. S.
¹⁴ Cf. Petrus Lombardus, Sent., 3, d. 6, c. 3, par. 3–4 and d. 7, c. 1, par. 94.
¹⁵ Ihesu MS.

nasius in Simbolo.[16] (5) Sicut anima rationalis et caro unus est homo, ita deus et[17] homo unus est Christus; verum tamen nec deitas informat carnem nec caro informat[18] deitatem, quod tamen requiritur ad compositionem phisicam et naturalem. Ita essentia[19] divina,[20] licet absolute considerata tantum sit essentia,[21] sicut equinitas tantum est equinitas, tamen per comparationem ad proprietates est pelagus[22] et fundamentum ipsarum, ut Damascenus in primo Sententiarum,[23] et istud esse pelagus[24] et habere in se talem fecunditatem. (6) Magister Petrus dicit bonitatem divinam sive essentiam constitui ex absolutione et inclinatione, quod quamvis improprie et inusitate loqui videatur, sensus bonus affirmatur, quod potest etiam dici et magis ad intellectum dicti magistri Petri, quod essentia potest accipi cum habitudine, et istud est constitui, et sine habitudine, et istud est non constitui. (7) Ita quod essentia divina potest considerari quadrupliciter: primo pro essentia sola; secundo essentia cum intellectu, et sic dicitur essentia cum absolutione; tertio essentia[25] cum intellectu et proxima dispositione ad actum generandi, et sic dicitur essentia[26] cum inclinatione;[27] quarto essentia cum intellectu proxima dispositione et omnibus requisitis ad actum generandi, et sic dicitur essentia cum fecunditate. Et istud est essentiam divinam constitui ex absolutione, inclinatione, et fecunditate ad habendum finem, idest, operationem instrinsecam. Et talis est intentio magistri Petri.

(8) Aliud in eodem libello invenimus, quod prima proprietas originatur seu pullulat in bonitate et de ipsa tota bonitate. Hoc aliqui trahunt ad hunc sensum, quod essentia[28] divina, que est prima bonitas, generaret, quod non sequitur nec secundum mentem theologorum nec ipsius Raymundi quia, licet filius generet de substantia sive ponatur patris sive non et secundum aliquos de substantia quasi de materia, non tamen concedent propter hoc quod essentia divina generet vel generetur. (9) Dicimus etiam quod "originatur" capitur pro "pullulat," quamvis Scotus[29] in primo,[30] distinctione XXVI,[31] in responsione ad sextum argumentum utatur isto vocabulo[32] in pullulatione dictarum proprietatum,[33] ac etiam distinctione XII[34] et distinctione VIII[35] utitur "originari" pro "naturari" et "signum

---

[16] Cf. Ps. Athanasius, *Symbolum Quicumque*, in *PG*, 28:1583B.

[17] et *om. S*.

[18] informat *om. S*; imformat *R*.

[19] esse *M*.

[20] diviva *R*.

[21] esse *M*.

[22] pelegus *RS*.

[23] Cf. Petrus Lombardus, *Sentent.*, 1, d. 27, c. 3, par. 2.

[24] pelegus *RS*.

[25] esse *M*.

[26] esse *M*.

[27] inclinatione . . . dicitur essentia cum *om. M*.

[28] esse *MR*.

[29] Scotus *om. M*.

[30] prima *RS*.

[31] 26 *R*.

[32] vocabulo *om. M*.

[33] Cf. John Duns Scotus, *Opus Oxoniense* 1, d. 26, n. 7 and n. 9 (in Duns Scotus, 10:297b and 299a).

[34] 12 *M*. Cf. ibid., 1, d. 12, q. 1 (in Duns Scotus, 9:853b and 857a).

[35] I was not able to find *originari* nor *signum originis* in the very long dist. 8 of *Opus Oxoniense*, 1.

originis" pro "signo nature," et sic salvatur dictum istius tractatus, quod prima
proprietas originatur seu pullulat in et de bonitate originaliter et fundamentaliter.

(10) Tertium dictum[36] in quo maior videtur[37] difficultas, quod pater et filius
dicuntur unum principium spirativum: "unum dico non numero nec discretione
numeri, sed tantum convenientie,"[38] cum ecclesia in consilio Lugdonensi sub
Gregorio Decimo determinaverit quod pater et filius sunt unum principium
spiritus sancti, et est hodie in sexto decretalium, et Augustinus idem voluerit in
quinto De trinitate, quod pater et filius sunt unum principium spiritus sancti. Et
sic potest dici ad sensum istius, quod nec auctoritas ecclesie nec Augustini dicit
unum numero vel plura numero.   (11) Scotus etiam in Reportationibus Parisien-
sibus in primo Sententiarum, distinctione 12, in[39] questione in qua queritur
utrum pater et filius sint duo spiratores, in secunda ratione ad conclusionem
habet ista verba: "Secundo probatur sic pater et filius sunt unum principium
spiritus sancti sicut dicit Augustinus. Non autem sunt unum principium quo
quia[40] suppositum non est principium quo,[40] sed quod agit."   (12) Pater ergo et
filius sunt unum principium quod respectu spiritus sancti."[41] Quod non est intel-
ligendum quod pater et filius sint unum principium quod numero cum sint due
persone realiter distincte, sed sunt unum principium convenientia, qua conveniunt in vi spirativa et spiratione.   (13) Et huic sententie videtur assentire
solemnis doctor Henricus de Gandavo in quinta, articolo v, questione prima,[42]
qui exponens auctoritatem Ricardi[43] tertio de trinitate,[44] capitulo secundo, quam
expositionem adducit Doctor Subtilis distinctione 12 primi libri questione in qua
queritur utrum pater et filius spirent spiritum sanctum in quantum omnino
unum vel in quantum aliquo modo distincti [qui habet].[45]   (14) Et secundum
hoc inspiratione spiritus sancti dupliciter consideranda est patris et filii distinctio:
uno modo ut intelliguntur sicut dicentes actum, alio modo ut intelliguntur esse
concordes in amore mutuo et in voluntate circa actum eliciendum ex distinctione
eius. Primo modo considerata, nullo modo dicendi sunt spirare ut plures (licet
enim sunt plures qui spirant, sed solum ex distinctione eorum).   (15) Secundo
modo considerata, et sic pater et filius non spirant spiritum sanctum in quantum
sunt plures in elicienda actione, licet concurrant in unam rationem, secundum
quam elicitur actio, sed ut plures in una voluntate, que est ratio eliciendi actum
concordando ad amorem suum in illa mutuitate.   (16) Et istud est dicere patrem
et filium esse unum principium non numero nec discretione numeri, sed unum
convenientia concordia ad spirandum spiritum sanctum[46] quia[47] sunt due persone distincte numero habentes eandem voluntatem et spirationem activam qua

---

[36] dictum *om. M.*

[37] maior videtur: est maior *M.*

[38] convenientia *RS.*

[39] in *om M.*

[40] quia . . . quo *om. M.*

[41] John Duns Scotus, *Reportata Parisiensia*, 1, d. 12, q. 2 (in Duns Scotus,
22:192b).

[42] prima *om. M.* Cf. Henry of Ghent, *Summa*, art. 55, q. 1 (Henry of Ghent,
2:ff. 106ⁿ–107ᵛ).

[43] Richardi *M.*

[44] Cf. Richard of St. Victor, 136–137.

[45] qui habet *secludo.* John Duns Scotus, *Reportata Parisiensia*, 1, d. 12, q. 1 (in
Duns Scotus, 22:191).

[46] spiritum sanctum spirandum *M.*

[47] qui *M.*

conveniunt et concordant. Et propter hoc aliqui dixerunt spiritum sanctum esse nexum, aliqui unionem, aliqui communionem patris et filii. (17) Et talis est sententia dicti magistri Petri, quam nos uniformiter laudamus.

Anthonius episcopus[48] Fanensis

Noyanus episcopus Cephalensis[49]

Ferdinandus Cordubensis, subdiaconus[50] domini nostri

Iohannes, abbas sancti Bernardi[51] Valentini

Iacobus Conil

Guillermus Bodovit[52]

---

[48] episcopns S.

[49] Xefalensis RS.

[50] subdiachonus RS.

[51] Bernatdi S.

[52] Guilermus Bodonit S.

APPENDIX 11

The Tomb of Fernando of Cordova
in S. Maria de Montserrat, Rome

The cloister of S. Maria de Montserrat is entered from via Giulia 151. As Denifle and Chatelain, 2:632 n. 5, state, the monument is to be found on the wall opposite the entrance to the cloister. See also Douie, 59. It is about 6 meters high and a little less than 3 meters wide. The top half is enclosed by a canopy covering a funeral bier which has in the middle of it the inscription "DOM" and upon which rests the reclining figure of Fernando, who is clean-shaven. The lower half has the inscription given below (bordered in each of the lower corners by the coat of arms described in note 29, page 7). The inscription has been published several times: Pérez Bayer in a note in Antonius, 2:321–22, who claims to have copied it when it was still in S. Giacomo degli Spagnuoli; Forcella, 3:216, num. 512, from MS BAV, Vat. lat. 7917, f. 60r; Bonilla y San Martín, 86, (from Forcella); and Havet, 315 (from Forcella). Forcella, or his source, was guilty of two errors, namely, making the abbreviation "DOM" ("domino optimo maximo") part of the inscription rather than of the bier and reading "OMNIVM" for "OMNI" in line 6. Pérez Bayer has exactly the same errors and also expands several abbreviations without noting the fact. For "DOM" see Kajanto, 24–26. The inscription reads as follows:

FERDINANDO CORDVBEN. PONT. MAX.
   HYPODIACONO
DISCIPLINAR. OMNIVM COGNITIONE INCLYTO
CVIVS INGENIVM AC DISSERENDI ACVMEN
CVNCTAR. GENTIVM GIMNASIA STVPVERE
VIRO OMNI VIRTVTVM GENERE ORNATISS.
MODESTIA VERO AC PROBITATE INSIGNI
QVI VITA SACRAR. LITTERAR. STUDIIS
INNOCENTISS. ACTA MVLTISQVE DOCTRINAE
MONVMENT. POSTERITATI RELICTIS
   HOMINEM EXVIT
ANNO AETATIS LXV SALVTIS CHRISTIAN.
   MCCCCLXXXVI
GEORGIVS CAR. PORTVGAL. BM
       POSVIT

BIBLIOGRAPHY

Adams, M. McCord. *William of Ockham*, 2 vols., Notre Dame, 1987.

Agricola, Rudolph. *De Inventione Dialectica Lucubrationes*, Cologne 1539 (reprt. Nieuwkoop, 1967).

Agrippa, Henricus Agrippa. *Opera*, 2 vols., Lyon, no date (reprt. Hildesheim, 1970).

Albertus Magnus. *De Animalibus*, ed. Fernando of Cordova, Rome: Nicola Cardella, 1478.

———. *Opera Omnia*, ed. E. Borgnet, 38 vols., Paris, 1890-1899.

Alexander of Aphrodisias. *In Aristotelis Metaphysica Commentaria*, ed. E. Hayduck (*CAG*, 1), Berlin, 1891.

Ammannati, I. *Diario consistoriale*, ed. E. Carusi, in *Rerum Italicarum Scriptores*, 2nd ed., vol. 23.3, Città di Castello, 1904.

Andres, M. *La teología española en el siglo XVI*, vol. 2, Madrid, 1977.

Anselm, *Opera Omnia*, vol. 1, ed. F. S. Schmitt, Edinburgh, 1946.

Antonius, N. *Bibliotheca Hispana Vetus*, 2 vols., Madrid, 1783-1788.

Aristotle. *Omnia quae extant opera . . . Averrois Cordubensis in ea opera omnes qui ad haec usque tempora pervenere commentarii*, 12 vols. in 14, Venice: Iunta Press, 1562; photographic reprint Frankfurt a. M., 1962.

———. *Aristotelis Opera ex Recensione Immanuelis Bekkeri*, ed. O. Gigon, 5 vols., Berlin, 1960-1961.

Asclepius. *In Aristotelis Metaphysicorum Libros A-Z Commentaria*, ed. M. Hayduck (*CAG*, 6.2), Berlin, 1888.

Aschbach, J. *Geschichte der Wiener Universität im ersten Jahrhunderte ihres Bestehens*, 2 vols., Vienna, 1865-1877.

Augustine. *De Trinitate Libri XV*, ed., W. J. Mountain and Fr. Glorie, 2 vols., Turnholt, 1968 (= CCSL, 50-50A).

Averroes. *Commentarium Magnum in Aristotelis de Anima Libros*, ed. F. Stuart Crawford, Cambridge, Mass., 1953.

———. *In Ea Opera [Aristotelis] Omnes Qui ad Haec usque Tempora Pervenere Commentarii*: see Aristotle (1562).

Avicenna Latinus, *Liber de Philosophia Prima sive Scientia Divina I-IV*, ed. S. Van Riet, introd. G. Verbeke, Louvain-Brill, 1977.

Avril, F. "Trois manuscrits napolitains des collections de Charles V et de Jean de Berry," *Bibliothèque de l'École des Chartres*, 127 (1969-1970):291-328.

Bandiera, I. N. *De Augustino Dato Libri Duo*, Rome, 1773.

Bandini, A. M. *Catalogus codicum latinorum Bibliothecae Mediceae Laurentianae*, 5 vols., Florence 1774-1778.

Batllori, M. "El lulismo en Italia (Ensayo de síntesis)," *Revista de filosofía*, 2 (1944): 253-313, 479-537, 495-99.

———. "El gran Cardénal d'Espanya à el lul-lista antilullià Fernando de Córdoba," *Estudios Lulianos*, 2 (1958):313-16.

Baudry, L. *La querelle des futurs contingents (Louvain 1465-1475). Texts inédits*, Paris, 1950.

Beltrán de Heredia, V. *Bulario de la Universidad de Salamanca (1219–1549)*, 3 vols. (= *Acta Salmanticensia.*, Historia de la Universidad, 12–14), Salamanca, 1966–1967.

Bett, H. *Johannes Scotus Erigena. A Study in Mediaeval Philosophy*, Cambridge, 1925.

Bianca, C. "Francesco Della Rovere: un francescano tra teologia e potere," in Miglio et al., 19–55.

Bignami Odier, J., with the collaboration of J. Ruysschaert. *La Bibliothèque Vaticane de Sixte IV à Pie XI*, (*Studi e testi*, 272) Vatican City, 1973.

Binder, K. "Zum Einfluss des Duns Scotus auf Theologen der mittelalterlichen Universität Wien," in *Deus et Homo ad mentem I. Duns Scoti. Acta Tertii Congressus Scotistici Internationalis, Vindebonae, 28 sept.–2 oct. 1970*, Rome, 1972, 749–60.

Biondo, Flavio. *Historiarum ab Inclinatione Romanorum Imperii Decades*, Venice, 1482.

Bonaventura, St. *Opera Omnia*, ed. A. C. Peltier, 15 vols., Paris, 1864–1871.

Bonilla y San Martín, A. *Fernando de Córdoba (?1425–1486¿) y los orígenes del Renacimiento filosófico en España*, Madrid, 1911.

Bonnefoy, J. F. "La question hypothétique «Utrum si Adam non peccasset . . .» au XIIIe siècle," *Revista española de teologia*, 14 (1954):327–68.

Bonner, A. ed. and tr. *Selected Works of Ramon Lull (1232–1316)*, 2 vols., Princeton, 1985.

Borchert, E. *Die Trinitätslehre des Johannes de Ripa*, 2 vols., Munich, 1974.

Boulay, E. du. *Historia Universitatis Parisiensis*, vol. 5, Paris, 1670.

Bracciolini, Poggio. *Opera Omnia*, ed. R. Fubini, 4 vols., Turin, 1964–1966.

Bracelli, G. *L'epistolario di Iacopo Bracelli*, ed. G. Balbi, Genoa, 1969.

Brandis, C.-A. *Scholia Graeca in Aristotelis Metaphysica*, Berlin, 1837 (reprt. in vol. 4 of Aristotle [1956]).

Buchowiecki, W. *Handbuch der Kirchen Roms*, 3 vols., Vienna, 1967–1974.

Calcidius. *In Timaeum*, ed. J. H. Waszink, London-Leiden, 1962.

Camporesi, P. *Il libro dei vagabondi: Lo "Speculum cerretanorum" di Teseo Pini, "Il vagabondo" di Rafaele Frianoro e altri testi di "furfanteria,"* Turin, 1973.

Campano, G. A. *Vita Pii II Pontificis Maximi*, ed. G. Zimolo, in *Rerum Italicarum Scriptores*, 2nd ed., 3.2, Bologna, 1964.

Cancellieri, F. *Descrizione di una copia all'encaustro della Scuola di Atene e di un codice membranaceo di Ferdinando Cordubense De consultandi ratione dedicato al Card. D'Ausia del Poggio arcivescovo di Monreale e poi posseduto dal Card. Girolamo Verallo*, Pesaro, 1826.

Cappizi, C. "Spigolature Bessarionee da fonti notarili inediti," *Studi albanologici, balcanici, bizantini e orientali in onore di Giuseppe Valentini, S. J.*, Florence, 1986, 204–46.

Cappuyns, M. *Jean Scot Erigène. Sa vie, son oeuvre, sa pensée*, Louvain, 1933.

Carreras y Artau, T. and J. *Historia de la filosofía española: Filosofía de los siglos XIII al XV*, 2 vols., Madrid, 1939–1943.

Ceruti, A. *Inventario Ceruti dei manoscritti della Biblioteca Ambrosiana*, 5 vols. (*Fontes Ambrosiani* 50, 52, 57, 60, 63), Milan, 1973–1979.

Chatelain, E. See Denifle, H.

Copinger, W.A. *Supplement to Hain's Repertorium Bibliographicum*, 2 vols., London, 1895–1902.

Corpus Iuris Canonici, ed. A. L. Richter and A. Friedberg, 2 vols., Leipzig, 1879 (repr. Graz, 1955).

F. Costa, "Motivi filosofici nel dissenso tra lo scotista B. Belluto e Scoto in merito alla "somma" grazia di Cristo," in C. Bérubé, ed., *La tradizione scotista veneto-padovana*, Padua, 1979, 113–33.

Cranz, F. E. "Alexander Aphrodisiensis," in *CTC* 1 (1960):77–135 and 2 (1971):411–22.

Croce, B. *La Spagna nella vita italiana durante la Rinascenza*, 4th ed., Bari, 1949.

Croci, E. "Gaetano Moroni e il suo Dizionario," in *Gregorio XVI*, 1:135–52.

Custerer, J. J. *Disertaciones Historicas del Beato Raymundo Lullio Dotor iluminado, y martir. Con un apendix de su vida*, Palma, 1700.

Dal Pra, M. "Il tempo e la problematizzazione dell' attualità della verità nel pensiero di Pietro De Rivo," in A. Banfi, ed., *La crisi dell' uso dogmatico della ragione*, Rome, 1953, 33–59.

Dallari, U. *I rotuli dei lettori legisti et artisti dello Studio Bolognese dal 1384 al 1799*, 4 vols., Bologna, 1888–1924.

Darricau, R. "Estouteville (Guillaume d')," *Dictionnaire de biographie française*, 73 (1971):126–28.

Dati, A. *Opera*, Siena, 1503.

De Clercq, C. *Catalogue des manuscrits du Grand Séminaire de Malines*. Catalogue général des manuscrits des bibliothèques de Belgique, vol. 4, Gembloux-Paris, 1937.

Deguí, Pere. *Metaphysica*, Seville: Stanislaus Polonus, 22 June 1500.

————. *Formalitates Breves*, (Seville: Stanislaus Polonus?), c. 1500.

Delisle, L. "Le formulaire de Clairmarais," *Journal de Savants*, unnumb. vol. (1899):172–95.

Della Campa, P. *Osservazioni sulla lettera di Francesco Cancellieri all' emo. e rmo. signore Cardinale Antonio Pallotta*, Modena 1826.

Denifle, H. and Chatelain, E., eds. *Auctarium Chartularii Universitatis Parisiensis*. Vols. 1–2: *Liber Procuratorum Nationis Anglicanae (Alemanniae) in Universitate Parisiensi (1333–1466)*, 2 vols., Paris, 1894–1897.

Dequekker, L. "Een XIVe-eeuwse bijbel vit het Arrascollege te Leuven nu op het Grootseminarie te Mechelen," *Handelingen van de koninklijke kring voor oudheidkunde, letteren en kunst van Mechelen* (= *Cercle archéologique, littéraire et artistique de Malines*), 70 (1966):113–41.

Di Camillo, O. *El humanesimo castellano del siglo XV*, Valencia, 1976.

Diago, F. *Historia de la provincia de Aragon de la Orden de Predicadores*, Barcelona, 1599.

Douie, Decima L. "Some Treatises Against the Fraticelli in the Vatican Library," *Franciscan Studies*, n. s., 38 (1978):10–80.

Du Plessis D'Argentré, C. *Collectio Judiciorum de Novis Erroribus*, 3 vols., Paris, 1728–1736.

Duns Scotus, John. *Opera Omnia*, 26 vols., Paris, 1894.

Durán, E. See Rogent and Durán.

Durandus a S. Porciano, *In Petri Lombardi Sententias Commentaria*, 2 vols., Venice, 1571 (reprt. Ridgewood, N. J., 1964).

Dykmans, M., ed., *L'Oeuvre de Patrizi de Piccolomini ou le cérémonial papal de la première Renaissance*, 2 vols. (*Studi e testi*, 293–94), Vatican City, 1980–1982.

Eijo Garay, L. "La finalidad de la Encarnación según el Beato R. Lulio," *Revista española de teologia*, 2 (1942):201–17.

Emden, A. B. *A Biographical Register of the University of Oxford to A.D. 1500*, 3 vol., Oxford, 1957–1959.

Epistolae Principum Rerumpublicarum ac Sapientium Virorum, Venice, 1574.

Epstein, S. R. *Alle origini della fattoria toscana: L'Ospedale della Scala di Siena e le sue terre (metà '200-metà '400)* (Florence, 1986).

Esposito Aliano, A. "Testamento e inventari per la ricostruzione della biblioteca del cardinale Guglielmo d'Estouteville," in C. Bianca, P. Farenga, G. Lombardi, A. G. Luciano, and M. Miglio, eds., *Scrittura, biblioteche e stampa a Roma nel Quattrocento: Aspetti e problemi. Atti del seminario 1–2 giugno 1979,* 2 vols., Rome, 1980, 308–42.

Eubel, C. *Hierarchia Catholica Medii Aevii,* vol. 2, 2nd ed., Münster, 1914.

Eustratius. *Eustratii et Michaelis et Anonyma in Ethica Nicomachea Commentaria,* ed. G. Heylbut (*CAG,* 20), Berlin, 1932.

Fabro, C. "Jean de Rupella," in *DTC,* 15 (Paris, 1938):208–52

———. *La nozione metafisica di partecipazione secondo S. Tommaso d'Aquino,* 2nd ed., Turin, 1950.

Fallmerayer, J. *Geschichte des Kaiserthums von Trapezunt,* Munich, 1827 (reprt. Hildesheim, 1964).

Fava, M. "Le *Appendices ad Hainii-Copingerii Repertorium bibliographicum* del prof. D. Reichling," *La Bibliofilia,* 12 (1910–11):176–204.

Federico, D. "Gregorio XVI Papa Umanista," in *Gregorio XVI,* 1:153–83.

Fernando of Cordova, See Albertus Magnus.

———. *De Iure Medios Exigendi Fructus Quos Vulgo Annatos Dicunt et Romani Pontificis in Temporalibus Potestate,* (Rome: Georgius Herolt, c. 1481).

Fioravanti, G. "Pietro de'Rossi: Bibbia ed Aristotele nella Siena del '400," *Rinascimento,* ser. 2, 20 (1980):87–159 (reprt. in his *Università e città*).

———. *Università e città: Cultura umanistica e cultura scolastica a Siena nel '400,* Florence, 1981.

Fisch, M. H. *Nicolaus Pol Doctor 1494, with a Critical Text of his Guaiac Tract Edited with a Translation* (the edition was prepared by D. M. Schullian), New York, 1947.

Fita, F. "Escritos de Fray Bernal Boyl, ermitaño de Monserrato," *Boletín de la Real Academia de la historia,* 19 (1891):267–348.

———. "Cartas inéditas de D. Arnaldo Descós en la colección 'Pascual'," *Boletín de la Real Academia de la historia,* 19 (1891):377–446.

Fois, M. *Il pensiero cristiano di Lorenzo Valla,* Rome, 1969.

Fontana, P. "Per la storia della censura pontificia: Il primo caso di sequestro di un libro a stampa," *Accademie e biblioteche d'Italia,* 4 (1932):470–75.

Forcella, V. *Iscrizioni delle chiese e d'altri edifici di Roma dal secolo XI fino ai giorni nostri,* 14 vols., Rome, 1861–1884.

Frati, C. *Dizionario bio-bibliographico dei bibliotecari e bibliofili italiani dal sec. XIV al XIX,* Firenze, 1934.

Frati, L. "Indice dei codici latini conservati nella R. Biblioteca Universitaria di Bologna," *Studi italiani di filologia classica,* 16 (1908):103–432 and 17 (1909):1–171.

Garosi, A. *Siena nella storia della medicina (1240–1555),* Florence, 1958.

Gasparrini-Leporace, T. and Mioni, E. *Cento codici bessarionei. Catalogo di mostra,* Venice, 1968.

Geiger, L. B. *La participation dans la philosophie de S. Thomas d'Aquin,* 2nd ed., Paris, 1952.

Gesner, C. *Bibliotheca Universalis . . . Aucta per Ioseam Simlerum,* Zurich, 1574.

Gigon, O. See Aristotle (1960–1961).

Gilson, É. *Jean Duns Scot: Introduction à ses positions fondamentales.* Paris, 1952.

———. *Le Thomisme: Introduction à la philosophie de saint Thomas d'Aquin,* 6th ed., Paris, 1965.

Goff, F. R. *Incunabula in American Libraries,* New York, 1964.

Gómez Canedo, L. *Un Español al servicio de la Santa Sede: Don Juan de Carvajal, Cardenal de Sant'Angelo, Legado en Alemania y Hungria (1399?–1469),* Madrid, 1947.

Grabmann, M. *Mittelalterliche lateinische Aristotelesübersetzungen und Aristoteles-kommentare in Handschriften spanischer Bibliotheken*, in Bayerische Akademie der Wissenschaften, *Sitzungsberichte. Philosophisch-philologische und historische Klasse. Jahrgang 1928. 5. Abhandlung*, Munich, 1928.

Gregorio XVI: Miscellanea commemorativa, 2 vols., Rome, 1948.

Grimm, J. and W. *Deutsches Wörterbuch*, ed. K. von Bahder and H. Sickel, vol. 13.1, Leipzig, 1922.

Grosseteste, Robert. *The Greek Commentaries on the Nicomachean Ethics of Aristotle in the Latin Translation of Robert Grosseteste, Bishop of Lincoln (+ 1253)*, ed. H. P. F. Merchen, vols. 1-, London, 1973-.

Gründel, J. "Johannes de Rupella," *Lexikon für Theologie und Kirche*, 5 (Freiburg: 1960):1077.

Guerra-Coppioli, L. "M. Pierleone da Spoleto, medico e filosofo: Note biogra-fiche con documenti inediti," *Bolletino della regia deputazione di storia patria per l'Umbria*, 21 (1915):387-431.

Guillemain, B. *La cour pontificiale d'Avignon, 1309-1376*, Paris, 1966.

Hain, L. *Repertorium Bibliographicum, in Quo Libri Omnes ab Arte Typographica Inventa usque ad Annum M. D. Typis Expressi Ordine Alphabetico Recensentur*, 2 vols. in 4, Stuttgart and Paris, 1826-38.

Haubst, R. "Das hoch- und spätmittelalterliche *Cur Deus homo*," *Münchener theologische Zeitschrift*, 6 (1955):302-13.

————. *Studien zu Nicolaus von Kues und Johannes Wenck aus Handschriften der Vati-kanischen Bibliothek*, Münster, 1955.

Havet, J. "Maître Fernand de Cordoue et l'Université de Paris au XVe siècle," *Mémoires de la Société de l'histoire de Paris et de l'Ile-de-France*, 9 (1882):193-222 (I used the reprint in Havet [1896], 310-38).

————. *Oeuvres de Julien Havet*, 2 vols., Paris, 1896.

Henry of Ghent. *Summae Quaestionum Ordinariarum*, 2 vols., Paris, 1520 (reprt. New York, 1953).

Hillgarth, J. N. *Ramon Lull and Lullism in Fourteenth Century France*, Oxford, 1972.

Hübl, A. *Catalogus Codicum Manu Scriptorum Qui in Bibliotheca Monasterii B. M. V. ad Scotos Vindobonae Servantur*, Vienna-Leipzig, 1899.

Iacometti, F. See Lisini, A.

Izbecki, T. M. *Protector of the Faith: Cardinal Johannes de Turrecremata and the Defense of the Institutional Church*, Washington, D.C., 1981.

Janer, Jaume (Iacobus Ianuarius). *Ars Metaphysicalis*, Valencia, Leonardus Hutz for Bartholomeus Gentil, 1506.

Jedin, H. "Juan de Torquemada und das Imperium Romanum," *Archivum Fratrum Praedicatorum*, 12 (1942):247-78

————. "Sanchez de Arevalo und die Konzilsfrage und Paul II," *Historisches Jahr-buch*, 73 (1954):95-119.

Jiménez Soler, A. *Itinerario del Rey Don Alfonso de Aragón y Nápoles*, Zaragoza, 1909.

Johnston, M. D. *The Spiritual Logic of Ramon Lull*, Oxford, 1987.

Kajanto, I. *Classical and Christian: Studies in the Latin Epitaphs of Medieval and Renais-sance Rome (Annales Academiae Scientiarum Fennicae*, ser. B, vol. 203), Helsinki, 1980.

Keil H. *Grammatici Latini*, vol. 3, Leipzig, 1860 (reprt. Hildesheim, 1961).

Kibre, P. See Thorndike and Kibre.

Kink, R. *Geschichte der kaiserlichen Universität zu Wien*, 2 vols., Vienna, 1854.

Kirsch, P. "Annates," in *DHGE*, 3 (Paris, 1924):307-15.

Kowalsky, N. *Inventario dell'Archivio storico della S. Congregazione "de Propaganda*

Fide." Neuen Zeitschrift für Missionswissenschaft. Schriftenreihe / Les Cahiers de la Nouvelle Revue de science missionaire, 17 (1961).

Kretzmann, N., Kenny, A., Pinborg, J., and Stump, E., eds. *The Cambridge History of Later Medieval Philosophy*, Cambridge, 1982.

Kristeller, P. O. *Il pensiero filosofico di Marsilio Ficino*, Florence, 1953.

————. *Iter Italicum: A Finding List of Uncatalogued or Incompletely Catalogued Humanistic Manuscripts of the Renaissance in Italian and Other Libraries*, 6 vols., London–Leiden, 1963–1992.

————. *Eight Philosophers of the Italian Renaissance*, Stanford, 1964.

Labowsky, L. *Bessarion's Library and the Biblioteca Marciana: Six Early Inventories*, Rome, 1979.

Lactantius. L. Caecilius. *Opera Omnia*, 2 vols. in 4 (*CSEL*, vols. 19 and 27), ed. S. Brandt and G. Laubmann, Vienna, 1890–1897.

Le Clercq, L. "La Bibliothèque du Séminaire en 1840," *Collectanea Mechliniensia*, n. s., 7 (1933):547–52.

Leclercq, H. "Pallium," in *Dictionnaire d'archéologie chrétienne et de liturgie*, 13 (Paris, 1937):931–40.

Leclerq, J. "L'idée de la royauté du Christ pendant le Grand Schisme et la crise conciliaire," *Archives d'histoire doctrinale et littéraire du moyen âge*, 24 (1949): 249–65.

Lee, E. *Sixtus IV and Men of Letters*, Rome, 1978.

Levot, P.-J. *Biographie Bretonne*, 2 vols., Vannes, 1852–1857 (reprt. Geneva, 1971).

Lhotsky, A. *Die Wiener Artistenfakultät 1365–1497*, in Österreichische Akademie der Wissenschaften, Philosophisch-historische Klasse, *Sitzungberichte*, 247.2. *Abhandlung*, Vienna, 1965.

Lisini, A. and Iacometti, F. *Cronache Senesi*, in *Rerum Italicorum Scriptores*, 2nd ed., vol. 15.6B, Bologna, n.d.

Lohr, C. H. "Medieval Latin Aristotle Commentaries," *Traditio*, 23–30 (1967–1974): passim.

————. "Renaissance Latin Aristotle Commentaries," *Studies in the Renaissance* 21 (1974):228–89; *Renaissance Quarterly*, 28–35 (1975–1982):passim.

Luger, F. *Die Unsterblichkeitsfrage bei Johannes Duns Scotus*, Vienna and Leipzig, 1933.

Lullus, Raymundus. *Opera Omnia*, ed. Ivo Salzinger et al., with introductions by F. Stegmüller, 10 vols., Mainz, 1721–42; (reprt. Frankfurt a. M., 1965).

Mahoney, E. P. "Metaphysical Foundations of the Hierarchy of Being according to Some Late Medieval and Renaissance Philosophers," in P. Morevedge, ed., *Ancient and Medieval Philosophers of Existence*, New York, 1980, 165–257.

Mancini, G. *Vita di Lorenzo Valla*, Florence, 1891.

Manteau-Bonamy, H. M. *Maternité divine et incarnation: Étude historique et doctrinale de Saint Thomas à nos jours*, Paris, 1949.

Marti, Berthe. *The Spanish College at Bologna in the Fourteenth Century: Edition and Translation of Its Statutes, with Introduction and Notes*, Philadelphia, 1966.

Marx, J. "Quatre documents relatifs à Guillaume d'Estouteville," *Mélanges d'archéologie et d'histoire*, 35 (1915):41–55.

Mauro, A. *Francesco del Tuppo e il suo "Esopo,"* Città di Castello, 1926.

Maximus episcopus Taurinensis, *Sermones*, ed. A. Mutzenbecher (*CCSL*, 23) Turnholt, 1962.

Mazzatinti, G. and Sorbelli, A., eds., *Inventari dei manoscritti delle biblioteche d'Italia*, vol. 70, Forlì and Florence, 1939.

Menéndez y Pelayo, M. *Historia de los heterodoxos españoles*, 3rd ed., 2 vols., Madrid, 1978.

Meuthen, E. "Zum Itinerar der deutschen Legation Bessarions 1460-1461," *Quellen und Forschungen aus italienischen Archiven und Bibliotheken*, 37 (1958): 328-333.

Michel, A. "Trinité. La théologie latine du VIe au XXe siècle," *DTC*, 15 (1946):1702-1830.

Miglio, M. "*Vidi thiaram Pauli pape secundi,*" *Bullettino dell' Istituto storico italiano*, 81 (1969):273-96.

M. Miglio et al., eds., *Un pontificato ed una città: Sisto IV (1471-1484)*, Vatican City, 1986.

Minges, P. *Ioannes Duns Scoti: Doctrina Philosophica et Theologica*, 2 vols., Quaracchi, 1930.

Minieri Riccio, C. "Alcuni fatti di Alfonso I. di Aragona dal 15 Aprile 1437 al 31 Maggio 1458," *Archivio storico per le provincie napoletane*, 6 (1881):195-308, (I used an offprint which begins with p. 1).

Mioni, E. See Gasparrini-Leporace and Mioni.

Mohler, L. *Kardinal Bessarion*, 3 vols., Paderborn, 1923-1942 (reprt. Aalen and Paderborn, 1967).

Molanus, Io. *Historiae Lovaniensium Libri XIV*, ed. F. X. De Ram, 2 vols., Brussels, 1861.

Monfasani, J. *George of Trebizond: A Biography and a Study of his Rhetoric and Logic.* Leiden, 1976.

———. "*Bessarion Latinus,*" *Rinascimento*, ser. 2, 21 (1981):165-209.

———. *Collectanea Trapezuntiana: Texts, Documents, and Bibliographies of George of Trebizond*, Binghamton, N.Y., 1984.

———. "The Fraticelli and Clerical Wealth in Quattrocento Rome," in J. Monfasani and R. Musto, eds., *Renaissance Society and Culture: Essays in Honor of Eugene F. Rice, Jr.*, New York, 1991, 177-95.

———. "A Theologian at the Roman Curia in the Mid-Quattrocento: A Bio-bibliographical Study of Niccolò Palmieri, O.S.A.," *Analecta Augustiniana*, 54 (1991):321-81; and 55 (1992):5-98.

Montfaucon, B. *Bibliotheca Bibliothecarum Manuscriptorum Nova*, 2 vols., Paris, 1739.

Moran, D. *The Philosophy of John Scottus Eriugena: A Study of Idealism in the Middle Ages*, Cambridge, 1989.

Moreau, E. *La Bibliothèque de l'Université de Louvain, 1636-1914*, Louvain, 1918.

Morel-Fatio, A. "Maître Fernand de Cordoue et les humanistes italiens du XVe siècle," *Mélanges Julien Havet*, Paris, 1895, 521-33.

Moroni, G. *Dizionario di erudizione storico-ecclesiastica*, 109 vols., Venice, 1840-97.

Nasalli Rocca, E. "Il card. Bessarione legato pontificio in Bologna (1450-1455)," *Atti e memorie della R. Deputazione di Storia Patria per le Romagne*, 20 (1931):1-64.

Naz, R. "Sous-diaconat," *Dictionnaire de droit canonique*, 7 (Paris, 1965):1074-78.

Nardi, P. *Mariano Sozzini, giureconsulto senese del Quattrocento*, Milan, 1974.

Nebrija, A. *Nebrissensia Biblica*, ed. P. Galindo and A. Ortiz, Madrid, 1950.

Nicolau, B. "El primado absoluto de Cristo en el pensamiento luliano," *Estudios lulianos*, 2 (1958):297-312.

Normore, C. "Future Contingents," in Kretzmann et al., 358-81.

O'Malley, J. W. *Praise and Blame in Renaissance Rome*, Durham, N.C., 1979.

Pastor, L. von. *The History of the Popes from the Close of the Middle Ages*, 5th ed., tr. F. I. Antrobus, vol. 2. I used the reprint of St. Louis, 1949.

Paz y Mélia, A. *Opúsculos literarios de los siglos XIV á XVI*, Madrid, 1892.

Pelzer A. *Codices Vaticani Latini. Tomus II. Codices 679-1134*, 2 vols., Vatican City, 1931-33.

Pérez Martínez, L. "El maestro Pedro Daguí y el Lulismo mallorquín de fines del siglo XV," *Estudios Lulianos*, 4 (1960):291–306.

Piana, Celestino. *Nuove ricerche sulle Università di Bologna e di Parma*, Quaracchi [Florence], 1966.

———. *Nuovi documenti sull'Università di Bologna e sul Collegio di Spagna*, 2 vols. Bologna, 1976.

Pius II, Pope. *Commentarii*, ed. A. Van Heck, 2 vols., Vatican City, 1984.

Platina. *Liber de Vita Christi ac Omnium Pontificum*, ed. G. Gaida, in *Rerum Italicarum Scriptores*, 2nd ed., vol. 3.1, Città di Castello, 1913–1932.

Platzeck, E. W. *Raimund Lull*, 2 vols., Düsseldorf, 1962.

———. "De tendentia beati Iohannis Duns Scoti respectu relationum tabellae a beato Raymundo propositae," *Antonianum*, 38 (1963):87–101.

Poppi, A. "L'Averroismo nella filosofia francescana," in Accademia Nazionale dei Lincei, *Convegno internazionale. L'Averroismo in Italia (Roma, 18–20 aprile 1977)*. Atti dei convegni Lincei, 40 (Rome, 1979):175–220.

Poupardin, R. "Deux ouvrages inconnus de Fernand de Cordoue," *Bibliothèque de l'École des Chartres*, 62 (1901):532–42.

Principum et illustrium virorum epistolae, Amsterdam, 1644.

Probst, J.-H. *Caractère et origine des idées du bienheureux Raymond Lulle*, Toulouse, 1912.

Publilius, Pseudo-. *Proverbia*, ed. O. Friedrich, Berlin, 1880 (reprt. Hildesheim, 1964).

Pugliese, A. "Annate e mezz'annate nel diritto canonico (evoluzione storica e natura giuridica)," in *Studi di storia e diritto in onore di Carlo Calisse*, 2 vols., Milan, 1940, 2:109–66.

Rashdall, H. *The Universities of Europe in the Middle Ages*, rev. ed., by P. M. Powicke and A. B. Emden, 3 vols., Oxford, 1936.

Redlich, V. *Tegernsee und die deutsche Geistesgeschichte im 15. Jahrhundert*, Munich, 1931.

Reichling, D. *Appendices ad Hainii-Copingeri Repertorium Bibliographicum, Additiones et Emendationes*, 7 parts, Munich, 1905–1911. *Supplement*, Munich, 1914 (reprt. in 2 vols., Munich, 1914).

Resta, G. "Antonio Cassarino e le sue traduzioni di Plutarco e Platone," *Italia medieovale e umanistica*, 2 (1959):207–83.

Richard of St. Victor. *De Trinitate*, ed. J. Ribaillier, Paris, 1958.

Rogent, E. and Durán, E. *Bibliografía des les impressions lul-lianes*, with a preface, additions, and index by R. D'Alós-Moner, Barcelona, 1927.

Rubió y Balaguer, J. "Investigacions lulianes en la biblioteca de Innichen," in Institut d'Estudis Catalans, *Anuari*, 5.2 (1913–1914, published in 1915):742–45.

———. "Los códices lulianos de la biblioteca de Innichen (Tirol)," *Revista de filología española*, 4 (1917):303–40.

Ruysschaert, J. "Nouvelles recherches au sujet de la bibliothèque de Pier Leoni, médecin de Laurent le Magnifique," in Académie royale de Belgique, *Bulletin de la classe des lettres et des sciences morales et politiques*, ser. 5, 46 (1960):37–65.

———. See also Bignami Odier.

Ryder, A. *The Kingdom of Naples under Alfonso the Magnanimous: The Making of a Modern State*, Oxford, 1976.

Sabbadini, R. *Cronologia documentata della vita di Lorenzo Della Valle detto il Valla*, in L. Barozzi, *Studi sul Panormita e sul Valla*, Florence, 1891 (also reprinted as an appendix in Valla [1962]).

———. "Note umanistiche," *Giornale ligustico di archeologia, storia e letteratura*, 18 (1891):299–306.

Sacchi, Bartolomeo. See Platina.

Sassi, R. *Documenti sul soggiorno a Fabriano di Nicolò V e della sua corte nel 1449 e nel 1450*, Ancona: Deputazione di Storia Patria per le Marche, 1955.

Samaran, C. and E. A. Van Moé, eds. *Auctarium Chartularii Universitatis Parisiensis*. Vol. 5: *Liber Procuratorum Nationis Gallicanae (Franciae)*, Paris, 1942.

Sbaraglia, G. G. *Supplementum et Castigatio ad Scriptores Trium Ordinis S. Francisci a Waddingo Aliisve Descriptos*, 3 parts, Rome, 1908–1936.

Schimmelpfennig, B. *Die Zeremonienbücher der römischen Kurie im Mittelalter*, Tübingen, 1973.

Schulemann, G. *Die Lehre von den Transcendentalien in der scholastischen Philosophie*, Leipzig, 1929.

Schulte, J. F. von. *Die Geschichte der Quellen und Literatur des canonischen Rechtes*, 3 vols. in 2, Stuttgart, 1875–1880 (reprt. Graz, 1956).

Schmitt, C. B. "Theophrastus," in *CTC*, 2 (1971):239–322.

Scotus Eriugena, John. *Periphyseon (De Divisione Naturae). Liber Primus*, ed. L. P. Sheldon-Williams, vol. 1, Dublin, 1968.

Seneca. *Opera Quae Supersunt. Supplementum*. ed. F. Haase, Leipzig, 1902.

Shirley, J. *A Parisian Journal 1404–1449*, Oxford, 1968.

Sikes, J. G. "Hervaeus Natalis: De Paupertate Christi et Apostolorum," *Archives d'histoire doctrinale et littéraire du Moyen Age*, 12–13 (1937–1938):209–97.

Sorbelli, A. See Mazzatinti and Sorbelli.

Soria, A. *Los humanistas de la corte de Alfonso el Magnanimo (según los epistolarios)*, Granada, 1956.

Stegmüller, F. *Repertorium Biblicum Medii Aevi*, 8 vols., Madrid, 1940–1976.

Steinschneider, M. "Alfarabi (Alpharabius), des arabischen Philosophen Leben und Schriften . . .," *Mémoires des l'Académie impériale des Sciences de St.-Pétersbourg*, VIIe sér., 13.4, St. Petersburg, 1869.

Steneck, N. H. *Science and Creation in the Middle Ages: Henry of Langenstein (d. 1397) on Genesis*, Notre Dame, 1976.

Stohr, A. *Die Trinitätslehre des hl. Bonaventura*, Munster i. W., 1923.

Strnad, A. A. "Francesco Todeschini-Piccolomini. Politik und Mäzenatentum im Quattrocento, *Römische historische Mitteilungen*, 8–9 (1964–65, 1965–1966): 101–425.

Thamiry, E. "Armes," *Dictionnaire de droit canonique*, 1 (Paris, 1935):1047.

Theeuws, P. "Jean de Turrecremata: Les relations entre l'Église et le pouvoir civil d'après un théologien du XVe siècle," *L'Organisation corporative du moyen âge à la fin de l'Ancien Régime. Études présentées à la Commission internationale pour l'histoire des assemblées d'états*, Louvain, 1943, 135–78.

Themistius. *In Aristotelis Metaphysicorum Libri Λ Paraphrasis Hebraice et Latine*, ed. S. Landauer (*CAG* 5.5), Berlin, 1902.

Thomas Aquinas. *Opera omnia*, vol. 22.2, fasc. 2, Rome, 1976.

Thorndike, L. *A History of Magic and Experimental Science*, vol. 4, New York, 1934.

Thorndike, L. and P. Kibre. *A Catalogue of Incipits of Medieval Scientific Treatises in Latin*, Cambridge, Mass., 1963.

Trame, R. *Rodrigo Sánchez de Arévalo, 1404–1470*, Washington, D.C., 1958.

Trithemius, Io. *Opera Historica*, 2 vols., Frankfurt a. M., 1601 (reprt. Frankfurt a. M., 1966).

———. *Annales Hirsaugienses*, 2 vols., St. Gall, 1690.

Ughelli, F. *Italia Sacra*, 2nd ed., ed. N. Coleti, 10 vols. in 9, Venice, 1717–21.

Uiblein, P. *Die Akten der theologischen Fakultät der Universität Wien (1396–1508)*, 2 vols., Vienna, 1978.

University of Vienna. *Die Matrikel der Universität Wien,* vol. 1, Graz and Cologne, 1956.

Valla, L. *Opera Omnia* "con premessa di Eugenio Garin," 2 vols., Turin, 1962 (= reprint of the 1540 *Opera Omnia* with new appendices).

———. *De Falso Credita et Ementita Constantini Donatione,* ed. W. Setz, Weimar, 1978.

———. *Epistolae,* ed. O. Besomi and M. Regoliosi, Padua, 1984.

Van Moé, A. See Samaran-Van Moé.

Vásquez, I. "La enseñanza del escotismo en España," in *De Doctrina Ioannis Duns Scoti. Acta Congressus Scotistici Internationalis, Oxonii et Edinburgi 11-17 Sept. 1966 Celebrati,* vol. 4, Rome, 1968, 191-220.

Victor, J. M. "The Revival of Lullism at Paris, 1499-1416," *Renaissance Quarterly,* 28 (1975):504-34.

Voigt, G. *Enea Silvio de' Piccolomini als Papst Pius der Zweite und sein Zeitalter,* 3 vols., Berlin, 1856-1863 (reprt. Berlin, 1967).

Wetter, F. *Die Trinitätslehre des Johannes Duns Scotus,* Münster, 1967.

William of Ockham. *Scriptum in Librum Primum Sententiarum. Ordinatio. Distinctiones IV-XVIII,* ed. G. I. Etzkorn, (= William of Ockham, *Opera Theologica,* vol. 3), St. Bonaventure, N.Y., 1977.

Wippel, J. "Essence and Existence," in Kretzmann et al., 385-410.

Wolter, A. B. *The Transcendentals and Their Function in the Metaphysics of Duns Scotus,* Washington, D.C., 1946.

Yates, F. *Lull and Bruno: Collected Essays,* vol. 1, London, 1982.

Zanetti, A. M. *Latina et Italica D. Marci Bibliotheca Codicum Manuscriptorum per Titulos Digesta,* Venice, 1741.

Zdekauer, L. *Lo Studio di Siena nel Rinascimento,* Milan, 1894.

Zippel, G. "L'autodifesa di Lorenzo Valla per il processo dell' inquisizione napoletana (1444)," *Italia medioevale e umanistica,* 13 (1970):59-94.

INDEX OF DOCUMENTS AND MANUSCRIPTS

Bologna, Archivio Arcivescovile, Ricuperi vari, num. 56: 64
——, Archivio di Stato, Rogati di Filippo Formaglini, busta 6: 64–65
——, Archivio di Stato, Rogati di Rolando Castellano, busta 23: 65–66
——, Biblioteca Universitaria, MS 1885: 67–68
Cremona, Biblioteca Governativa, MS 132: 93
Florence, Biblioteca Laurenziana, MS 20, 40: 93
——, Biblioteca Nazionale Centrale, MS Magl. XXXI, 17: 27n., 42–43nn., 89–92
——, Biblioteca Riccardiana, MS 162: 36n.
Louvain, Katholieke Universiteit, Faculteit der Godgeleerdheid, MS Seminarie
    Mechelen 1: 93
Madrid, Biblioteca Nacional, MS 9250: 26n.
Mainz, Stadtbibliothek, MS I 121: 71–82
Milan, Biblioteca Ambrosiana, MS N 240 sup.: 52n.
——, Biblioteca Ambrosiana, MS N 250 sup.: 95
Montserrat, MS 882: 24n.
Oxford, Merton College, MS 281: 1
Paris, Bibliothèque Nationale, MS lat. 3169: 36n.
——, Bibliothèque Nationale, MS lat. 4152: 36n.
Rome, Biblioteca Vallicelliana, MS I 22: 24–25
San Candido/Innichen, Biblioteca della Collegiata/Kapitelbibliothek, MS VIII b
    9: 95
Siena, Archivio di Stato, Fondo Concistorio, filza 1667: 69n.
Vatican City, ASV, Armadio XXXIX, 16: 51
——, ASV, Reg. Suppl. 379: 17n.
——, ASV, Reg. Suppl. 423: 57
——, ASV, Reg. Suppl. 528: 60
——, ASV, Reg. Suppl. 536: 62
——, ASV, Reg. Suppl. 540: 61–62
——, ASV, Reg. Suppl. 542: 62
——, ASV, Reg. Vat. 390: 59–60
——, ASV, Reg. Vat. 410: 57–59
——, ASV, Reg. Vat. 492: 62–63
——, ASV, Reg. Vat. 508: 61
——, ASV, Reg. Vat. 542: 62
——, BAV, MS Barb. lat. 1493: 45n.
——, BAV, MS Chis. A. IV. 113: 25n.
——, BAV, MS Regin. lat. 1773: 48n.
——, BAV, MS Urb. gr. 49: 47n.
——, BAV, MS Vat. lat. 1056: 34n.
——, BAV, MS Vat. lat. 1127: 38n., 83–88
——, BAV, MS Vat. lat. 1128: 45n.
——, BAV, MS Vat. lat. 3177: 26n.
——, BAV, MS Vat. lat. 3495: 45n.

————, BAV, MS Vat. lat. 5739: 89–92
————, BAV, MS Vat. lat. 7917: 100
Venice, Biblioteca Marciana, MS Zan. lat. 142 (= 1669): 39n.
————, Biblioteca Marciana, MS Zan. lat. 481 (= 1915): 26n.
Vienna, Österreichische Nationalbibliothek, MS Phil gr. 189: 47n.
————, Schottenkloster, MS 407: 71, 73–82
————, Universitätsarchiv, Acta Facultatis Artium, Libri II–III:

Lost: MS of Fernando of Cordova's *De Consultandi Ratione*: 43–45

INDEX OF NAMES AND SUBJECTS

Abbazia Monte Oliveto Maggiore, 68n.
Aeschines, 92
Agricola, Rudolph, 29-31
Agrippa, Henricus Cornelius, 27n.
Albert the Great, 6, 14n., 34n., 49-50, 81n.
Alexander VI, Pope, 53n.
Alexander of Aigai, 47n.
Alexander of Aphrodisias, 27n., 46-47
Alexander of Hales, 5
Alexander of Neckham, 10-11n.
Alfarabi, 27n., 31n.
Alfonso of Aragon, King, 3, 8-9, 16, 68, 69-70
Algazel, 27n., 31n.
Alvari, Garsias, 62
Alyngdon, Robert de, 78
American Council of Learned Societies, ix
American Philosophical Society, ix
Anselm, Saint, 32
Anti-Christ, 1, 13
Antonius de Pina, 66
Antonius de Portugallia, 65-66
Apollo, 15n., 18
Arabic, 4, 10, 49
Arabs, 91
Aramaic, 4, 10
Arcimboldi, Cardinal Giovanni, 51n.
Aristotle, 14nn., 15, 21n., 26, 27n., 29, 35, 46, 47, 50, 73-74, 77
Armenia, King of, 91n.
Arnaldus de Villanova, 67
Asclepius, Aristotelian commentator, 47
Astigia, Church of S. Ioannes, 61
Athanasius, Saint, 96-97
Atza, diocese of Osma, 5n.
Augustine, Saint, 6, 20, 21n., 34n., 74-77, 80n., 98
Augustinian-Franciscan School, 5-6, 21n., 34
Auxias de Podio, Cardinal, 43-44
Averroes, 6, 14n., 34n., 74, 77
Avicenna, 34n.

Barbut, Gui, 48-49
Bartholomaeus de Stabia, 36n.
Bartholomeus de Corduba, 65-66
Basil the Great, Saint, 27n.
Beltrán de Heredia, V. 57
Benignus, Georgius, 34, 36

Bernardino of Siena, Saint, 67
Bernardus Petri, 62-63
Bessarion, Cardinal, 23-26, 31, 34n., 35-39, 41, 42, 49, 50, 93-94
Bianca, Concetta, 17n., 57, 59
Biondo, Flavio, 46
Bodovit, Guillermus, 52, 98
Boethius, 29
Bologna, University of, 6-8, 9n., 17-18n., 23, 64
Bonaventure, Saint, 5, 21n., 33, 77
Bonet, Nicholas, 34
Boniface IX, Pope, 46
Bonilla y San Martín, A., 5, 16, 31
Bourgeois de Paris, 10-12nn.
Bowsky, William, 67, 68n.
Brabant, letter to the chancellor of, 4-6nn., 10-13nn.
Bracciolini, Poggio, 9-10, 23
Bracelli, Giacomo, 4n., 6n., 11n., 14
Brenden, Baptista, 36n.
Burgos, 57, 59

Calcidius, 81n.
Calixtus III, Pope, 67
Canacia, Antonius, 36n.
Cancellieri, F., 44nn.
Carafa, Cardinal Oliverio, 51n.
Caramania, Prince of, 91n.
Cardella, Nicola, 49n.
Carreras y Artau, T. and J., 29, 32n.
Carvajal, Cardinal Juan, 7, 17-19, 21, 57, 68, 71-72
Caselles, Guillem, 52
Cassarino, Antonio, 14
Cesarini, Cardinal Giuliano, 89, 93-94
Chaldean, 4
Châlons-sur-Marne, municipal archives, 5n., 10-12nn.
Charles VII, King of France, 11
Chastellain, Georges, 4n., 12-13nn.
Chatelain, E., 17
Cicero, Marcus Tullius, 40n., 46
Cimeriis, Tomasinus, 65
Cineas, 69
Clement V, Pope, 8n.
College of Saint Bernard, Paris, 12-13; student of, 4n., 10-12nn., 26

Cologne, 13
Congregation of the Propagation of the Faith, 44n.
Conil, Jaume, 52–53, 98
Cordova, 7, 17, 57, 62, 64–65
Corvinus, Matthias, King of Hungary, 37
Costa, Cardinal Jorge de, 51n., 53, 100
Cuenca, 24, 59–60, 62
Cuna, 68
Curlo, Iacopo, 14n.
Cyrus the Great, 69

Dalmatii, Petrus, 59–60
Dardanus, 46
Dati, Agostino, 11n., 14n., 15
Deguí, Pere, 35, 51–53, 95–99
Della Campa, P., 44nn.
Della Rovere, Francesco. See Sixtus IV, Pope
Demosthenes, 50, 92
Denifle, H., 17
Descós, Arnaldo, 35
D'Escouchy, Mathieu, 4n., 11–12nn.
D'Estouteville, Cardinal Guillaume, 38–40, 48, 83–86
Didaci, Sancius, 62
Diego de Avellaneda, 51n.
Dionysius the Areopagite, pseudo-, 28
Dominicans, 6, 51–52
Dominici, Domenico, 36n.
Dominici, Iacoba, 67
Dominici, Ioannes, 67
Donation of Constantine, 39n., 40, 45n.
Dooley, John, 93
Dorcas, 87
Duns Scotus, John, 5, 15, 20, 32–35, 97–98 (see also Scotism)
Durand of Saint-Pourain, 43

Edlawer, Hermannus, 19n.
Egypt, 46
England, 13–14; King of, 8, 68
Eriugena, John Scotus, 28
Eruli, Bernardus, 59
Euclid, 46
Eugenius IV, Pope, 17
Eusebius of Caesarea, 27n., 42n., 46
Eustratius, 47–48

Favaroni, Agostino, 39
Ferdinand, King of Aragon, 51, 53n., 95
Ferezinos, Church of S. Martha, 62
Fernando, Juan, 9
Fernando of Cordova, date of birth, 4–5; education, 5–8; clerical status and ecclesiastical benefices, 8–9, 17, 23–24, 38, 41–43, 50, 57–63; family, 7n.; professor-

ship, 5, 23–24; sepulchral monument, 3, 5, 7n., 53; skill in martial exercises, 11; skill in music and art, 11; tried for heresy and diabolical possession, 13; authentic and unauthentic writings (in short title): *Adversus Hereticos*, 38–40, 41, 55, 83–88; *An Licita Sit cum Saracenis Pax*, 37–38, 55; *Approbatio Libelli Petri Dagui*, 35, 51–53, 56, 95–99; *Commentarii in Apocalypsin*, 12, 56; *Commentarii in Ptolemaei Almagestum*, 12, 48, 56; *De Animalibus*, 49–50, 56; *De Artificio*, 26–35, 37, 38, 48, 56; *De Consultandi Ratione*, 43–45, 55; *De Differentiis*, 26n., 37n., 56; *De Discretione Spirituum*, 49, 55; *De Duabus Philosophiis*, 25–26, 37, 55; *De Eucharistia*, 37, 55; *De Haereticis*, 56; *De Iure Medios Exigendi Fructus*, 27n., 28n., 42, 45–48, 49, 50, 55; *De Laudibus Platonis*, 24–25, 27n., 37, 38, 55, 89n.; *De Misterio Pallii*, 27n., 41–43, 49, 55, 89–92; *De Modis Quibus Decollaratur Ecclesia*, 40, 55; *De Secretis*. 48–49, 55; *Dialectica*, 37, 55; *Dialectical Practica*, 37, 56; Letter to the King of France, 10n., 56; *Propositiones*, 6, 19–21, 55, 71–82; *Sermo de s. Augustino*, 56; *Treatise on the Ephod*, 43, 56; Two treatises on future contingents, 35–37, 55
Fernando of Medina, 6–8, 9n., 17–18n., 64–66
Fernandus Alfonsi, 17
Ficino, Marsilio, 28
Fonseca, Alfonsus de, 61
Fontanelle, 3n.
Forcella, V., 100
France, 13n., 14
Franciscans, 39, 40n.
Francisco of Toledo, 36n.
Fraticelli, 25n., 38–40, 83–88
Frederick, III, Emperor, 18–19

Gallus, 16n.
Gaza, Theodore, 49
Genoa, 4, 6n., 13–14
George of Trebizond, 24–26, 37
Georgia, Duke of, 91n.
Germany, 7, 13–14, 17, 35, 57, 92
Gerponus, Iosephus, 44n.
Gesner, Conrad, 37n.
Ghent, 13
Giberto da Correggio, 67
Gilbert, Moses, 91n.
González de Mendoza, Cardinal Pedro, 50
Gorgias of Leontini, 14–15n.
Greek, 4, 10, 49
Gregory I, Pope, 98
Gregory XVI, Pope, 44

Gregory Nazianzenus, 27n., 91
Gregory of Nyssa, 27n., 91
Grosseteste, Robert, 47–48
Guazzalotti, Andrea, 25n.
Guglielmi di Vulci, Marchese Benedetto, 44n.
Gundisalvus Fernandi de Poria, 61
Gundisalvus de Saavedra, 61–62

Hebrew, 4, 10, 43, 46
Henry of Ghent, 98
Henry of Langenstein, 42, 43n., 90n.
Herolt, Georgius, 45n.
Hippias of Elis, 11
Hungary, 17

Iacobus de Portugallia, 64–65
Iacobus de Sarina (de Sarris), 65–66
IJsewijn, Jozef, 93–94
Innocent VIII, Pope, 53
Ioachim of Lerma, 36n.
Ioannes, Abbot of St. Bernard, Valencia, 52, 98
Ioannes de Francia, 66
Ioannes de Rupecissa, 67
Ioannes de Salas, 65–66
Isabella, Queen of Castile, 50–52
Isocrates, 92

Janer, Jaime, 35
Jesus Christ, 20, 38–40, 73, 78–79 (see Trinity), 83–88, 90
Jews, 46
John XXII, Pope, 39n.
John Philoponus, 27n., 46–47
John of Damascus, 91, 96–97
John of Ripa, 21n., 68
John of Rupella, 43
Joseph of Arimathaea, 87
Josephus, 46
Jouffroy, Cardinal Jean, 40n.
Juan II, King of Castile, 9–10

Kristeller, Paul Oskar, ix

Lactantius, 84n.
L'Aquila, 3n.
Latin, 4, 10, 49–50
Lavinheta, Bernardo de, 35
Lazarus, 87
Leo I, Pope, 91
Leo X, Pope, 57
Leon, 24
Leonardus of Siena, 4n., 8, 15, 17, 67–68
Leoni, Pier, 48n., 49, 89

Levet, Petrus, 95
Lidenses, 91
Lisias, 92
Liutprand of Cremona, 46
Livy, 46
López, Alfonso, 57
Louvain, University of, 35, 50, 93–94; Heilige Geestcollege, 93
Lucena, Juan de, 18
Lull, Ramon, 27, 31–32, 51–52, 95–97
Lullism and Lullists, 27, 48, 95–99

Macrobius, 46
Majorca, 16, 51–53
Marigenero, Petrus, 65
Marinus, Petrus, 64–65
Martha, 87
Martini, Ioannes, 65
Mary, the Virgin, 51n., 87
Mauro, Alfredo, 9
Maximus the Confessor, 46n.
Maximus of Turin, 46n.
Medici, Lorenzo de', 49
Medina Azzahra, 7
Menéndez y Pelayo, M., 29, 32n.
Milan, 14
Minieri Riccio, Camillo, 8–9
Mithridates, King of Persia, 69
Moroni, Gaetano, 44
Morvecus, Ioannes, 62
Moses, 50
Moslems, 38, 46
Moya, 60, 61

Naples, 3–4, 5n., 8–10, 16, 40, 68
Nebrija, Antonio, 90n.
Nicholas V, Pope, 17, 21, 23, 57–60, 67
Nicholas of Cusa, 89
Nicholas of Lyra, 46, 90n.
Nominalists, 6, 20–21
Noya, Franciscus de, 52–53, 99

Ochon, Luppi, 65–66
Ockham, William of, and the Ockhamists, 8, 20, 21n., 37, 80, 93
Origen, 91
Ospedale di Santa Maria della Scala, 68
Ottoman Turks, 38

Padua, 14
Palmieri, Niccolò, 24–25, 37, 61
Palotta, Cardinal Antonio, 44
Pannartz, A., 90n.
Paris, University of, 5, 12–13, 17, 19, 26, 35, 42, 43, 49, 53n., 95
Parmenides, 28

Patrizi, Francesco, 47
Patrizi-Piccolomini, Agostino, 41
Paul II, Pope, 24n., 37, 41
Paulus de Colonia, 95
Pelayo, Alvaro, 88
Pérez Bayer, F., 100
Pericles, 92
Persia, King of, 91n.
Pescara, 3n.
Peter, Saint, 91
Peter Lombard, 42-43, 80n., 97
Petrus de Iaen, 89
Petrus de Sancto Sebastiano, 66
Philip the Good, Duke of Burgundy, 12-13
Piana, Celestino 7n., 64
Piccolomini, Enea Silvio. See Pius II, Pope
Pico della Mirandola, Giovanni, 1, 11
Pignerolio, Antonius de, 52, 98
Pius II, Pope, 19, 23-24, 91-92
Pius III, Pope, 41-42, 60-63, 89-92
Platina, 46
Plato, 6, 15, 21, 26, 27n., 28, 29, 47-48, 50, 81-82, 84
Plato-Aristotle Controversy, ix, 1, 24-26
Platonism and Neoplatonism, 6, 21n., 29, 32
Pletho, Georgius Gemistus, 26n.
Pliny, 46
Polonus, Stanislaus, 95
Posa, Petrus, 95
Primum in aliquo genere, 28
Priscian, 46
Ptolemaeus de Corduba, 66
Ptolemy, 12, 48
Punic, 4
Pyrrhus, King of Epirus, 69

Quentell, Peter, 95

Ram, R. X., 93
Rangone, Cardinal Gabriele, 51
Richard of St. Victor, 98
Rivo, Petrus de, 35-37, 50
Rome, University of, 23, 61; S. Giacomo degli Spagnuoli, 53, 100; S. Maria Maggiore, 86; S. Maria de Montserrat, 53, 100
Rossi, Pietro, 15
Rovicrus, Sancius, 61-62

Salamanca, University of 5-6
Salomon, 73, 75, 77
Sánchez de Arévalo, Rodrigo, 39
Sanctius de Sanzano, 66
Santri, Antonius, 61
Saria de Galicia (Portugal), 65
Saronii, 91

Scotism and Scotists, 6, 20-21, 32-35, 51-52
Seguenza, 59
Seneca, 46, 85
Servius, 46
Seville, 17, 58, 61
Siena, 4, 6, 25, 7, 8, 11n., 13-16, 17, 67-70
Sierra de Yeguas, 61
Sigismund, Duke of Austria, 19
Silber, Eucharius, 51, 95
Simler, J., 37
Sixtus IV, Pope, 36, 41-42, 45, 50-53, 96
Sorrento, 3n.
Sozzini, Mariano, 14-15
Spaeth, Paul J., 95
Spanish College, Bologna, 6-7, 17-18n., 64-66
Spoleto, 21
State University of New York, ix
Suetonius, 46
Sweynheim, C., 90n.

Themistius, 27n., 46-47
Thimodeus, 66
Thomas Aquinas, 5-6, 28, 32, 34n., 43n., 51n., 52, 81n.
Thomism and Thomists, 20-21, 34n., 51-52
Todeschini-Piccolomini, Francesco. See Pius III, Pope.
Toledo, 65
Torquemada, Cardinal Juan, 39
Trebizond, Emperor of, 91n.
Trebizond, George of. See George of Trebizond
Trinity, 73-80
Trithemius, John, 12n., 16, 27n.
Tudel, Georg, of Giengen, 19-20, 71-73

Vadel, Pedro, 35n.
Valenza, Fernando, 9
Valla, Lorenzo, 3-4, 8-10, 23, 40
Van de Velde, J. Fr., 94
Venice, 14, 26, 37
Verallo, Girolamo, 44n.
Vienna, 93; University of, 4, 5, 6, 18-21, 42, 71-73
Villa I Tatti, Florence, ix
Virgil, 46

Wyclif, John, 78n.

Yanes, Fernandus, 62-63

Zambelli, Paola, 16n.
Zoemeren, Henricus de, 35-36, 93-94

www.ingramcontent.com/pod-product-compliance
Lightning Source LLC
Chambersburg PA
CBHW080928100426

42812CB00007B/2407

* 9 7 8 0 8 7 1 6 9 8 2 6 1 *